THE CARLTON SPORTS GUIDE

FORMULA ONE 2019

This edition printed in 2019
by Carlton Books Limited
20 Mortimer Street
London W1T 3JW

ISBN 978-1-78739-211-3

Editorial Director: Martin Corteel
Design Manager: Luke Griffin
Design: RockJaw Creative
Picture Research: Paul Langan
Production: Ena Matagic
Assistant Editor: David Ballheimer

Printed in Spain

**Opposite: Sebastian Vettel started the year well but faded and will be seeking
consistency in 2019.**

THE **CARLTON SPORTS** GUIDE

FORMULA ONE 2019

BRUCE JONES

CARLTON
BOOKS

CONTENTS

4

Right: Max Verstappen shows his sheer delight after winning the Austrian GP at the Red Bull Ring as Red Bull Racing got up to speed and he began to impose himself as team leader.

Lewis Hamilton is in huge demand wherever he goes and knows that it's expected that he will make time to sign autographs, which isn't always easy.

ANALYSIS OF THE 2019 SEASON

There was hope last year that Ferrari would take the battle to Mercedes, but its challenge fell apart as Lewis Hamilton drove the silver arrows back to the front. The rising star at season's end was Max Verstappen, but Red Bull Racing will use Honda engines in 2019 and it remains to be seen if these will be good enough for the team to take the battle to Mercedes.

The season ahead brings considerable change as the driver merry-go-round has been given its most vigorous spin for many a year. Better still in this shuffling of the pack, there are a handful of the best of last year's F2 drivers joining the fray to add an air of the unknown.

The question asked most frequently by fans is how to make overtaking more likely and the sport's brains trust has produced changes to the front and rear wings to reduce the effect of aerodynamic turbulence to the front and open the slot more in the rear wing to enhance the effect of the Drag Reduction System.

F1's official tyre supplier, Pirelli, has come up with a sensible change. Although it will continue to make five or six compounds of

dry weather tyres, it will make it easier for fans to identify which of the three compounds it selects for that meeting by giving them white, yellow or red markings in descending order of hardness, i.e. hard, medium and soft.

Mercedes keeps the same driver line-up of now five-times World Champion Lewis Hamilton and Valtteri Bottas. While Hamilton's speed has never been doubted, he displayed extra steeliness to achieve his goals last year. Alongside him, Bottas's best chance not to be consigned to the role of support player, or "wing man" as Toto Wolff described him last year, is to bag some early season wins.

Ferrari's signing of Charles Leclerc from Sauber could be a revelation, as Ferrari has seldom offered a ride to a driver with so

little F1 experience. But what the Monegasque ace showed in his rookie season is more than enough to make it likely that he will keep Sebastian Vettel on his toes, something that the team needs after he made a few slip-ups last year.

Red Bull Racing will be led by Max Verstappen and will be hoping that they can get him to maintain his form and perhaps round off the rough edges. One factor that will be different is that the team's longstanding deal with Renault has ended and the cars will be powered by Honda units from now on. There's a new second driver, with Pierre Gasly being promoted from Scuderia Toro Rosso.

It will seem strange not to have Daniel Ricciardo in a Red Bull after his five years with the team, but a failure to agree terms led to the Australian joining Renault where he will find a stern challenge from Nico Hulkenberg in a team that is very much on an upward trajectory.

There's no change at Haas F1, as Romain Grosjean and Kevin Magnussen stay on board.

McLaren has replaced one Spaniard with another, bringing Carlos Sainz Jr across to fill the seat vacated by Fernando Alonso as he heads off to his sabbatical. Alonso will race in other great events rather than struggle in F1's midgrid when it's wins and titles that he wants at this stage in his career. The second seat introduces F2 frontrunner Lando Norris, a driver that McLaren has been mentoring since spotting his form in the junior categories.

Racing Point, the team formerly known as Force India until Lawrence Stroll bought it out of bankruptcy last summer, will have a fresh livery but fortunately the same personnel, including Sergio Perez. The second driver is the new owner's son Lance, who will want to bounce back from a torrid year with struggling Williams.

Sauber has pulled off the biggest coup in landing one of its old boys, Kimi Raikkonen, as he knew he was being moved on from Ferrari, but didn't want to stop doing what he likes best: driving an F1 car. Antonio Giovinazzi has been pushed by Ferrari, as part of its engine deal, to drive the second car.

Scuderia Toro Rosso is another team that has an all-new line-up, with Daniil Kvyat being brought back from the F1 wilderness to the team with which he started in 2014. He is joined by Alex Albon, the British-born Thai-representing driver, who showed strong enough form in F2 last year to take over from Brendon Hartley.

F1 fans ought to rejoice at the Williams line-up for 2019, as it is all change and not only introduces runaway F2 champion George Russell but has brought back one of F1's thwarted talents: Robert Kubica. Yes, the latter is a risk, due to the dreadful injuries he suffered to his right forearm in a rallying accident. Yet, they wouldn't have signed him if they weren't sure that he was almost back to full strength, sure that he could get back to his previous, prodigious best. They need one other thing: a good car.

The deck has been shuffled, so let's see who comes out top.

MERCEDES-AMG PETRONAS

Another year, another title was Mercedes' story last year, but its five constructors' titles in a row shows why the unchanged team starts favourite to remain at the top of F1 in 2019 and why Lewis Hamilton must be favourite for individual honours.

Lewis Hamilton rose to new heights last year as he took his fifth F1 title, but knows the challenge from Red Bull's Max Verstappen is growing.

When Mercedes-Benz arrived in Formula 1 in 1954, it set a new standard, then dominated in 1955, with Juan Manuel Fangio and Stirling Moss its flag bearers. All rivals were cowed, but then, following the Le Mans disaster in 1955 in which a Mercedes flew into the crowd and killed more than 80 spectators, a decision was taken to withdraw from the sport and the rest of F1 was spared Mercedes' efforts for another five decades.

When Mercedes came back to F1, it did so not by starting from scratch but by adopting the more sensible approach of taking over an established team and moulding it into its own identity. The team in question was Brawn GP, but this wasn't the team's starting point. That was BAR, or British American Racing, to give it its full name.

The BAR story started with Jacques Villeneuve and his former PE teacher Craig Pollock. With Pollock using the 1997 World Champion to attract the backing of cigarette company British American Tobacco, they elected to start their own team. It was

a big risk for Villeneuve to quit Williams to do so, but the budget was healthy and they decided to do it, starting in 1999. With a new base established at Brackley, near

Silverstone, they were right in the arc of motorsport industry excellence and so attracted top people. Their first year results with Villeneuve and Ricardo Zonta were

THE POWER AND THE GLORY

JAMES ALLISON
A Cambridge engineering graduate, James joined Benetton's aerodynamic department in 1991. After being head of aerodynamics at the Larrousse team, he returned to a similar position at Benetton, then joined Ferrari in 2000. A third spell at Benetton followed from 2005 to 2013, albeit now racing as Renault and he became the team's technical director. A man in demand, he was headhunted by Ferrari in 2013, before leaving in 2016 and taking over as Mercedes' technical director in 2017 after Paddy Lowe's departure.

HAVING TO STEP UP TO THE CHALLENGE
Last season, it was clear that Mercedes was going to have to face its most powerful challenge in recent seasons, as Ferrari had stepped up its engine development. Lewis Hamilton failed to win until the fourth round. Valtteri Bottas did his best but was gradually left behind as Hamilton took on and overhauled Ferrari's Sebastian Vettel. Behind the scenes, John Owen was appointed engineering director, and Loic Serra performance director.

2018 DRIVERS & RESULTS

Driver	Nationality	Races	Wins	Pts	Pos
Lewis Hamilton	British	21	11	408	1st
Valtteri Bottas	Finnish	21	0	247	5th

FOR THE RECORD

Country of origin:	England
Team base:	Brackley, England
Telephone:	(44) 01280 844000
Website:	www.mercedes-amg-f1.com
Active in Formula One:	As BAR 1999-2005, Honda Racing 2006-08, Brawn GP 2009, Mercedes 2010 onwards
Grands Prix contested:	365
Wins:	87
Pole positions:	101
Fastest laps:	66

nowhere near those predicted when they launched. However, 2000 was way better and it ranked fourth equal overall as great strides were made with Honda engines. In 2001, two podium finishes were achieved.

A major change followed for 2003, when David Richards' Prodrive concern took over. Jenson Button recorded four second-place finishes to rank BAR second, behind only Ferrari in 2004 – he was third in the Drivers' Championship – but it was to be the high point.

For 2006, with increased involvement from engine-provider Honda, the team became Honda Racing. On a day of mixed weather at the Hungarian GP, Button gave the team its first win. The next two seasons were not so competitive. Then, with the world economic slump hitting, Honda closed the team at the end of 2008. However, at the 11th hour, technical director Ross Brawn saved it and the team became Brawn GP for 2009. Amazingly, the team found a technical loophole and stole a lead with its cars benefitting from double-decker diffusers, allowing Button to win six of the first seven

rounds. Team-mate Rubens Barrichello collected a pair and the team landed both the drivers' and constructors' titles in an extraordinary year.

Mercedes had long been an engine supplier, most notably to McLaren, but it wanted to run a team in its own right, so it bought Brawn and put up the money for Michael Schumacher to return to F1 as its team leader for 2010. The results took a while to come, with Nico Rosberg claiming victory in the 2012 Chinese GP.

However, it was the arrival of Lewis Hamilton in 2013 that really propelled the team forward to end the season second only to Red Bull Racing, with the silver cars coming out of Brackley showing technical excellence thanks to the input of technical chief Paddy Lowe and Bob Bell.

The year that the second age of the silver arrows really came to fruition was 2014 as Hamilton and Rosberg won the first 10 rounds and Hamilton went on to land the title, with Mercedes taking its first Constructors' Cup too – this element of F1 hadn't existed in the mid-1950s. Hamilton then won the 2015,

THE TEAM

Non-executive chairman:	Niki Lauda
Head of Mercedes-Benz Motorsport:	Toto Wolff
Technical director:	James Allison
MD, Mercedes-AMG High Performance Powertrains:	Andy Cowell
Technology director:	Geoff Willis
Engineering director:	John Owen
Performance director:	Loic Serra
Sporting director:	Ron Meadows
Chief race engineer:	Andrew Shovlin
Chief track engineer:	Simon Cole
Test driver:	Esteban Ocon
Chassis:	Mercedes F1 W10
Engine:	Mercedes V6
Tyres:	Pirelli

2017 and 2018 drivers' titles, with Rosberg pipping him in 2016 before promptly quitting. Rosberg had raised his game in response to the challenge from Hamilton, but his sudden departure left the team struggling for a replacement, with Valtteri Bottas filling the slot admirably, although not usually being quite as close to the British driver's pace.

> "Last year, Lewis was the best Lewis Hamilton that I've seen in six years. He has driven better and he has been better out of the car. He has been very, very complete."
> **Toto Wolff**

Toto Wolff appreciates Valtteri Bottas's acceptance of his supporting role to Lewis Hamilton.

LEWIS HAMILTON

If the challenge from Ferrari's Sebastian Vettel had grown in 2017, it did so even more last year and Lewis really had to fight for his fifth crown. The bad news for his rivals is that Lewis is still hungry for more and all set for the season ahead.

Lewis is one of those rare drivers who was famous before reaching F1. His pace made him stand out, but it was his cheek that earned him a dream break. Attending a ceremony to collect a karting trophy from McLaren F1 boss Ron Dennis, he asked Ron to back him. After a little consideration, Ron decided he would. This took the weight off the shoulders of Lewis's father Anthony, as car racing would have been beyond their means.

Lewis won the British Formula Renault title for Manor at his second attempt in 2003. F3 was also a two-year project and Lewis took the 2005 European F3 crown by winning 15 races. It was clear that Lewis was gaining momentum, and still with McLaren assistance, he won the 2006 GP2 title at his first attempt, so the team rewarded him with his F1 break in 2007.

Few drivers ever start with a top team – and McLaren was still a top team back then – but Lewis made the most of it, by becoming a winner on his sixth outing. He fell one point short of the world championship as he and team-mate Fernando Alonso ended up on 109 points; Ferrari's Kimi Raikkonen clinched the title with a final-round victory.

Lewis enjoyed last year's battle, that really made him work with his team to hit the top.

Lewis became McLaren team leader for 2008 after Alonso left in a huff and landed the title. A gradual loss of form for McLaren encouraged Lewis to join Mercedes in 2013 and he got his timing right as he won the title in 2014 and has since added three more.

TRACK NOTES

Nationality:	BRITISH
Born:	7 JANUARY 1985, STEVENAGE, ENGLAND
Website:	www.lewishamilton.com
Teams:	McLAREN 2007-12, MERCEDES 2013-19

CAREER RECORD

First Grand Prix:	2007 AUSTRALIAN GP
Grand Prix starts:	229
Grand Prix wins:	73

2007 Canadian GP, United States GP, Hungarian GP, Japanese GP, 2008 Australian GP, Monaco GP, British GP, German GP, Chinese GP, 2009 Hungarian GP, Singapore GP, 2010 Turkish GP, Canadian GP, Belgian GP, 2011 Chinese GP, German GP, Abu Dhabi GP, 2012 Canadian GP, Hungarian GP, Italian GP, United States GP, 2013 Hungarian GP, 2014 Malaysian GP, Bahrain GP, Chinese GP, Spanish GP, British GP, Italian GP, Singapore GP, Japanese GP, Russian GP, United States GP, Abu Dhabi GP, 2015 Australian GP, Chinese GP, Bahrain GP, Canadian GP, British GP, Belgian GP, Italian GP, Japanese GP, Russian GP, United States GP, 2016 Monaco GP, Canadian GP, Austrian GP, British GP, Hungarian GP, German GP, United States GP, Mexican GP, Brazilian GP, Abu Dhabi GP, 2017 Chinese GP, Spanish GP, Canadian GP, British GP, Belgian GP, Italian GP, Singapore GP, Japanese GP, United States GP, 2018 Azerbaijan GP, Spanish GP, French GP, German GP, Hungarian GP, Italian GP, Singapore GP, Russian GP, Japanese GP, Brazilian GP, Abu Dhabi GP

Poles:	83
Fastest laps:	41
Points:	3018

Honours: 2008, 2014, 2015, 2017 & 2018 F1 WORLD CHAMPION, 2007 & 2016 F1 RUNNER-UP, 2006 GP2 CHAMPION, 2005 EUROPEAN F3 CHAMPION, 2003 BRITISH FORMULA RENAULT CHAMPION, 2000 WORLD KART CUP & EUROPEAN FORMULA A KART CHAMPION, 1999 ITALIAN INTERCONTINENTAL A CHAMPION, 1995 BRITISH CADET KART CHAMPION

IT'S FIVE ALIVE FOR LEWIS

Ferrari made Lewis dig really deep to get to the front last year. Then, once he had got ahead of Sebastian Vettel, he seemed to relax and drive all the better because of it. With no wins until the fourth round of the season – on the streets of Baku – Lewis felt a lot better when he won next time out as well, in Spain. However, Red Bull Racing's drivers also were in the mix and, with wins being shared between the top three teams, it took longer for Lewis to claw back Vettel's points advantage than it would have done in a more typical two-horse race. Retirement in Austria let Vettel back ahead, but Lewis enjoyed a great run in to F1's summer break by finishing second at Silverstone then winning both the German and Hungarian GPs to give him a 24-point lead. Resuming with second place at Spa-Francorchamps, Lewis stretched his legs by winning four grands prix in a row from Monza to Suzuka. then fourth place in the Mexican GP was enough for his fifth F1 crown.

VALTTERI BOTTAS

Given a one-year extension on his Mercedes contract, this sporting Finn won't want to play a supporting role to Lewis Hamilton again, but it's hard to see how things will play out any differently to the way they have for the past two years.

Team players are rare in F1, but that is what Valtteri has had to be at various points on his way up racing's ladder to the top.

Valtteri spent seven years in Finland's national karting squad, his best year being 2006, when the 16-year-old won three titles. It encouraged him to step up to car racing in 2007. Valtteri finished third in the Northern European Countries Formula Renault series, a title that he'd win in 2008. However, his main prize in his second year of Formula Renault was the European title, with his five wins putting him ahead of Daniel Ricciardo.

The next step was F3 and, after ranking third in 2009, Valtteri wanted the title in 2010, but had to settle for third again as Edoardo Mortara became champion.

Without sufficient financial backing to advance to GP2, Valtteri moved only slightly upwards to race in GP3 in 2011. Fortunately, his career momentum continued by winning the title and then shining in the champion's prize of a Williams F1 test run. The team liked him too, and signed Valtteri to be their reserve driver for 2012, when he attended the grands prix and provided sound feedback

Valtteri showed strong pace in the second half of last year but in a supporting role.

when he ran in the Friday morning practice sessions and often outperformed Pastor Maldonado and Bruno Senna.

Many would have found it tricky to play this supporting role, wanting instead to be the star, but Valtteri earned the team's

respect as he simply got on with the job.

Valtteri's reward was a full race seat for 2013, but the team was having a slump. His second year was a huge improvement as Williams changed to Mercedes power and Valtteri finished fourth in the Drivers' Championship, with second-place finishes in the British and German GPs.

Very much seen as a rising star, there was talk of Valtteri replacing Kimi Raikkonen at Ferrari, but that never happened. Then, at the end of 2016, his big break came from nowhere, as Nico Rosberg surprised everyone by retiring after he clinched the drivers' title. And so Valtteri joined Mercedes, his reward a first win - at Sochi - and third overall after winning twice more.

TRACK NOTES

Nationality:	FINNISH
Born:	28 AUGUST 1989, NASTOLA, FINLAND
Website:	www.valtteribottas.com
Teams:	WILLIAMS 2013-16, MERCEDES 2017-19

CAREER RECORD

First Grand Prix:	2013 AUSTRALIAN GP
Grand Prix starts:	118
Grand Prix wins:	3
2017 Russian GP, Austrian GP, Abu Dhabi GP	
Poles:	6
Fastest laps:	10
Points:	963
Honours:	2011 GP3 CHAMPION,
	2009 & 2010 FORMULA 3 MASTERS WINNER,
	2008 EUROPEAN & NORTHERN EUROPEAN
	FORMULA RENAULT CHAMPION

A YEAR OF BEING THWARTED

Valtteri may not have seen a black cat crossing the road in front of him, but he clearly must have hit one as his 2018 season was dogged by the bad luck that this is supposed to bring. Time and again a top finish was denied him and it was a mark of Valtteri's sanguine resilience that he contained the anger that it must surely have triggered. Often almost a match to World Champion elect team-mate Lewis Hamilton, Valtteri reached the summer break, after 12 of the 21 grands prix, without a win, while Hamilton had four. Add to that the throwaway comment from Mercedes F1's frontman Toto Wolff made at the German GP about Valtteri being "the perfect wingman" for Hamilton and you can imagine how deflating that must have felt for the Finn. At least he had a one-year contract extension to remain with F1's top team, but Valtteri must be looking to see what might come next, as no driver wants to spend their career in a supporting role.

SCUDERIA FERRARI

Ferrari was a team on the up last year, but there's a new dynamic as Sebastian Vettel has a new team-mate to keep him sharp as he takes another tilt at the title, with the arrival of Charles Leclerc. This could be the impetus Ferrari needs.

Things looked rosy for Ferrari with first and third in Australia last year, but Mercedes came good, so the team has to have learnt the lessons.

Ferrari has a history longer than any other F1 team, having contested the inaugural World Championship in 1950. However, it has seldom championed young drivers across the intervening decades, so Charles Leclerc's signing represents great change.

When Enzo Ferrari ran the team from behind a pair of dark sunglasses, there appeared to be an air of mystery, but the team seldom did anything unexpected. In truth, once Enzo died and an increasing number of management types descended from parent company Fiat, and latterly Chrysler, the decisions have been far more unpredictable as automotive manufacturers and racing teams don't work in the same way.

In many ways, Ferrari's early years were its glory years, as Enzo's cars started

THE POWER AND THE GLORY

LOIC BIGOIS
Like many technical chiefs, this 58-year-old French engineer has been around a bit. He worked in aerospace before joining the Ligier F1 team in 1990. He tried other teams and Ligier again before becoming head of aerodynamics at Minardi in 2001. Williams landed Loic in 2003 and he stayed there until 2007 before joining Honda. His greatest accolade came in 2009 when the team was resurrected as Brawn GP and won both titles. He stayed through the early Mercedes years then left in 2012 to join Ferrari.

ON THE PACE BUT NOT QUITE IN THE RACE
The SF71H was Ferrari's most competitive car for years, but it failed to deliver a drivers' title for Sebastian Vettel or a constructors' title for the team. Much of the blame has to lie at the team's door as it didn't manage its strategy well, thus letting Mercedes back into the battle. The sudden death of Ferrari supremo Sergio Marchionne last July also forced a change of dynamic in the team, with further change when chief designer Simone Resta left for Sauber.

2018 DRIVERS & RESULTS

Driver	Nationality	Races	Wins	Pts	Pos
Sebastian Vettel	German	21	5	320	2nd
Kimi Raikkonen	Finnish	21	1	251	3rd

FOR THE RECORD

Country of origin:	Italy
Team base:	Maranello, Italy
Telephone:	(39) 536 949111
Website:	www.ferrari.com
Active in Formula One:	From 1950
Grands Prix contested:	970
Wins:	234
Pole positions:	219
Fastest laps:	247

THE TEAM

President:	Louis Camilleri
Team principal:	Mattia Binotto
Technical director:	tba
Chief designer:	tba
Chief designer, power unit:	Lorenzo Sassi
Head of aerodynamics:	Loic Bigois
Director of aero development:	Enrico Cardile
Sporting director:	Claudio Albertini
Head of race activities:	Jock Clear
Operations director:	Gino Rosato
Test driver:	tba
Chassis:	Ferrari SF72H
Engine:	Ferrari V6
Tyres:	Pirelli

winning in 1951 then, after a change in the regulations, dominated 1952 and 1953 in the hands of Alberto Ascari. Mercedes raised the bar when it arrived in 1954 but Ferrari was back at the front in 1956 after Mercedes withdrew, helping Juan Manuel Fangio to the title. Two years later, it just resisted the Vanwall charge for Mike Hawthorn to be crowned champion.

A rule change for 1961, to engines of just 1,500cc, favoured Ferrari and Phil Hill gave the team its fifth title. However, the British teams fought back. With greater ingenuity, BRM's Graham Hill came top in 1962 then Lotus's Jim Clark in 1963. John Surtees' doggedness landed the 1964 title for Ferrari, but the team wasn't producing the technical ingenuity to stay at the front.

The breakthrough came when Niki Lauda made the team try harder and Luca di Montezemolo kept the parent company at bay. But for his burns at the 1976 German GP, Niki might have won three titles in a row, rather than just in 1975 and 1977.

Lauda moved on, but Enzo signed Gilles Villeneuve to dazzle and Jody Scheckter to deliver, with the latter taking the 1979 crown after Mauro Forghieri's team got to grips with ground-effects technology.

After that, despite several years in the early 1980s when Harvey Postlethwaite revamped the technical side and it took the constructors' crown, Ferrari's challenge wasn't strong enough as McLaren and Williams dominated until 2000, which made life barren for Ferrari's fans, the *tifosi*.

Ferrari's best years have come when British brains have run its technical division, and John Barnard was followed by Ross Brawn in the late 1990s. This, in conjunction with the management skills of Jean Todt and the signing of Michael Schumacher, made all the difference, and, from 2000, the titles began to flow again. In fact, Michael won five consecutive drivers' crowns, several of which were near total domination – with 11 wins in 2002 bettered by his 13 in 2004. This form seemed so good that surely it could never end, but it did.

After Michael left at the end of 2006, Kimi Raikkonen pipped McLaren's Fernando Alonso and Lewis Hamilton to the 2007 title by a point, but neither Alonso nor Sebastian Vettel have since managed to land the drivers' crown as Red Bull Racing

and Mercedes have assumed the mantle of being F1's most competitive team.

Ferrari, though, appears to be back on the boil, its engines the best of all in 2018 and Sergio Marchionne's firm hand on the tiller that allowed the team to act as a team rather than as a marketing tool. Sadly, he died after an operation and the winter marked a power battle from within.

"If you have to make a choice about the future of the team, then I think that in signing Charles [Leclerc] we made the right one for us and the right one for Kimi [Raikkonen]."
Maurizio Arrivabene
(former team principal)

The famous fluffed photo finish at the 2002 US GP, with Barrichello pipping Schumacher.

SEBASTIAN VETTEL

Sebastian's four F1 titles now feel quite a long time ago. The most recent was in 2013 and so this German ace's strong form at the start of last year raised his hopes of adding a fifth. If Ferrari stays strong, he might get it in 2019.

Sebastian was European and German junior kart champion in 2001. Then, with the money found to try car racing in 2003, he was immediately on the pace. Runner-up in his first year of Formula BMW, he took the title in 2004 with an incredible 18 wins in 20 races. He then also spent two years in F3, but was beaten to the 2006 European title by Paul di Resta.

However, this didn't slow his progress, as Sebastian took his Red Bull backing to Formula Renault 3.5 in 2007 and took a win at the second round. But then his life changed very rapidly, as Robert Kubica was injured in the Canadian GP and the Sauber team elevated Sebastian from his testing role to a racing one for the United States GP. Eighth place was impressive, but then Kubica returned.

Yet, Toro Rosso snapped Sebastian up three races later after it dropped Scott Speed and he took fourth in the Chinese GP to secure his drive for 2008. Red Bull Racing was eager to take its first F1 win but Sebastian beat them to it with the junior team, Toro Rosso, when he won from pole in the Italian GP. The senior team snapped him up for 2009 and Sebastian rattled off four

Sebastian made some mistakes last year, so will be looking to atone for this in 2019.

wins to be second behind Jenson Button.

Then, with a late-season charge, Sebastian grabbed the 2010 F1 title, and the next three. Since joining Ferrari in 2015, Sebastian has always been a front-runner, but never a champion.

RACING AND WINNING, BUT NO TITLE

Sebastian finished his 20-race 2017 campaign 46 points behind Lewis Hamilton, so he knew that there needed to be a step up from Ferrari for 2018. From the very start of the season, it was clear that his wish had been granted, for he rattled off wins in the first two grands prix. The third race, in China, was a setback as Sebastian finished only eighth after being hit by Max Verstappen, but it was clear that this could be a good season for the team from Maranello. Further wins followed in the Canadian and British GPs, boosted by a smattering of pole positions, but he blew his chance of victory in his home race at Hockenheim when he crashed out in the wet. However, Lewis Hamilton began to hit his stride for Mercedes as the midpoint in the season approached and took the championship lead. Despite winning in Belgium, Sebastian wasn't to win again as his season rather tailed off through the last few grands prix. It was a case of what might have been.

TRACK NOTES

Nationality:	GERMAN
Born:	3 JULY 1987, HEPPENHEIM, GERMANY
Website:	www.sebastianvettel.de
Teams:	BMW SAUBER 2007,
	TORO ROSSO 2007-08,
	RED BULL RACING 2009-14, FERRARI 2015-19

CAREER RECORD

First Grand Prix:	2007 UNITED STATES GP
Grand Prix starts:	220
Grand Prix wins:	52

2008 Italian GP, 2009 Chinese GP, British GP, Japanese GP, Abu Dhabi GP, 2010 Malaysian GP, European GP, Japanese GP, Brazilian GP, Abu Dhabi GP, 2011 Australian GP, Malaysian GP, Turkish GP, Spanish GP, Monaco GP, European GP, Belgian GP, Italian GP, Singapore GP, Korean GP, Indian GP, 2012 Bahrain GP, Singapore GP, Japanese GP, Korean GP, Indian GP, 2013 Malaysian GP, Bahrain GP, Canadian GP, German GP, Belgian GP, Italian GP, Singapore GP, Korean GP, Japanese GP, Indian GP, Abu Dhabi GP, United States GP, Brazilian GP, 2015 Malaysian GP, Hungarian GP, Singapore GP, 2017 Australian GP, Bahrain GP, Monaco GP, Hungarian GP, Brazilian GP, 2018 Australian GP, Bahrain GP, Canadian GP, British GP, Belgian GP

Poles:	55
Fastest laps:	36
Points:	2745
Honours:	2010, 2011, 2012 & 2013 F1 WORLD CHAMPION, 2006 EUROPEAN FORMULA THREE RUNNER-UP, 2004 GERMAN FORMULA BMW ADAC CHAMPION, 2001 EUROPEAN & GERMAN JUNIOR KART CHAMPION

CHARLES LECLERC

No driver who is less than excellent reaches F1. Yet, some are that little bit better, and Charles has all the hallmarks of being very special indeed. Ferrari loved what he did at Sauber last year and now want him to push Sebastian Vettel.

Although Charles came from a car racing family, it took the intervention of Ferrari in 2016 to keep his career on track once he reached the expensive upper echelons of single-seater racing. This was when it signed the 18-year-old Monegasque to its Driver Academy to ensure he could do GP3.

Charles's father Herve used to contest the annual F3 race supporting their home grand prix in Monaco, and his involvement with a local kart track ensured that all of his three sons cut their teeth in racing at an early age. Charles proved the best, but the youngest, Arthur, showed good speed too in French F4 last year.

After winning the French cadet kart title in 2009, Charles won local and national junior titles and peaked with the 2011 world KF3 title. Moving to more senior categories, Charles finished second to Max Verstappen in the world KZ series in 2013.

Nicolas Todt's ARM driver management company propelled Charles into car racing in 2014 when he was 16 and he finished second in a regional Formula Renault series. F3 followed in 2015 and Charles showed his form by winning a race at the opening round of the European series and

Charles' form for Sauber last year suggests he could shine now that he's joined Ferrari.

ending the year fourth overall against more experienced rivals.

GP3 followed in 2016 and Charles won the title easily with ART Grand Prix and also showed good pace in his F1 test debut with Sauber. He landed the F2 title in 2017 at a

canter, with seven wins for Prema Racing and tested for Ferrari.

Charles's skill set was apparent from the opening round at which he qualified on pole position at Sakhir. With no seat available to advance to F1 with the Italian team, Charles was placed with Sauber for 2018 as part of the deal in which Sauber used F1 engines. Having a more competitive car than the Swiss team usually provides certainly helped Charles to state his case.

TRACK NOTES

Nationality:	MONEGASQUE
Born:	
	16 OCTOBER 1997, MONTE CARLO, MONACO
Website:	www.charles-leclerc.com
Teams:	SAUBER 2018, FERRARI 2019

CAREER RECORD	
First Grand Prix:	2018 AUSTRALIAN GP
Grand Prix starts:	21
Grand Prix wins:	0 (best result: 6th, 2018 Azerbaijan GP)
Poles:	0
Fastest laps:	0
Points:	39
Honours:	2017 FIA F2 CHAMPION, 2016 GP3 CHAMPION, 2015 MACAU F3 RUNNER-UP, 2014 FORMULA RENAULT ALPS RUNNER-UP, 2013 WORLD KZ KART RUNNER-UP, 2012 UNDER 18 WORLD KART CHAMPIONSHIP RUNNER-UP & EURO KF KART RUNNER-UP, 2011 ACADEMY TROPHY KART CHAMPION, 2010 JUNIOR MONACO KART CUP CHAMPION, 2009 FRENCH CADET KART CHAMPION

PUSHING SAUBER EVER FORWARDS

With Mercedes, Ferrari and Red Bull Racing drivers almost invariably filling the top six point-scoring places, the drivers for the remaining seven teams had the minor scores as their victories. Sauber hasn't traditionally been a team that has provided a car capable of this in recent seasons, but its increasingly competitive Ferrari engines gave its drivers a chance last year and Charles helped himself, finishing in the points ten times. His best result was sixth place at the Azerbaijan GP. Amid this display of consistent promise, Charles survived a scare at the Belgian GP when Nico Hulkenberg launched Fernando Alonso's McLaren onto him at the first corner, with his Sauber's halo saving him from serious injury or worse. Four seventh place finishes in the late season grands prix at Sochi, Mexico City, Interlagos and Abu Dhabi really marked Charles out as something special, a driver who was not just impressively rapid but one who was consistent too.

Slick pitstop choreography is a must for every team, with Ferrari showing how you can do it even before the drivers have arrived at the circuit. Practice makes perfect.

RED BULL RACING

Red Bull got close to the pace with Renault engines in 2018 but never set it until the end of the year. Whether that will change now it has Honda power remains to be seen. Max Verstappen is team leader but newcomer Pierre Gasly will be looking to challenge.

Daniel Ricciardo beat Ferrari and Mercedes at Monaco last year, but it was Max Verstappen who rose to become the team leader for 2019.

Midway through the first decade of this millennium, this team was thought of as a broom that had had several handles, with its new identity as Red Bull Racing still sitting uneasily. This, after all, was the third name under which it had raced in F1. However, the sponsorship from the energy drink manufacturer has remained firm and so the name has stuck. Better than that, it has four constructors' titles to its name, so it must have been doing something right.

In the late 1980s, Jackie Stewart and his elder son Paul decided to form their own team to help Paul go racing. He advanced and it grew, shining in F3 for many years and stepping up to the then level below F1: F3000. Paul then quit the cockpit and they elected to advance to the top step of racing's ladder, entering F1 as Stewart Grand Prix for 1997, with more than a little help from Ford. Rubens Barrichello bagged second at Monaco, but this was an unusual result.

By 1999, the team had gained form and Johnny Herbert delivered its first

win in a rain-affected European GP at the Nurburgring. Inspired by this, Ford pressed to buy out the Stewarts to use the team to add image to one of its premier brands: Jaguar.

THE POWER AND THE GLORY

CHRISTIAN HORNER
Many F1 fans will have no idea that Red Bull Racing's team principal was once a racer. Christian competed in Formula Renault, then F3, before stepping up to F3000 in 1997. He didn't win races, but his family team, Arden Motorsport, showed potential and Christian changed role to run other drivers, with Bjorn Wirdheim landing the team the 2003 F3000 title before Vitantonio Liuzzi repeated the feat. When Red Bull Racing was created from Jaguar Racing, Christian was given the helm and has been one of F1's top bosses ever since.

THERE OR THEREABOUTS, HOLDING ON
Last season won't go down as one of Red Bull's greatest years, as the engine development achieved by Ferrari and Mercedes left it in the shade. With their relationship having soured before it ended at season's close, Max Verstappen and Daniel Ricciardo were left to give chase and hope the top two teams stumbled. Ricciardo's win at Monaco, when short on power, was the highlight, but his name wasn't so rosy when he announced that he was joining Renault.

Remaining headquartered in Milton Keynes, the team's metallic green cars showed flashes of speed, most notably in the hands of Eddie Irvine, then Mark

2018 DRIVERS & RESULTS

Driver	Nationality	Races	Wins	Pts	Pos
Daniel Ricciardo	Australian	21	2	170	6th
Max Verstappen	Dutch	21	2	249	4th

FOR THE RECORD

Country of origin:	England
Team base:	Milton Keynes, England
Telephone:	44) 01908 279700
Website:	www.redbullracing.com
Active in Formula One:	As Stewart GP 1997-99, Jaguar Racing 2000-04, Red Bull Racing 2005 onwards
Grands Prix contested:	381
Wins:	59
Pole positions:	60
Fastest laps:	60

THE TEAM

Chairman:	Dietrich Mateschitz
Team principal:	Christian Horner
Chief technical officer:	Adrian Newey
Chief engineering officer:	Rob Marshall
Chief engineer, aerodynamics:	Dan Fallows
Chief engineer, car engineering:	Paul Monaghan
Chief engineer, performance engineering:	Pierre Wache
Team manager:	Jonathan Wheatley
Chief engineer:	Giullaume Roquelin
Test driver:	tba
Chassis:	Red Bull RB15
Engine:	Honda V6
Tyres:	Pirelli

Webber, but there was a rapid turnover of management as Ford's corporate people interfered. This all changed for 2005, though, when the team gained its third identity, painted in a new multi-coloured livery, as Red Bull Racing.

Better still, David Coulthard enticed F1's top designer Adrian Newey to follow him from McLaren for 2007.

One of the ideas behind the team was to be the pinnacle of a Red Bull-funded enterprise that developed the best young drivers and then chose the cream of the crop for its F1 team. The backing went down to the level of Formula Renault, but those thought not quite good enough were discarded quite brutally. However, Red Bull's scholarship produced some gems and a problem arose as the team became ever more competitive, the leap became too great for young drivers stepping up to F1. To get around this, Red Bull company co-founder Dietrich Mateschitz bought another F1 team, the former Minardi, and used it as the F1 starting point for its rising stars.

The most famous graduate from this was Sebastian Vettel, who was promoted for 2009, and he and team-mate Webber shone in the second half of the year as the team closed in on Brawn GP.

Red Bull Racing blossomed in 2010, with Webber and Vettel in the title hunt all the way to the final round, where Vettel came from behind to take the championship and the team the constructors' crown. Powered by Renault engines, this was the first of Vettel's four consecutive drivers' crowns and Red Bull Racing was riding high, but then the Mercedes charge began and the team has had to work ever harder just to stay in the hunt, always there or thereabouts, but seldom setting the absolute pace, particularly now that Ferrari's resurgence has made it competitive again.

In the past few years, in Daniel Ricciardo and Max Verstappen, it had grand prix winners, but beating Lewis Hamilton's Mercedes or Vettel's Ferrari has been generally a step too far, something that team principal Christian Horner has increasingly blamed on its Renault engines. The blame game hasn't worked, though, and the longstanding partnership has ended, to be replaced by a new engine deal with Honda.

"There's huge anticipation about the new partnership with Honda and integrating a new power unit into the car for the first time in a long time. Pierre went very well last year and deserves his opportunity here."
Christian Horner

Max Verstappen surprised everyone at the 2016 Spanish GP when he won on his debut.

MAX VERSTAPPEN

There was no escaping the fact that Red Bull Racing wasn't quite a match for Mercedes and Ferrari in 2018. This year, though, it will be pinning its hopes on Honda power, while Max is in the new position of being the clear team leader.

Few drivers have stepped up from karts to car racing with as many championship titles under their belt as Max, with the 2013 world crown the pick of the crop. However, few drivers have reached F1 without winning any car racing titles. Max didn't. Then again, he spent only one year in cars before reaching F1. Think about that, as it's mad. Yet, he has proved many times that he's more than good enough.

Max's single season of car racing before F1 was in F3, already a level higher than most karting stars chose for their step into cars. The year was 2014 and Max raced to third place in the European F3 Championship, taking 10 wins from 33 rounds when Esteban Ocon was cock of the roost.

With a former F1 racer, Jos, as his father and a mother who also came from a racing family, Max was never short of advice and he displayed uncanny raw speed.

Already backed by Red Bull, it came as no surprise that it found an F1 ride for him in 2015, with Scuderia Toro Rosso, and Max belied the fact that he had become F1's youngest driver, at 17, by collecting a pair of fourth places. This would have been fair with a top team, but Toro Rosso wasn't at that level.

Max showed last year that he is prepared to take no prisoners in his quest to be top.

Staying on with Toro Rosso in 2016, Max had to shift up a gear before the fifth round in Spain as Red Bull Racing swapped him with the underperforming Daniil Kvyat. In his first outing with Red Bull's senior team, Max only went and won ...

Ranked fifth at year's end thanks to bolstering that surprise win with four second-place finishes, Max has become a Red Bull Racing fixture and he doubled his 2016 win tally in 2017, triumphing in Malaysia and, most impressively, in Mexico. However, the Mercedes and Ferraris were just that little bit more competitive so Max and Daniel Ricciardo were heading for fifth and sixth places in the rankings - except for mishaps ahead of them - and it was the Australian who finished ahead.

TRACK NOTES

Nationality:	DUTCH
Born: 30 SEPTEMBER 1997, HASSELT, BELGIUM	
Website:	www.verstappen.nl
Teams:	TORO ROSSO 2015-16, RED BULL RACING 2016-19

CAREER RECORD

First Grand Prix:	2015 AUSTRALIAN GP
Grand Prix starts:	81
Grand Prix wins:	5
2016 Spanish GP, 2017 Malaysian GP, Mexican GP, 2018 Austrian GP, Mexican GP	
Poles:	0
Fastest laps:	4
Points:	670
Honours:	2013 WORLD & EUROPEAN KZ KART CHAMPION, 2012 WSK MASTER SERIES KF2 CHAMPION, 2011 WSK EURO SERIES CHAMPION, 2009 BELGIAN KF5 CHAMPION, 2008 DUTCH CADET KART CHAMPION, 2007 & 2008 DUTCH MINIMAX CHAMPION, 2006 BELGIAN ROTAX MINIMAX CHAMPION

STILL LEARNING HOW TO WIN A TITLE

Such was the explosion of Max onto the F1 scene that some thought that he might be World Champion by now. However, there is more to success than simply being blindingly fast and prepared to take risks to get to the front. There's the small matter of being in the most competitive car/engine combination. And, even though Red Bull Racing still builds great chassis, its TAG Heuer-badged Renault engine seemed to lose ground to the Ferrari and Mercedes units through 2018, making his push to be the best more of a challenge than it might have been. There were internal pressures, too, with a degree of friction growing between Max and team-mate Daniel Ricciardo. However, Max came on really strongly and showed race-winning pace again in Mexico and then in Brazil. Although, at the latter, he lost victory when he had an unfortunate collision when Esteban Ocon was attempting to unlap himself. He was furious but ought to have learnt from that experience.

PIERRE GASLY

Fourth place at last year's second grand prix, at Sakhir, was impossible for Red Bull Racing to ignore when it was forced to look for a replacement for Daniel Ricciardo. Expect this impressive French driver to step up to the mark.

Some drivers have that little bit of edge about them, that almost infinitesimal margin of superiority that ensures that when the going gets tough the tough get going. One look at this 22-year-old Frenchman's career record is proof that he is one such driver, as he has a string of single-seater titles to his name.

Finishing as runner-up in the European KF3 karting championship in 2010 showed that he could drive, but it was what happened when he reached car racing that showed that he was one to really watch. This didn't happen straight away, as Pierre's 10th place in the 2012 European Formula Renault series wasn't that impressive. Winning it the following year was, with regular rival Esteban Ocon third.

Red Bull signed Pierre up as one of its scholars and this enabled the driver from Normandy to bypass F3 and GP3 to move up to Formula Renault 3.5 in 2014. He starred in these more powerful cars, ending the year as runner-up to Carlos Sainz Jr.

After a trial season of GP2 with the DAMS team in 2015, and then a few F1 test runs, Pierre returned in 2016 and won the title – thanks to four victories for Prema

Pierre knows that he has been given his big break and expect him to push Max hard.

Racing – just outscoring Antonio Giovinazzi. However, there were no race seat openings in F1 and Red Bull decided that it would really be best for Pierre to keep racing rather than have him lose touch with his cutting edge by serving simply as a reserve

driver for its secondary F1 team: Scuderia Toro Rosso.

Instead, Red Bull entered him in Japan's Super Formula series and Pierre nearly did the unthinkable in beating the long-established regulars on circuits he'd never visited before.

The first potential fly in his ointment was a call-up from Toro Rosso to replace Daniil Kvyat. He impressed and there was a question-mark over whether he would race in the United States GP or go to the final Super Formula for a tilt at the crown. The latter was chosen, but the event was rained off, leaving him second at season's end.

TRACK NOTES

Nationality:	FRENCH
Born:	7 FEBRUARY 1996, ROUEN, FRANCE
Website:	www.pierregasly.com
Teams:	TORO ROSSO 2017-18,
	RED BULL RACING 2019

CAREER RECORD	
First Grand Prix:	2017 MALAYSIAN GP
Grand Prix starts:	26
Grand Prix wins:	0
	(best result: 4th, 2018 Bahrain GP)
Poles:	0
Fastest laps:	0
Points:	29
Honours:	2017 JAPANESE SUPER
	FORMULA RUNNER-UP, 2016 GP2 CHAMPION,
	2014 FORMULA RENAULT 3.5 RUNNER-UP, 2013
	EUROPEAN FORMULA RENAULT CHAMPION,
	2010 EUROPEAN KF3 KART RUNNER-UP

MAKING AN INSTANT IMPRESSION

With five grands prix under his belt with Toro Rosso in the latter stages of the 2017 World Championship, Pierre started his first full F1 campaign knowing a little of what to expect. However, no one would have predicted his remarkable performance in the second race of 2018, in Bahrain. On a day when one Ferrari and both Red Bulls failed to go the distance, he was best of the rest, finishing fourth. This was heady, especially as the team was using the Honda engines reviled by McLaren in 2017. Seventh place in Monaco also stood out, but sixth in the Hungarian GP was better still as he was again the best of the rest behind the top three teams on a day when Toro Rosso used a clever tyre strategy. Before the season's end, Pierre's promotion to one of these top three teams was accelerated by Daniel Ricciardo's shock decision not to remain with Red Bull Racing. Many has been the time a driver has had to wait too long to be promoted from Toro Rosso. Not this time.

RENAULT

Daniel Ricciardo has pinned his hopes on a move from Red Bull Racing to Renault to revive his career, confident that the team will continue to find its form. With Nico Hulkenberg in the other car, the team should go forward if the car proves competitive.

Nico Hulkenberg will have a challenge from within with the arrival of Daniel Ricciardo, but his fifth place in Germany showed he can fight.

Like Mercedes and Racing Point, this British team is one that has had many names across the decades. It started life as Toleman back in 1981 and has raced under three guises since, using the Renault name twice. To add to the confusion, when this team races in F1 as Renault, it has nothing to do with the French manufacturer's team that operated out of a French base from 1977 to 1985.

Toleman stepped up from running cars in junior single-seater categories to shine in F2. Having ranked first and second in F1's feeder formula in 1980, with Brian Henton beating Derek Warwick, team owner Ted Toleman gave the green light for a move up to F1.

This first campaign wasn't a success, but designer Rory Byrne produced ever more competitive chassis and the combination of Hart engines with an F1 rookie made the team shine in 1984, coming within a whisker of winning the Monaco GP. That rookie was Ayrton Senna. Sadly, he moved on to Lotus

and the team's form dipped.

It came back in 1986 under a new name, clothing manufacturer Benetton having bought the naming rights. Operating out of Enstone in Oxfordshire, it made giant strides when the cars were fitted with BMW engines – when turbocharged engines were at their most powerful - which helped

THE POWER AND THE GLORY

REMI TAFFIN
The man in charge of Renault's F1 engine programme joined Renault Sport back in 1999, looking after the engines for Arrows, BAR and Benetton as well as Renault's F1 outfit. A highlight has been engineering Fernando Alonso to the world title in both 2005 and 2006. Remi then took a more senior role and enjoyed assisting in Sebastian Vettel's run to four titles between 2010 and 2013. Then in 2015, Remi took charge of all the engineers at Viry-Chatillon to work in tandem with Nick Chester running the team's chassis programme.

A TEAM THAT'S REDISCOVERING ITS FORM
After a year of mixed results, Renault made solid strides back towards the front of the field last year. It had excellent drivers in Nico Hulkenberg and Carlos Sainz Jr, with both of them peaking with a fifth-place finish, effectively as high up as they could hope for against Mercedes, Ferrari and Red Bull Racing. Reliability woes were fewer than in 2017, but they continued to hamper the gathering of points, although the team still did enough to win the battle to end the year fourth overall.

2018 DRIVERS & RESULTS

Driver	Nationality	Races	Wins	Pts	Pos
Nico Hulkenberg	German	21	0	69	7th
Carlos Sainz Jr	Spanish	21	0	53	10th

FOR THE RECORD

Country of origin:	England
Team base:	Enstone, England
Telephone:	(44) 01608 678000
Website:	www.renaultsport.com
Active in Formula One:	As Toleman 1981-85, Benetton 1986-2000, Renault 2002-11 & 2016 onwards, Lotus 2012-15
Grands Prix contested:	634
Wins:	48
Pole positions:	34
Fastest laps:	54

THE TEAM

Managing director:	Cyril Abiteboul
President:	Jerome Stoll
Executive director:	Marcin Budkowski
Team chassis technical director:	Nick Chester
Team engine technical director:	Remi Taffin
Sporting director:	Alan Permane
Chief aerodynamicist:	Pete Machin
Operations director:	Rob White
Chief engineer:	Ciaron Pilbeam
Team manager:	Paul Seaby
Test driver:	tba
Chassis:	Renault RS19
Engine:	Renault V6
Tyres:	Pirelli

the team not just to flame-spitting pole laps but also to a first win, when Gerhard Berger took the chequered flag at the 1986 Mexican GP.

The biggest moment in Benetton's F1 history hinged on the signing of Michael Schumacher in 1991, after he'd made a surprise and very impressive F1 debut for Jordan. That was in the Belgian GP and, having moved fast, he was a Benetton driver for the next race, at Monza. It took him precisely one year to become a grand prix winner, at Spa-Francorchamps. Then, being armed with increasingly competitive machinery thanks to technical director Ross Brawn and design chief Byrne, Schumacher did just enough in 1994 to deny Williams's Damon Hill the drivers' title, although the team came under suspicion for having trick electronics to boost their getaways from the standing race starts, although it was never proved that the team had used them... Then, after changing from Ford engines to Renaults, Schumacher added the 1995 crown.

After Brawn, Byrne and Schumacher all headed to Ferrari, the team continued but no longer at the front of the field. Then, for 2002, it gained extra finance and, with it, a third name: Renault. Like with the signing of Schumacher, the promotion of Fernando Alonso from its test team for 2003 was pivotal. He scored his first win for the team that year, then won the drivers' title in both 2005 and 2006 to mark the end of Schumacher's title run. With team-mate Giancarlo Fisichella also winning races, Renault added constructors' series crowns in both seasons.

Alonso then left for a troubled year with McLaren, in which he ended up one point short of landing a third drivers' title before returning, as many of the team's longstanding technical staff have done across the decades, but the team had fallen down F1's pecking order and this was one of the reasons that its value seemed to plummet.

Thus arrived the team's fourth name when it was renamed Lotus for 2012. Like when this team assumed the Renault name in 2002, this had nothing to do with the original Lotus team from Norfolk, which was all a little unnecessarily confusing. It was, essentially, a branding exercise. With the team not firing on all cylinders, it took a reversion to the Renault name, and another welcome injection of cash from the French manufacturer, for the team to start its bounce back towards the top. With manufacturer interest increasing, that can only help its push to get into the top three.

> "Signing Daniel pushed the team on. It will help with development. It's a big deal to show everybody that Renault believes in us enough to get a top-line driver."
> **Nick Chester**

Ayrton Senna propelled Toleman to new heights in 1984 in the first of the team's iterations.

DANIEL RICCIARDO

Having felt increasingly that Red Bull Racing was favouring Max Verstappen over him, this popular Australian surprised the F1 paddock last summer when he declined to sign a contract extension and elected to join Renault instead.

Daniel's father was mad about racing, which explains why he was happy to travel considerable distances from Western Australia to take Daniel racing. First stop was the Asian Formula BMW series in 2006, with Sepang being as close as the east coast Australian tracks he'd have been racing on had he done an Australian series.

Next up was Formula Renault in Europe, with sixth in the 2007 Italian series earning the attention of Red Bull's talent scouts. Picked as a rising star, Daniel finished second in the European series in 2008, pipped by Valtteri Bottas.

Daniel joined Carlin for 2009 and blitzed the British F3 championship. He then stepped up to Formula Renault 3.5 for 2010 and ended the year as runner-up. Having returned in 2011, Daniel's year took a twist midseason when Narain Karthikeyan left struggling HRT and Red Bull pushed him through the door into F1 as his replacement.

Red Bull placed him with Scuderia Toro Rosso for 2012. In 2013, the race was on to see whether he or team-mate Jean-Eric Vergne might be promoted to Red Bull Racing to fill the seat vacated by Mark

Daniel is hoping to find more support from Renault than he did during 2018 at Red Bull.

Webber, and it was Daniel who won.

That Daniel then outscored Sebastian Vettel in 2014, helped by winning in Canada, Hungary and Belgium, was a massive feather in his hat. Then, when the

four-time World Champion left for Ferrari in 2015, Daniel became team leader, but it was a difficult year and he was pipped on points by his new team-mate Daniil Kvyat.

Things went far better in 2016, but a new thorn in his side arrived at the Spanish GP: Max Verstappen. The Dutch teenager stepped up from Toro Rosso and won first time out. Over the course of the year, Daniel finished ahead and matched his 2014 feat of ranking third overall. He finished ahead of him again in 2017, but the pressure was on.

TRACK NOTES

Nationality:	AUSTRALIAN
Born:	1 JULY 1989, PERTH, AUSTRALIA
Website:	www.danielricciardo.com
Teams:	HRT 2011, TORO ROSSO 2012-13, RED BULL RACING 2014-18, RENAULT 2019

CAREER RECORD

First Grand Prix:	2011 BRITISH GP
Grand Prix starts:	150
Grand Prix wins:	7
2014 Canadian GP, Hungarian GP, Belgian GP, 2016 Malaysian GP, 2017 Azerbaijan GP, 2018 Chinese GP, Monaco GP	
Poles:	3
Fastest laps:	13
Points:	986
Honours:	2010 FORMULA RENAULT 3.5 RUNNER-UP, 2009 BRITISH FORMULA THREE CHAMPION, 2008 EUROPEAN FORMULA RENAULT RUNNER-UP & WESTERN EUROPEAN FORMULA RENAULT CHAMPION

A YEAR OF FEELING UNLOVED

Perception can be based on facts or hunches, or both, and it was something that played on Daniel's mind last year. He felt that Red Bull Racing was favouring team-mate Max Verstappen. Occasions like the Azerbaijan GP when they clashed and the team blamed him despite the race officials reckoning both were to blame. Yet, it was thought that this could be ironed out and a new contract signed for 2019. Then Daniel caught everyone off guard last August by announcing that he was leaving to join Renault. It might have been the kneejerk reaction of a driver who, at that point, had won two races to Max's one or it might have been carefully thought through. What made the fact that all was other than sweetness and light somewhat perplexing was that Daniel had put in some blinding performances and his overtaking was second to none. The race that drew the most praise was the Monaco GP, not just because he won it, but because he won it despite having to nurse a car that was down by 160bhp for the last 50 laps as its MGU-K had failed.

NICO HULKENBERG

Last year was a good second campaign with Renault for Nico and he probably had done enough to establish himself as team leader. However, the applecart was upset when Daniel Ricciardo announced that he was joining the team for 2019.

F1 fans can enjoy their viewing much more if they watch the junior single-seater formulae. It allows them the chance to pick out stars who may break into F1 in the years ahead and also gives an insight into their personalities. Nico is the sort of driver who'd have been easy to identify as a perennial winner.

German junior and senior karting titles were his calling card, and he delivered on that when he advanced to cars. Eight wins in his debut season landed Nico the 2005 German Formula BMW title. Fifth place in German F3 in 2006 might not sound much, but he was in an unfancied chassis and showed that he was the real deal when he topped the times at an A1GP test then delivered Germany the 2006-07 title.

Third in European F3 in 2007, he was champion in 2008, scoring almost twice as many points as his closest rival. Nico then trashed the idea that GP2 needs to be a two-year programme by landing the title at his first attempt.

This earned him an F1 ride for 2010, with Williams no less. Points were hard to come by, but Nico took pole in Brazil. Dropped for 2011,

Nico has a new yardstick to compare himself against with the arrival of Daniel Ricciardo.

when Pastor Maldonado's money bought the seat, he was back in 2012, with Force India. A year spent with Sauber followed, but Nico rejoined Force India in 2014 and ranked ninth

overall, a feat he matched in 2016. Anxious to join a works team, Nico moved to Renault in 2017.

For a driver of Nico's talent, not winning races has been wearing. So, he jumped at the chance to have a tilt at something else in 2015: the Le Mans 24 Hours. Porsche was delighted to welcome him to its fold and he came away with the top prize after winning with Earl Bamber and Nick Tandy. His F1 rivals were impressed at the adulation, and Fernando Alonso certainly took note.

TRACK NOTES

Nationality:	GERMAN
Born:	19 AUGUST 1987, EMMERICH, GERMANY
Website:	www.nicohulkenberg.net
Teams:	WILLIAMS 2010, FORCE INDIA 2012 & 2014-16, SAUBER 2013, RENAULT 2017-19

CAREER RECORD

First Grand Prix:	2010 BAHRAIN GP
Grand Prix starts:	158
Grand Prix wins:	0 (best result: 4th, 2012 Belgian GP, 2013 Korean GP, 2016 Belgian GP)
Poles:	1
Fastest laps:	2
Points:	474
Honours:	2015 LE MANS 24 HOURS WINNER, 2009 GP2 CHAMPION, 2008 EUROPEAN F3 CHAMPION, 2007 F3 MASTERS WINNER, 2006/07 A1GP CHAMPION, 2005 GERMAN FORMULA BMW ADAC CHAMPION, 2003 GERMAN KART CHAMPION, 2002 JUNIOR KART CHAMPION, 2003 GERMAN KART CHAMPION, 2002 JUNIOR KART CHAMPION

A YEAR OF HIGHS WITH A FEW LOWS

A run that included a seventh place then a pair of sixth place finishes was a great start to last year's championship, with the tall German marking himself out as the best of the rest as he kicked off his second season for Renault. That is to say that he was proving himself to be the best of the drivers not armed with a Mercedes, Ferrari or Red Bull. Other strong results followed through the course of the season, but there were quite a few retirements too, which was frustrating. However, Nico remained as the dominant force in the team, managing usually to keep Carlos Sainz Jr in check. Another reminder of Nico's speed was when he finished in fifth place in his home grand prix at Hockenheim. However, he then blotted his copybook by slamming into Fernando Alonso's McLaren at the first corner of the Belgian GP, with his 10-place grid penalty for the next race making it a double whammy. Two sixth place finishes in the United States and Mexican GPs gave Nico a late-season boost, but he will have spent the winter aware that his team-mate for 2019 has done something he hasn't: won a grand prix.

There is no doubting which country turns out in the most force to support one of its own: the Netherlands, with the orange army applauding Max Verstappen's every move.

HAAS F1

This American team looks ever more solid since it made its sensational dive into the F1 pond in 2016 by scoring points on its debut, with its continuity of drivers for a third year sure to boost its hopes of podium finishes with its Ferrari engines.

Last year's Austrian GP was a highlight as Romain Grosjean and Kevin Magnussen came fourth and fifth. They are team-mates again in 2019.

Getting into Formula 1 is no insignificant feat, but staying there is. Gene Haas didn't take the risks required to cross motor racing cultures from NASCAR into motor racing's top category just to get in to stay there. He made the leap with the aim of winning. This hasn't happened yet and may never happen, but his team is now healthily in the midfield, scoring points at roughly every second race. So, it's a success, and one that is all the more remarkable as most insiders reckoned that his bid would fall flat on its face.

Gene is an engineer by training and made a considerable fortune from his machine tool manufacturing company. To promote it across the United States, he took to running a NASCAR team. Starting in a small way in 2002, it began to do acceptably well. However, it took until joining forces with top racer Tony Stewart's team, as Stewart-Haas Racing, at the end of 2008 for the wins to start to flow before Stewart landed the team the 2011 title. Last year's team - comprising Kevin Harvick, Aric Almirola, Kurt Busch and Clint Bowyer - was right at the front end of the NASCAR field, running Ford Fusions.

Buoyed by the success not just in sporting terms but also in marketing terms, Haas began to look to F1 to spread the Haas Automation brand worldwide. In 2014, he

THE POWER AND THE GLORY

GUNTHER STEINER

The name is Germanic, but Gunther is Italian, and he has spent life criss-crossing the globe working in racing. He worked as an engineer on Mazda's World Rally Championship programme in the late 1980s, then joined Jolly Club and Prodrive before becoming technical director of M-Sport. Then F1 beckoned and Gunther joined Jaguar Racing in 2001, then went back in 2006 after it became Red Bull before basing himself in the US where he built a composites company until he and Haas decided to join forces to form Haas F1.

FERRARI POWER PROPELS TEAM TO FIFTH

Ferrari's engine was a fabulous unit in 2018 and it gave Haas F1 the opportunity to run closer to the front than before. With the budgets of F1's leading three teams being so much larger, it meant aiming to be the best of the rest. While qualifying tended to be a strong point, Haas's strategy wasn't always an asset. When it could keep its tyres sweet, Romain Grosjean and Kevin Magnussen achieved great results, such as Romain's fourth in Austria and Kevin's two fifths.

2018 DRIVERS & RESULTS

Driver	Nationality	Races	Wins	Pts	Pos
Romain Grosjean	French	21	0	37	14th
Kevin Magnussen	Danish	21	0	56	9th

FOR THE RECORD

Country of origin:	USA
Team bases:	Kannapolis, NC, USA & Banbury, England
Telephone:	(1) 704 652 4227
Website:	www.haasf1team.com
Active in Formula One:	From 2016
Grands Prix contested:	62
Wins:	0
Pole positions:	0
Fastest laps:	1

THE TEAM

Team owner:	Gene Haas
Team principal:	Gunther Steiner
Chief operating officer:	Joe Custer
Technical director:	Rob Taylor
Vice-president of technology:	Matt Borland
Team manager:	Dave O'Neill
Chief aerodynamicist:	Ben Agathangelou
Group leader aerodynamicist:	
	Christian Cattaneo
Head of logistics:	Peter Crolla
Chief engineer:	Ayao Komatsu
Test driver:	Pietro Fittipaldi
Chassis:	Ferrari VF-19
Engine:	Honda V6
Tyres:	Pirelli

applied for a licence to join F1. The plan was to run the team from a building alongside the one from which Stewart-Haas Racing operates at Kannapolis, North Carolina. That set F1's insiders talking, as no team from outside F1's European heartland had ever worked in F1 before and certainly not one based in the USA.

Yet, Haas employed former Jaguar Racing F1 technical chief Gunther Steiner and said that the team would have a European base to operate from during the Euro-centric middle part of the campaign. Best of all, though, Haas F1 would be using Ferrari engines fitted to the back of chassis designed by Dallara. This meant the team wouldn't spend its learning year in F1, 2016, sorting technical problems of its own making.

Still, not much was expected, so everyone was caught out when Romain Grosjean finished sixth on the team's first outing, then fifth on its second. Points were harder to come by after that, but the team was seen to be doing things sensibly and not making novice errors as it claimed eighth place in the constructors' end-of-season rankings.

Grosjean was joined by Kevin Magnussen for 2017, in place of Esteban Gutierrez, and the pair consistently finished in the minor points-scoring positions as Haas F1 again ranked eighth overall. That might be seen as a lack of progress over its first World Championship campaign, but as this was its first year using a car of its own design, it wasn't. In fact, preserving position tends to be something of an achievement, as incoming F1 teams have far longer to focus on their first campaign than they do on their second and so many drop down the rankings in their second year.

There was pressure on Haas from America's race fans and media to insert a driver of their own to give the team a more American image, but Gene and Gunther have resisted this so far, indeed having elected to keep Grosjean and Magnussen together for a third season. In time, though, if a suitably competitive American driver can be found, you can be sure that Haas certainly won't turn his back on the publicity that this would bring. Such a move, though, would never come at the expense of potentially collecting fewer of the prized championship points that dictate how much prize money the team would receive at season's end; he's too much of a businessman for that.

First F1 race, first points for Romain Grosjean and Gene Haas on the team's debut in 2016.

"It's not a coincidence that in their second year as team-mates that Haas F1 had its best year. So, by keeping Romain [Grosjean] and Kevin [Magnussen] together, we aim to do even better in 2019." **Gunther Steiner**

KEVIN MAGNUSSEN

He started last year on an equal footing with Romain Grosjean at Haas F1, but rose to become the de facto team leader and won many new fans with his no nonsense approach. Expect even more steps forward in the season ahead.

Perhaps it's because his father Jan was a racer of repute, and because he was brought up around the racing scene, but Kevin has a way deeper love of racing than most second-generation drivers. He just wants to get out there and drive and doesn't care for the fripperies.

His success started early, as he stepped up from karts to cars when he was 15, winning the 2008 Danish Formula Ford series in a year of double success for the family as his father won the GT1 category of the American Le Mans Series for Corvette.

Formula Renault came next and Kevin was ninth in the European series and runner-up in the Western Europe Cup but decided that he was ready to move on. So it was F3 in 2010, and he ranked third in Germany before he went on to Jan's most famous stamping ground: British F3. Kevin didn't take the title with 14 wins from 18 races, as his father had, but he finished second behind Felipe Nasr.

The next step up was to Formula Renault 3.5 and he won the title at his second attempt, ending the 2013 season easily ahead of Stoffel Vandoorne.

Kevin continues to be good for points when his car is competitive enough.

Having had several test outings for McLaren, Kevin felt ready for F1 and McLaren agreed, making him Jenson Button's team-mate in 2014. He shocked everyone by finishing second on his debut in Australia, but this was the first race for a raft of new technical rules and when the season settled down he could rank only 11th overall.

When Honda and Fernando Alonso arrived in 2015, Kevin dropped back to being a test driver. However, Renault snapped him up for 2016, but the team was in turmoil and could offer him only a one-year deal, so he was delighted to join Haas F1 in 2017 and he hasn't looked back since. As Haas F1 gets ever stronger with Ferrari engines and assistance, so does Kevin. Whereas Jan was silky smooth and very fast, Kevin is rapid but aggressive too, and his results are getting ever better.

TRACK NOTES

Nationality:	DANISH
Born:	5 OCTOBER 1992, ROSKILDE, DENMARK
Website:	www.kevinmagnussen.com
Teams:	McLAREN 2014, RENAULT 2016, HAAS F1 2017-19

CAREER RECORD

First Grand Prix:	2014 AUSTRALIAN GP
Grand Prix starts:	82
Grand Prix wins:	0 (best result: 2nd, 2014 Australian GP)
Poles:	0
Fastest laps:	1
Points:	137

Honours: 2013 FORMULA RENAULT 3.5 CHAMPION, 2011 BRITISH FORMULA THREE RUNNER-UP, 2009 FORMULA RENAULT NORTHERN EUROPE RUNNER-UP, 2008 DANISH FORMULA FORD CHAMPION

A RACER WITH OLD SCHOOL STYLE

Kevin is not a driver to be pushed around and his no holds barred approach reaped dividends last year as he continued to give 100 percent at all times, something that you need to do when you're racing in F1's midfield, fighting for every position. He was no doubt helped by the Haas F1 team's ever improving level of competitiveness. Fifth place at the season's second round, in Bahrain, was a huge fillip, then Kevin added a pair of sixth-place finishes in the Spanish and French GPs before taking a second fifth place at the Red Bull Ring. Any finish higher than this required several of the runners from the top three teams – Mercedes, Ferrari and Red Bull Racing – not to finish. All Kevin could keep doing was to qualify as high up the grid as he could and then go for it. Which, of course, he did. He and team-mate Romain Grosjean enjoyed a healthy level of intra-team competitiveness, but the points margin between them showed how Kevin gradually pulled ahead across the 21-round season to reverse their finishing order at the end of 2017.

ROMAIN GROSJEAN

It seems incredible that it was as long ago as 2009 that Romain made his F1 debut as he still makes occasional errors to undo his good work. Yet, and no one can deny this, he can be one of the quickest drivers when he's in the mood.

In the year that Lewis Hamilton won the European F3 Championship, Romain won the French Formula Renault title. That was in 2005 and two years later, by which time Lewis was tilting for the F1 title in his first season with McLaren, Romain was following in his wheeltracks by winning that same European F3 crown.

However, Romain didn't quite make the same rapid steps to the big time. He too stepped up to GP2 but, unlike Lewis, didn't win the title at his first attempt. Instead, he ranked fourth so returned for a second crack. Yet, suddenly, he was given his F1 shot towards the end of 2009 when Nelson Piquet Jr was dropped by the Renault team for his part in fixing the outcome of the previous year's Singapore GP.

Sadly, this golden opportunity didn't work for Romain and it took until 2012 for him to be offered another shot at F1, after he had taken the brave step to go back to GP2 in 2011. He had to win the title and did.

Romain's second shot at F1 came with Lotus, which was the same team as he had raced for before, simply running under a different name. His speed was clear for all

Romain is now one of F1's elder statesmen, but it's a long time since his last podium.

to see, but so were the accidents as he took too many risks. The other drivers felt concerned when he was around them. Yet, a second and two thirds helped him to rank eighth. Romain then cemented that

form by ranking one place higher in 2013.

The 2014 and 2015 seasons proved to be more difficult as the team lost form, so the announcement of an all-new team for 2016 gave Romain a new opportunity. This was the Haas F1 team and he's been with the American outfit ever since. The start of 2016 could not have been much more of a fairytale as he scored points first time out, finishing sixth in Australia, and then again at the second race. Since then, the flashes of speed have been part of his make-up, along with occasional brain fade.

TRACK NOTES

Nationality:	FRENCH
Born:	17 APRIL 1986, GENEVA, SWITZERLAND
Website:	www.romaingrosjean.com
Teams:	RENAULT 2009, LOTUS 2012-15, HAAS F1 2016-19

CAREER RECORD	
First Grand Prix:	2009 EUROPEAN GP
Grand Prix starts:	145
Grand Prix wins:	0 (best result: 2nd, 2012 Canadian GP, 2013 United States GP)
Poles:	0
Fastest laps:	1
Points:	381
Honours:	2012 RACE OF CHAMPIONS CHAMPION, 2011 GP2 CHAMPION, 2010 AUTO GT CHAMPION, 2008 & 2011 GP2 ASIA CHAMPION, 2007 FORMULA THREE EUROSERIES CHAMPION, 2005 FRENCH FORMULA RENAULT CHAMPION, 2003 SWISS FORMULA RENAULT 1600 CHAMPION

SCORING A MOUNTAINOUS HIGH

Fourth place in the Austrian GP at the lofty Red Bull Ring proved to be the high point of a mixed third season with Haas F1. Certainly, Ferrari's power unit was more competitive than before, and this really put the Haas F1 drivers up among lofty company, especially in qualifying. All too often, however, there would be reasons why points got away, with the spectre of driver penalties hanging ever more ominously over Romain's head. After the Singapore GP, he knew that one more penalty would lead to a one-race ban. There was a time midway through the season when team-mate Kevin Magnussen assumed the upper hand, but then Romain would respond with a performance from the top drawer. Yet, the suggestion that he still struggles to keep his emotions in check rose again when he was heard race after race complaining about things over the radio, making some question his focus. He would do himself a favour if he learnt to keep those reactions to himself and just let his driving do the talking.

McLAREN

The excuse had been that the team had been held back by Honda engines, but last year's switch to Renault power brought no real improvements, making it hard to relate the current team to the one that was a class leader a dozen years ago.

Fernando Alonso drove hard for few results, but this year there's a new line-up as Carlos Sainz Jr is joined by rookie Lando Norris.

Bruce McLaren was a racer, an engineer, a motivator and a man of vision, but it was after his death in an accident at Goodwood in 1970 that the team took off. The result was eight constructors' titles and 12 drivers' titles up to Lewis Hamilton's success in 2008. For a spell, it was right with Ferrari at the top of the all-time F1 wins lists, but those days now seem a long time ago. Yes, McLaren makes astonishingly good supercars for the road and track, but its racing side has gone off the boil.

Bruce was a make-do-and-mend racer in the 1950s, as all New Zealanders had to be as they were so far from suppliers of spare parts. He was quick, too, and was rewarded with passage to Europe to progress. After winning grands prix for Cooper, he followed Jack Brabham's lead and built his own racing cars. After introducing his first F1 car in 1966, others followed, all financed by the marque's considerable success in the CanAm sportscar arena. The first win, taken by Bruce, came in 1968.

However, it took the combination of the creation of the M23 chassis and the arrival of Emerson Fittipaldi in 1974 to give the team its first drivers' and constructors' titles, with James Hunt becoming champion two years later.

The team's greatest days came after Ron Dennis took over the helm and not only did

THE POWER AND THE GLORY

GIL DE FERRAN
This effervescent yet cerebral Brazilian could be the man to help McLaren to rediscover its mojo as he has experience both behind the wheel and from a management perspective. He came up to Europe to race in Formula Ford. After becoming British F3 champion in 1992, he was a winner in F3000, but didn't get his F1 break, so headed to Indycars and became champion for Penske in 2000 and 2001, winning the Indy 500 in 2003. Gil joined Honda's F1 team as sporting director in 2005, but left in 2007 and ran his own sportscar team.

NOT QUITE THE TURNAROUND EXPECTED
The best that McLaren could aspire to in its first year with Renault engines was to finish next after the top three teams, yet this was seldom achieved, despite Fernando Alonso's efforts. Thus, it was no surprise that the axe was wielded. Technical director Tim Goss was ousted in April. Last summer, race director Eric Boullier resigned, with Gil de Ferran becoming sporting director, James Key technical director and Pat Fry director of engineering.

2018 DRIVERS & RESULTS

Driver	Nationality	Races	Wins	Pts	Pos
Fernando Alonso	Spanish	21	0	50	11th
Stoffel Vandoorne	Belgian	21	0	12	16th

FOR THE RECORD

Country of origin:	England
Team base:	Woking, England
Telephone:	(44) 01483 261900
Website:	www.mclaren.com
Active in Formula One:	From 1966
Grands Prix contested:	843
Wins:	181
Pole positions:	154
Fastest laps:	154

THE TEAM

Executive director:	Zak Brown
Chief operating officer, McLaren Group:	
	Jonathan Neale
Chief operating officer, McLaren Racing:	
	Simon Roberts
Technical director:	James Key
Performance director:	Andrea Stella
Sporting director:	Gil de Ferran
Director of design & development:	
	Neil Oatley
Operations director:	Simon Roberts
Director of engineering:	Pat Fry
Chief engineer, aerodynamics:	
	Peter Prodromou
Chief aerodynamicist:	Marianne Hinson
Team manager:	Paul James
Test driver:	Oliver Turvey
Chassis:	McLaren MCL34
Engine:	Renault V6
Tyres:	Pirelli

he get multiple champion Niki Lauda and hotshot Alain Prost to drive his cars, but he got the TAG group to fund their engines. The result was two title doubles in 1984 and 1985, with Prost drivers' champion again in 1986.

The greatest years came from 1988 when Ayrton Senna joined as Prost's team-mate. Their relationship was explosive, but having the two fastest drivers in the fastest car - the Honda-powered MP4/4 - meant 15 wins from 16 grands prix that year. Senna took the title, then it was Prost's turn in 1989 before he moved to Ferrari and left the way clear for Senna for the next two campaigns. It was hard to imagine anyone touching the red and white McLarens, the fastest cars prepared by F1's most meticulous team. But nothing stands still forever, and Williams dominated in 1992, then Honda withdrew at the end of that year, leaving McLaren to make do with less competitive Ford engines.

Key to McLaren's next great age was forming a partnership with Mercedes. This took a few years to gel, but Mika Hakkinen and David Coulthard enjoyed 1998 and 1999 very much in the now silver-liveried McLarens as the Finn took two titles. Chief designer Adrian Newey deserves a major share of the plaudits.

Always there or thereabouts through the next decade, either Fernando Alonso or rookie team-mate Lewis Hamilton could have won the 2007 crown, but they both fell a point short and let former McLaren racer Kimi Raikkonen win for Ferrari. Then Hamilton landed his first and the team's most recent title the following year.

Since then, McLaren gradually lost ground as the Mercedes team dominated.

There was hope that starting a second spell with Honda as engine supplier would take the team back to the top, especially with Alonso back as team leader, but this turned out not to be the case. Although much of the blame was on Honda not getting to grips with the new rules, Dennis's leadership was lacking, as he'd concentrated so much of his focus for a decade on building the exquisite McLaren Technical Centre. It's a beautiful work of architecture, but it would be far more attractive to F1 folk if it was the home of a team good enough to win races again.

It was all smiles in 2007 as Alonso was joined by Hamilton, but things became fraught.

"We have to be careful that we don't set the bar so high for Lando that by FP1 in Australia we have all come to conclusions about whether he is the next superstar or not." **Zak Brown**

McLaren has replaced one Spanish driver with another, with Carlos moving across from Renault to take the McLaren seat vacated by compatriot Fernando Alonso. On last year's form, it's hard to tell whether this will be a step forward or back.

Carlos Jr is a driver who has always shown a good turn of speed. He reached F1 by 20, and is now set for his fifth year at the sport's most senior category but he has yet to find a regular home. Indeed, his move to McLaren for 2019 makes it the Spaniard's third team at this level.

With a multiple World Rally Champion as a father, it might have been expected that Carlos Jr would follow in his dust storm. However, it was clear from early on that tarmac was more his taste than gravel or snow. Thus Carlos Jr's first celebrations in Monaco were not for emulating his father's wins on the Monte Carlo Rally but for winning the Monaco Kart Cup in 2009.

He enjoyed a strong maiden season of car racing, ranking fourth in the 2010 European Formula BMW series. Then Red Bull made Carlos Jr one of its junior stars for a season of European Formula Renault. Second place in that pleased them and Carlos Jr added 10 victories to win the lesser Northern European series.

Formula 3 beckoned for 2012 and Carlos Jr ranked fifth, but matters became less rosy in 2013 when he was classified only 10th in GP3. This would have him worried

Carlos Jr arrives from Renault to take over as team leader from fellow Spaniard Alonso.

about keeping his Red Bull backing, but he tried Formula Renault 3.5 and felt comfortable in these more powerful cars so he raced them in 2014 and blossomed, winning seven races en route to the title.

Red Bull gave him his F1 break with

Scuderia Toro Rosso in 2015. Fifteenth was followed by 12th in 2016, including three sixth places. Carlos Jr might have thought that this would earn him promotion to Red Bull Racing, but Daniil Kvyat's poor form for the senior team had opened the door for his team-mate Max Verstappen to beat him to it.

In 2017, Carlos Jr raced to fourth at Sepang, but there appeared to be no likelihood of an opening at Red Bull Racing for 2018. Luckily, Renault decided on a late-season driver change and he at least stepped up to a team further up the grid.

TRACK NOTES

Nationality:	SPANISH
Born:	1 SEPTEMBER 1994, MADRID, SPAIN
Website:	www.carlossainzjr.com
Teams:	TORO ROSSO 2015-17,
	RENAULT 2017-18, McLAREN 2019

CAREER RECORD	
First Grand Prix:	2015 AUSTRALIAN GP
Grand Prix starts:	81
Grand Prix wins:	0 (best result: 4th,
	2017 Singapore GP)
Poles:	0
Fastest laps:	0
Points:	171
Honours:	2014 FORMULA RENAULT 3.5
	CHAMPION, 2011 EUROPEAN FORMULA
	RENAULT RUNNER-UP & NORTHERN
	EUROPEAN FORMULA RENAULT CHAMPION,
	2009 MONACO KART CUP WINNER, 2008
	ASIA/PACIFIC JUNIOR KART CHAMPION, 2006
	MADRID CADET KART CHAMPION

PUSHING HULKENBERG HARD

When Carlos Jr moved from Scuderia Toro Rosso to Renault to take over from Jolyon Palmer for the final four rounds of 2017, he might have thought that this was a golden opportunity to become a team leader at last. However, in those grands prix and the 21 that followed through 2018, the Spanish racer has found Nico Hulkenberg a harder nut to crack than he might have expected. Fifth place at the Azerbaijan GP early in the championship was encouraging, but that was a race of relatively high attrition among the frontrunning drivers. There were other races that could have yielded similar results, most notably when he was denied a likely sixth place in the French GP by MGU-K failure. That said, Carlos Jr's German team-mate also suffered mechanical reliability failures but did end the year ahead on points. So, perhaps Fernando Alonso's decision to take a break from F1 has come to his rescue as he moves away from Renault and tries to establish himself as McLaren's team leader.

Some names are up in lights from their early days and Lando's form in kart racing was so exceptionally good that he was tipped for the very top. McLaren paid attention, took him under its wing and is now taking the 19-year-old to F1.

Look at video footage of Lando when he started to make a name for himself and two things stand out. The first was his pure speed and ability in traffic. The second was that he was smaller even than the standard, jockey-sized karting hopeful. He's still not a giant, but he's in F1, so he must have been doing something right...

The key to Lando's progress has been firm family support through karting and then a massive helping hand from McLaren after it spotted his potential.

Having been a European junior karting champion at the age of 13, when he ranked fourth in the world junior series, Lando became a full world kart champion the following year, 2014. However, he also developed car racing awareness in 2014 by competing in the Ginetta Junior series, taking to these small sportscars with enough aplomb to rank third overall.

It was all cars from then on for Lando, as he stormed to eight wins and the MSA Formula single-seater category in 2015, also racing in F4 to gain more experience.

Having turned 16 just before the start of the season in early 2016, Lando headed down to contest the Formula Toyota Series

Lando has been under McLaren's tutelage for a few years and must grab his chance.

in New Zealand and kept his momentum by winning that, then returning home and winning the European Formula Renault title.

Always looking ahead, Lando tried a few F3 outings in 2016 in preparation for a full assault in 2017, and this worked as nine

wins with Carlin made him a clear European champion and he also tried a couple of F2 races to gear himself for his 2018 campaign.

At the end of 2016, Lando won the coveted McLaren Autosport BRDC Award for young drivers and shone on the F1 test with McLaren that was part of its prize, encouraging the team to give him some Friday F1 practice outings through last year; that helped cement his race seat for 2019 once it was clear that team lead driver Fernando Alonso would be taking time out from F1.

TRACK NOTES

Nationality:	BRITISH
Born:	13 NOVEMBER 1999, GLASTONBURY, ENGLAND
Website:	www.landonorris.com
Team:	McLAREN 2019

CAREER RECORD	
First Grand Prix:	2019 Australian GP
Grand Prix starts:	0
Grand Prix wins:	0
Poles:	0
Fastest laps:	0
Points:	0
Honours:	2018 F2 RUNNER-UP, 2017 EUROPEAN F3 CHAMPION, 2016 EUROPEAN FORMULA RENAULT CHAMPION & FORMULA RENAULT NEC CHAMPION & TOYOTA RACING SERIES CHAMPION, 2015 MSA FORMULA CHAMPION, 2014 WORLD KF KART CHAMPION, 2013 EUROPEAN KF KART CHAMPION & KF JUNIOR SUPER CUP WINNER

A TALE OF BATTLING BRITS

The 2018 FIA F2 Championship was one of fierce contest between the best young drivers beneath F1 and it was a battlefield full of British talent. The chief jousting was between Lando and George Russell, but Alexander Albon and Jack Aitken were in the mix too, with all of them winning races. Lando was competing for Carlin, the team with which he'd made his first steps in single-seaters in 2015 and then won the European F3 crown in 2017. He started the year in a style that suggested he might be heading for his fifth single-seater title in four years, by winning the opening race at Sakhir from pole. Since then, though, there were podium results galore but no further wins. From the Belgian GP on, though, Lando was honoured to be given the Friday morning practice session at grands prix, and it was after the second of these that it was announced that he rather than Stoffel Vandoorne would be filling McLaren's second race seat for 2019.

RACING POINT*

The new owners of the team that was Force India, now Racing Point, will bring not just welcome stability but also the extra backing that this fine midfield team requires to keep it batting above its weight as it returns with its fifth identity.

The team's greatest result in recent years came on the streets of Baku last year when Sergio Perez finished third, a result he'll aim for again.

Eddie Jordan was a racer who dreamt of the big time, but was never blessed with quite enough talent or enough cash to take himself to a top team. So, at the start of the 1980s, after giving F2 a brief go, he turned to running cars for others. Famously, Martin Brundle very nearly overhauled Ayrton Senna in an epic battle for the 1983 British F3 Championship in one of his cars.

Eddie Jordan Racing then moved up to F3000 and enjoyed great success with Johnny Herbert and Martin Donnelly, before Jean Alesi landed the title for the team in 1989. This gave EJ ambitions of moving on to F1 and these were realised when he found the money to do so in 1991.

The team's first F1 car was designed by Gary Anderson and it was clearly spot-on from the start, pushing for podium results and ending the team's first year in the big time, ranked fifth overall. However, landing the money to keep going and factor in the required development was a major struggle, with some engine deals being done for the sake of expediency rather than for outright performance, like its one with Yamaha for 1992.

This hurt Jordan's chances, but Eddie always kept an eye on up and coming talent and found two gems in Rubens Barrichello and Eddie Irvine who pushed the team as far forward as it would go over the next

THE POWER AND THE GLORY

LAWRENCE STROLL
This self-made Canadian businessman loves cars and loves racing, owning a string of Ferraris and even the former home of the Canadian GP – Mont Tremblant in Quebec – thanks to the fortune he made from bringing the Pierre Cardin, Ralph Lauren and Tommy Hilfiger fashion labels to Canada. He raced a Ferrari, then oversaw son Lance's rise through karting and single-seaters to reach F1 by the time he was 18. Having bought a share in Williams, he then headed the consortium that took over the Force India team last summer.

CHANGING NAME AND MAYBE FORTUNES
Team owner Vijay Mallya spent the first half of 2018 embroiled in financial investigations before selling the team to a consortium led by Lawrence Stroll. Then, with the deal being approved, the team was forced to drop all its points from before the Belgian GP, tipping it from sixth overall to last, in order to be allowed to change its name for 2019. Yet, so good was Sergio Perez and Esteban Ocon's form that it bounced back to seventh place by the end of the season.

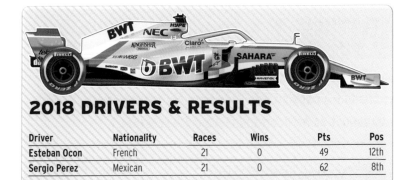

2018 DRIVERS & RESULTS

Driver	Nationality	Races	Wins	Pts	Pos
Esteban Ocon	French	21	0	49	12th
Sergio Perez	Mexican	21	0	62	8th

FOR THE RECORD

Country of origin:	England
Team base:	Silverstone, England
Telephone:	(44) 01327 850800
Website:	www.forceindiaf1.com
Active in Formula One:	As Jordan 1991-2004, Midland 2005-06, Spyker 2007, Force India 2008-18, Racing Point 2019
Grands Prix contested:	497
Wins:	4
Pole positions:	3
Fastest laps:	7

THE TEAM

Team principal:	Otmar Szafnauer
Technical director:	Andrew Green
Sporting director:	Andy Stevenson
Production director:	Bob Halliwell
Chief designers:	Akio Haga & Ian Hall
Aerodynamics director:	Simon Phillips
Chief engineer:	Tom McCullough
Operations manager:	Mark Gray
Test driver:	tba
Chassis:	Racing Point
Engine:	Mercedes V6
Tyres:	Pirelli

few seasons. The pair made their first podium appearance together at the 1995 Canadian GP and Jordan would continue to harry the top teams in its youthful and rebellious way until its day of days at the 1998 Belgian GP when, not only did Damon Hill win with Mugen Honda power, but Ralf Schumacher made it a one-two.

The next campaign for the team headquartered just across the road from the main entrance to Silverstone was better still, with Heinz-Harald Frentzen winning twice to help the team to a career-high ranking of third overall, behind only Ferrari and McLaren. The team was never as close to the front again, though Giancarlo Fisichella did score a surprise win in the 2003 Brazilian GP.

As F1 became ever more expensive, though, Jordan couldn't afford to stay in the hunt and Eddie sold up to Alex Shnaider in 2005. The name then changed again in 2007, from Midland to Spyker, and then once more to Force India in 2008 after Indian industrialist and occasional racer Vijay Mallya gave it a proper rebranding.

The team's biggest step forward in years came when it landed an engine supply deal with Mercedes for 2009, and this propelled the cars back towards the sharp end of the field, with starring performances from Fisichella - who finished second in the 2009 Belgian GP - Paul di Resta, Adrian Sutil, Nico Hulkenberg and Sergio Perez.

The team's bright light in 2018 was Esteban Ocon, although the battle between him and Perez became a little too competitive at times, costing the team points and infuriating the man at the helm, Otmar Szafnauer.

One key to the team continuing to be one of the best run in the business is that it is a team that exists solely to go racing. It doesn't build hybrid road cars, super cars or manufacture high-end engineering parts. It simply goes racing. Better still, despite the many changes of ownership, it has kept a remarkably low turnover of staff, so people know what they are supposed to be doing and get on with it, with their results far more likely to be affected adversely by a lack of money in the coffers.

Last year's late summer takeover by Lawrence Stroll saved around 400 jobs and kept one of F1's true teams in business. (See Talking Point feature on page 58).

* Racing Point name may change in 2019.

"I'm delighted we have investors who believe in us. Our expertise and commitment has meant that we have always punched above our weight and this new investment ensures that we have a bright future."
Otmar Szafnauer

Jordan's breakthrough came at Spa in 1998 when Damon Hill led home a one-two finish.

SERGIO PEREZ

This feisty Mexican took to the courts last year, not to resolve a disagreement with team-mate Esteban Ocon, with whom he had tussled, but with his team for unpaid bills. Thus Force India has become Racing Point and Sergio team leader.

Sergio's family invested in his career by sending him to race cars in the United States' Barber Dodge series at the incredibly young age of 14 in 2004. But the next step, the following year, was a far greater one as it took Sergio to Europe to contest the Formula BMW ADAC series in what must have seemed a far more alien environment.

Sergio didn't stand out in 2005 but he ranked sixth in 2006. Fortunately for him, there was a revival in interest in motor racing in Mexico and he gained attention by being the number two driver in Mexico's A1GP team and this helped to attract sponsorship from Telmex to let him try F3. It was in 2007 that Sergio claimed the only title he would land on his way to F1, and this was for the National class of the British championship, rather than the overall title. Racing for outright honours in 2008, Sergio ranked fourth, as Jaime Alguersuari took the title.

Sergio was a revelation as he stepped up to GP2, taking a couple of wins in the Asian series, but this was good only for seventh overall. Racing in the main GP2

Sergio should revel in being undisputed leader in his sixth year with the team.

series, he showed flashes of speed, but not enough consistency, and was only 12th. In 2010, though, Sergio grabbed five wins in the main championship and ended the year as runner-up to Pastor Maldonado.

Sauber decided to give Sergio an F1 test, perhaps with an eye on his Mexican sponsors, and he impressed with his speed, landing his F1 break for 2011. Sergio developed a reputation for being light on his tyres and this nearly yielded one of F1's most surprising wins early in his second year when he harried Ferrari's Fernando Alonso in the Malaysian GP but spun and ended up second.

That zenith earned Sergio a McLaren ride in 2013, but it didn't work out and so he joined Force India for 2014 and he has been with the team ever since, with seventh overall in 2016 and 2017 being his best ranking.

TRIGGERING A REVOLUTION

Third place in the Azerbaijan GP on the streets of Baku was an incredibly impressive result, albeit one that was helped by a tangle between the Red Bulls and Valtteri Bottas's Williams having a puncture. However, the most historically notable thing that Sergio did last year was to take out an injunction against Force India for non-payment of his wages. This action forced the team into administration and enabled those waiting to take over the team to spring into action to hopefully give the team new life. On track, the battles he had with team-mate Esteban Ocon in 2017 continued into 2018, thankfully with less of an edge, but Sergio gradually seemed to fall behind, although both drivers came good together in tricky conditions in qualifying for the Belgian GP where they locked out the second row and Sergio went on to finish in fifth place. Sergio continued to show his trademark ability of being easy on his car's tyres, an attribute that has always been a key to achieving a good result, particularly in a midfield car.

TRACK NOTES

Nationality:	MEXICAN
Born:	26 JANUARY 1990, GUADALAJARA, MEXICO
Website:	www.sergioperezf1.com
Teams:	SAUBER 2011-12, McLAREN 2013, FORCE INDIA 2014-18, RACING POINT 2019

CAREER RECORD

First Grand Prix:	2011 AUSTRALIAN GP
Grand Prix starts:	155
Grand Prix wins:	0 (best result: 2nd, 2012 Malaysian GP & Italian GP)
Poles:	0
Fastest laps:	4
Points:	529
Honours:	2010 GP2 RUNNER-UP, 2007 BRITISH FORMULA THREE NATIONAL CLASS CHAMPION

LANCE STROLL

Change of year, change of team for this 20-year-old Canadian, with his father's investment in the team now competing as Racing Point enabling Lance to move on from Williams to a team more likely to provide him with a competitive car.

Lance was like any infatuated 10-year-old when he took up kart racing in his native Canada, urged on by his car-mad father Lawrence. As he gained experience and spread his wings, Lawrence was there to support him, but it was the level of support that always marked Lance out as different to his rivals. Lawrence is a billionaire, made rich through the fashion industry.

So, only the best would do and his form when racing in Italy attracted the attention of the Ferrari Driver Academy. Fittingly, Lance made his car debut in the Ferrari-approved Florida Winter Series when he was 15, with Max Verstappen among his rivals. Pleased with this start, Lance then won the Italian F4 title in 2014 easily.

Diving down to the southern hemisphere summer, he then won the Toyota Racing Series in New Zealand and then stepped up to the European F3 Championship. Although he won a race at the final round and ranked fifth overall against more experienced rivals, Lance gained a reputation as a driver who took more risks than most and often crashed.

This was certainly a reputation he had to

Lance will be fired up by being with a team starting midgrid rather than from the back.

shed and he did so in dominant fashion in 2016 by becoming European F3 champion at his second attempt, his 14 wins giving him almost double the score of his closest rival. His speed attracted attention from

Williams and Lance enjoyed his first taste of F1. Another new experience was racing a sports-prototype, finishing fifth in the Daytona 24 Hours for Chip Ganassi Racing.

Then, with father Lawrence investing in financially-strapped Williams, Lance bypassed F2 and became a Williams F1 driver in 2017. In a wise move, he was mentored by the experienced Felipe Massa and after enduring a torrid start of three straight retirements, he settled down and shocked everyone by being third to the finish in an extraordinary Azerbaijan GP. His next best finish was sixth in Mexico and the fact that he ended the year just three points behind Massa was impressive.

TRACK NOTES

Nationality:	CANADIAN
Born: 29 OCTOBER 1998, MONTREAL, CANADA	
Website:	www.lancestroll.com
Teams: WILLIAMS 2017-18, RACING POINT 2019	

CAREER RECORD

First Grand Prix:	2017 AUSTRALIAN GP
Grand Prix starts:	41
Grand Prix wins:	0 (best result: 3rd, 2017 Azerbaijan GP)
Poles:	0
Fastest laps:	0
Points:	46
Honours:	2016 FIA EUROPEAN FORMULA THREE CHAMPION, 2015 TOYOTA RACING SERIES CHAMPION, 2014 ITALIAN FORMULA FOUR CHAMPION

POINTS WERE HARD TO COME BY

Lance's first year of F1, in 2017, had some peaks to balance out the odd slip-ups as he learnt. Unfortunately, last year offered fewer highs as Williams provided him with a car that was clearly not much good at all, a point made all the more obvious by the fact that it had Mercedes power and yet trailed behind fellow Mercedes customer team Force India. There were points along the way, but only twice, for Lance's eighth place in the Azerbaijan GP and for ninth at Spa-Francorchamps. The fact that his Baku result was five places lower than he had managed there a year earlier showed just how far Williams's form had slid, even though that had been a freak result in 2017. Perhaps the team would have fared better had it had a more experienced driver in the other seat, rather than rookie Sergey Sirotkin, especially in terms of chassis development through the year. However, it was a sad situation for this once proud team and Lance is fortunate that his huge family wealth has found him a way out to a more competitive team.

SAUBER

Driver changes are the big difference at Sauber, as the return of Kimi Raikkonen is an interesting move that should fire up the team. Also, the team's promotion of Italian hotshot Antonio Giovinazzi, at Ferrari's urging, is a positive as well.

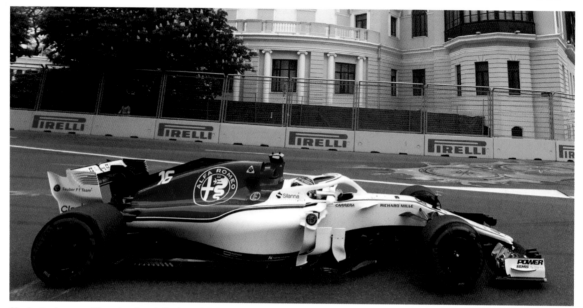

Charles Leclerc raced to a stunning sixth place at Baku and this and other strong results earned him his driver swap with Kimi Raikkonen.

One of the main changes in F1 in 2018 was the improving form of Sauber and the fact that its drivers, most notably Charles Leclerc, finishing in the points was no longer seen as a shock. This was a team that, perhaps, could start looking back to the splash it made when it arrived in F1 in 1993 and even its glory days when BMW gave it huge assistance, peaking in 2008.

Sauber is rare in that it didn't spring from a team with a single-seater background or take the opposite approach of being created by a motor manufacturer. Instead, this is a team that came to F1 from sports-prototype racing, masterminded by a Swiss racer turned car builder, Peter Sauber.

He started contesting hill-climb events, then moved onto the international sportscar racing scene. What turned out to be a game-changer was when he started building sportscars for others, with his C5 design showing promise in the late 1970s. The Saubers got ever closer to the front of the field in the World Sportscar Championship in the 1980s, especially when Mercedes began offering covert support. This helped the team to expand and take the battle to Jaguar, with Sauber Mercedes beating it to the 1989 title in a year that included a one-two finish in the Le Mans 24 Hours.

Sauber decided that it was time to try F1, with Mercedes as a partner, as it had been in

THE POWER AND THE GLORY

SIMONE RESTA

Growing up in Imola when his local circuit hosted the San Marino GP will most likely have given Simone a love of racing. After graduating as an engineer, he joined the Minardi team, moving on to Ferrari in 2001. With his star in the ascendancy, he rose from design engineer to head of R&D before becoming deputy chief designer in 2012 and chief designer in 2014. With Alfa Romeo involvement on the up, this is a great time to become technical director.

GETTING INTO THE POINTS MORE OFTEN

Sauber's 2018 season was one of promise, not just because Charles Leclerc became no stranger to scoring points. Marcus Ericsson found form too in the other car in the second half of the campaign. Furthermore, an increasingly competitive engine from Ferrari moved the team up the order. However, change was at hand when Jorg Zander's long reign as technical director came to an end last May. Former Ferrari chief designer Simone Resta replaced him as the team showed that it is indeed intent on moving up to the front of the midfield.

2018 DRIVERS & RESULTS

Driver	Nationality	Races	Wins	Pts	Pos
Marcus Ericsson	Swedish	21	0	9	17th
Charles Leclerc	Monegasque	21	0	39	13th

FOR THE RECORD

Country of origin:	Switzerland
Team base:	Hinwil, Switzerland
Telephone:	(41) 937 9000
Website:	www.sauberf1team.com
Active in Formula One:	From 1993
	(as BMW Sauber 2006-10)
Grands Prix contested:	464
Wins:	1
Pole positions:	1
Fastest laps:	5

THE TEAM

Chairman:	Pascal Picci
Team principal:	Frederic Vasseur
Technical director:	Simone Resta
Chief designer:	Eric Gandelin
Head of aerodynamics:	
	Nicolas Hennel de Beaupreau
Head of engineering:	Giampaolo Dall'ara
Head of track engineering:	Xevi Pujolar
Head of aerodynamic development:	
	Mariano Alperin-Bruvera
Head of aerodynamic research:	
	Seamus Mullarkey
Head of vehicle performance:	
	Elliot Dason-Barber
Team manager:	Beat Zehnder
Test driver:	Marcus Ericsson
Chassis:	Sauber C38
Engine:	Ferrari V6
Tyres:	Pirelli

its sportscar programme, but Mercedes didn't commit and the team went to F1 anyway.

F1 was much simpler back in 1993 but, even so, JJ Lehto claiming the team's first points with fifth place in the opening round at Kyalami was extremely impressive.

The arrival of Mercedes engines for 1994 was expected to move the team forward, but didn't, and the German manufacturer moved on to McLaren for 1995, leaving Sauber to run Ford units and rank seventh overall for the next three years. Rebadged Ferrari engines failed to improve things in 1999 and 2000. Then, in 2001, there was a leap forward when the best efforts of Nick Heidfeld and rookie Kimi Raikkonen helped it to rank fourth. This was a distant fourth, though, and the major advancement came after the arrival of BMW in 2006.

The BMW Sauber team came on strongly through 2007 and ended the year second overall, albeit with only half of the points tally of champions Ferrari in a season that peaked with Heidfeld's second place in the Canadian GP.

Robert Kubica went one better to win the same race 12 months later, with Heidfeld chasing him home on the team's day of days.

Since BMW pulled out at the end of 2010, Sauber has run with Ferrari engines and an increasing degree of engineering assistance. However, having Ferrari power probably held back Sergio Perez when he challenged Fernando Alonso for the lead at Sepang in 2012, as the Spaniard was driving a Ferrari and overtaking it might have harmed the relationship...

A constant problem for Sauber has been first attracting, then keeping, leading designers and engineers, as most are settled working for the many British-based F1 teams, but current team principal Frederic Vasseur has made a concerted effort to overcome this and also to boost the size of the team's workforce. Having Alfa Romeo branding on the cars has been a huge help in finding the money to pay for them, and the upswing of form in 2018 over 2017 has augmented the team's reinstatement into F1's midfield.

Late last summer, the team received an approach from Kimi Raikkonen's manager Steve Robertson, the man who brought Kimi into F1 with the team back in 2001. Raikkonen wasn't staying at Ferrari, but he still wanted to race in F1, and his involvement has given the team a real buzz. In return, Kimi will relish racing without the corporate pressure he operated under at Ferrari.

> "Most people expected Kimi to retire and go and sit on his yacht, but he loves driving F1 cars. Once we knew he wasn't going to stay at Ferrari, he wanted to do a deal." **Steve Robertson**

Robert Kubica and founder Peter Sauber after the team's only win so far, in Canada in 2008.

KIMI RAIKKONEN

This 39-year-old Finn isn't like most other drivers. When his time at Ferrari came to an end last year, it had been thought he would slip into retirement. Not a bit of it, as Kimi plans to race on with Sauber for at least this year and next.

Kimi's racing career history remains an extraordinary one, as it has a blink-and-you-missed-it passage from karts to F1 of just 23 races, then an F1 career that is all set for its 300th outing in its 17th year.

McLaren established its own annual scholarship in the 1990s, picking the best from the junior single-seater categories. By the end of the decade, some driver managers started scouting the pick of kart racers. David Robertson thought Kimi looked worth a shot at Formula Renault. He won the British series at his first attempt and Robertson then talked Sauber into giving him a test in which his raw speed shocked them. Despite not even doing F3, Kimi was offered an F1 ride for 2001. Even better he finished sixth in the opening round, silencing all doubters. In fact, McLaren, a front-running team back then, signed him for 2002.

Having finished second to Ferrari's Michael Schumacher in 2003, Kimi was second again in 2005, then joined Ferrari in Schumacher's place in 2007 and won the title at the final round after a

Kimi started his F1 career with Sauber in 2001 and aims to finish it with the team too.

gripping three-way battle with McLaren's Fernando Alonso and Lewis Hamilton.

Yet one thing about Kimi that always marked him out as different is his total disregard for PR. He wants to race, that's it. This is why he moved to the less pressured World Rally Championship in 2009 before coming back to F1 in 2012, even winning two races for Lotus before rejoining Ferrari in 2014.

TRACK NOTES

Nationality:	FINNISH
Born:	17 OCTOBER 1979, ESPOO, FINLAND
Website:	www.kimiraikkonen.com
Teams:	SAUBER 2001 & 2019, McLAREN 2002-06, FERRARI 2007-09 & 2014-18, LOTUS 2012-13

CAREER RECORD

First Grand Prix:	2001 AUSTRALIAN GP
Grand Prix starts:	294
Grand Prix wins:	21
	2003 Malaysian GP, 2004 Belgian GP, 2005 Spanish GP, Monaco GP, Canadian GP, Hungarian GP, Turkish GP, Belgian GP, Japanese GP, 2007 Australian GP, French GP, British GP, Belgian GP, Chinese GP, Brazilian GP, 2008 Malaysian GP, Spanish GP, 2009 Belgian GP, 2012 Abu Dhabi GP, 2013 Australian GP, 2018 United States GP
Poles:	18
Fastest laps:	46
Points:	1816
Honours:	2007 FORMULA ONE WORLD CHAMPION, 2003 & 2005 FORMULA ONE RUNNER-UP, 2000 BRITISH FORMULA RENAULT CHAMPION, 1999 BRITISH FORMULA RENAULT WINTER SERIES CHAMPION, 1998 EUROPEAN SUPER A KART RUNNER-UP, FINNISH & NORDIC KART CHAMPION

STILL QUICK, STILL IN SUPPORT

The Ferrari was a competitive package in 2018, and this ought to have given Kimi a chance of a final shot at victory in what was always going to be his final campaign with the Italian team. However, that has never been his role since returning to Ferrari in 2014. His role was to drive hard and frustrate the opposition, but never to trouble the team leader. Support player was the designated role. At this, he was good, but not as good as in the past, save for qualifying in which he was seen as most useful at giving Sebastian Vettel a tow, until Monza where it went his way. As long as Vettel had a chance of the title, Kimi was expected to support him. He knew too that his place in the team was going to end at the close of the season, with Charles Leclerc lined up to replace him. Then, pleasingly, Kimi did get to visit the top step of a podium one more time when he produced a brilliant drive to win the United States GP. This performance was thrown into an extra positive light by the fact that he ended the season more strongly than Vettel did.

ANTONIO GIOVINAZZI

Sponsorship from Alfa Romeo has encouraged Sauber to demote well-backed Marcus Ericsson to a reserve driver role for 2019 and give his seat to this well-considered Italian who had two grand prix outings for the team in 2017.

Having been a front-running kart racer, Antonio went to the Far East to start his single-seater car racing career and he immediately won the Formula Pilota China title in 2012, as well as grabbing some Formula Abarth wins in Europe.

For 2013, Antonio contested the British F3 Championship, finishing as runner-up in this admittedly declining series. He then raced in the European F3 series in 2014, collecting a couple of wins en route to sixth place overall for the Carlin team. His team-mate that year was Indonesian driver Sean Gelael, who became a great friend, and the pair would race together again at the end of the following year.

For 2015, Antonio focused on European F3 again and won six times to finish as runner-up to the experienced Felix Rosenqvist. He also won the standalone F3 Masters event at Zandvoort.

Gelael and Antonio then teamed up to try sports-prototype racing, winning two rounds of the Asian Le Mans Series.

For 2016, Antonio stepped up to GP2, and he and Pierre Gasly were way clear of the rest but, despite collecting five

Antonio is highly considered by the team and could spring a surprise or two in 2019.

wins, Antonio was pipped to the title at the final round in Abu Dhabi. Still inspired by sportscar racing, Antonio contested a couple of rounds of the World Endurance Championship in the secondary LMP2

class for Extreme Speed Motorsports.

With support from Ferrari, Antonio was then placed with Sauber as its third driver for 2017 as part of the team's engine supply deal. Although expecting a year spent on the sidelines, he was then given a surprise F1 race debut at the opening round in Australia after Pascal Wehrlein had failed to recover from a back injury suffered in an accident in the close-season multi-discipline Race of Champions. Antonio competed in the following race in China too, before reverting to his expected role on the sidelines, looking and learning.

TRACK NOTES

Nationality:	ITALIAN
Born:	14 DECEMBER 1993, MARTINA FRANCA, ITALY
Website:	www.antoniogiovinazzi.com
Teams:	SAUBER 2017 & 2019

CAREER RECORD	
First Grand Prix:	2017 AUSTRALIAN GP
Grand Prix starts:	2
Grand Prix wins:	0 (best result: 12th, 2017 Australian GP)
Poles:	0
Fastest laps:	0
Points:	0
Honours:	2016 GP2 SERIES RUNNER-UP, 2015 FORMULA 3 EUROPEAN CHAMPIONSHIP RUNNER-UP, 2013 BRITISH FORMULA 3 CHAMPIONSHIP RUNNER-UP, 2012 FORMULA PILOTA CHINA CHAMPION

FINDING OTHER THINGS TO DO

The life of an F1 reserve driver isn't one that involves a great deal of action, mainly comprising simulator work, the odd test here and there, plus the possibility of the occasional Friday practice session at a grand prix, along with helping the PR team fulfil its duties of putting drivers in front of the media for interviews. Fortunately for Antonio, he did get to race in 2018 after all, competing in the Le Mans 24 Hours in an AF Corse works Ferrari that he shared with Felipe "Pipo" Derani and Toni Vilander to finish fifth in the GTE Pro class. This was ideal, as it gave Antonio plenty of track time and a chance to keep his competitive juices flowing. While focusing on his "day job", though, Antonio had to pray that there would be an F1 race seat opening up for 2019, and he found out in late September that pressure from title sponsor Alfa Romeo had landed him the second Sauber F1 race seat ahead of the well-funded Swedish incumbent Marcus Ericsson who had the backing of the team's majority shareholder.

Charles Leclerc boosted Sauber considerably
as the Swiss team took giant strides in 2018,
helping it score almost 10 times as many
points as in 2017.

SCUDERIA TORO ROSSO

Bringing back Daniil Kvyat might not be seen as a way of bringing on young talent – the modus operandi for this team – but it will give Scuderia Toro Rosso a welcome degree of experience as it enters its second season with Honda power.

Scuderia Toro Rosso had a number of promising results last year, most notably in Bahrain, and its two new drivers will be optimistic about 2019.

For years, Scuderia Toro Rosso was described as "the team that used to be Minardi", but those days are long behind us and it's more usually acknowledged as the junior team to Red Bull Racing, a team that can occasionally pull off a strong result on days when the top teams stumble.

Giancarlo Minardi ran a team in the lower reaches of the Italian single-seater ladder before stepping up to F2 in 1974. Ferrari became involved, but its engines weren't competitive and Minardi only began to shine in F2 when it entered its own chassis in the early 1980s, most notably in the hands of Alessandro Nannini.

The team stepped up to F1 in 1985, but it was only after it replaced its Motori Moderni engines in 1988 that it scored its first point. Two years later, Minardi's nephew Pierluigi Martini delivered one of the all-time shock F1 results. This happened at the United States GP on a street circuit in Phoenix when there was a tyre war in F1 and Martini found his Pirelli tyres good enough to help him qualify on the front row alongside Gerhard Berger's McLaren. In the race, though, they fell away and Martini finished seventh.

Based in Faenza in Italy's industrial heartland, Minardi operated a policy of bringing on rising Italian stars and Giancarlo Fisichella and Jarno Trulli had cause to thank the team for giving them

THE POWER AND THE GLORY

JODY EGGINTON
Jody broke into F1 as a junior in Tyrrell's design department. What expanded his brief as a design engineer was what followed, stints with the Xtrac automotive engineering company, then time with both Opel's and Aston Martin's motorsport divisions. A return to F1 with Force India in 2005 was followed by a move to Caterham as chief engineer in 2010. When that team folded, Jody joined Scuderia Toro Rosso and rose to be head of vehicle performance and, last year, to deputy technical director.

STARTING WITH A BANG, ENDING WITH A WHIMPER
It was all-change for Toro Rosso last year, with the team acting as guinea pig for Red Bull Racing by swapping from Renault to Honda power. When Pierre Gasly finished fourth in the second round, it was a hugely positive surprise. However, other good results proved hard to come by and, despite Gasly landing sixth in Hungary, he and Brendon Hartley were more often out of the points. In July, it was announced that technical director James Key was leaving for McLaren.

2018 DRIVERS & RESULTS

Driver	Nationality	Races	Wins	Pts	Pos
Pierre Gasly	French	21	0	29	15th
Brendon Hartley	New Zealander	21	0	4	19th

FOR THE RECORD

Country of origin:	Italy
Team base:	Faenza, Italy
Telephone:	(39) 546 696111
Website:	www.scuderiatororosso.com
Active in Formula One:	As Minardi
	1985-2005, Toro Rosso 2006 onwards
Grands Prix contested:	588
Wins:	1
Pole positions:	1
Fastest laps:	1

THE TEAM

Team owner:	Dietrich Mateschitz
Team principal:	Franz Tost
Technical director:	tba
Deputy technical director:	Jody Egginton
Chief designers:	Paolo Marabini &
	Mark Tatham
Head of aerodynamics:	Brendan Gilhome
Head of vehicle performance:	
	Guillaume Dezoteux
Team manager:	Graham Watson
Team co-ordinator:	Michele Andreazza
Chief engineer:	Marco Matassa
Chief race engineer:	Jonathan Eddols
Test driver:	tba
Chassis:	Toro Rosso STR14
Engine:	Honda V6
Tyres:	Pirelli

their F1 break. Although not Italian, so too did Fernando Alonso and Mark Webber. Minardi's predominantly black and yellow cars were viewed with affection, the fans appreciating these perennial underdogs.

Yet, finances were always stretched and the F1 power race of the early 21st century magnified the difference, so it was no surprise that when Red Bull founder Dietrich Mateschitz was looking around to create a feeder team for Red Bull Racing, a place to test and develop drivers for his number one squad in F1 conditions, that he took his cheque book to Minardi.

The deal was done for 2006 and the first year of Toro Rosso - Italian for Red Bull - was helped by having a chassis not far removed from the previous year's Red Bull design.

Results began to improve, but even Sebastian Vettel's growing army of fans wouldn't have tipped him to qualify on pole in the wet at Monza in 2008 and they certainly couldn't have dreamt that he would then convert that into the team's first and, thus far, only F1 win. Imagine the mixed feelings that the shock result triggered, as Red Bull Racing had yet to put any of its drivers onto the top step of an F1 podium.

Vettel moved up to Red Bull Racing for 2009 and this has remained the pattern for the team ever since, with any driver who manages to shine at Toro Rosso, under the intensely critical gaze of Red Bull's talent spotter Helmut Marko, being in with a good chance of promotion. The flip side of this has been several drivers being kept in this "waiting room" when there were no openings for several years at Red Bull Racing and then being overlooked, while others have simply been ejected for not being deemed to have made the mark.

Neither Daniel Ricciardo nor Max Verstappen can have any cause for complaint though, as they both used Toro Rosso as a springboard to Red Bull Racing and the wins soon followed. Last year, with Ricciardo's surprise announcement that he would be quitting Red Bull for Renault in 2019, Pierre Gasly became the latest driver to be given the chance to step up from Toro Rosso and, on last year's form, he looks likely to be able to take hold of the opportunity with both hands, especially as he has a year of racing experience with Honda's F1 engines that Red Bull Racing adopts this year.

Pierluigi Martini gave Minardi its day of days in 1990 by qualifying on the front row in Phoenix.

"Daniil is a highly skilled driver with fantastic natural speed. There were some difficult situations that he had to face but, having had time to mature as a person, these will help him show his undeniable capabilities."
Franz Tost

DANIIL KVYAT

Being dropped by Scuderia Toro Rosso in 2017 wasn't the greatest vote of confidence, but Daniil has been brought back to have another crack at F1, coming back older and hopefully wiser after a year spent watching from the sidelines.

Look back over this Russian driver's career and it might be said that Red Bull's driver scholarship scheme brought him to the top of the sport before he was quite ready for this most exacting of challenges, as it introduced him to the sport's top category in 2014 when he was not quite 20.

His racing record to that point was impressive, as he had gone well in karts before finishing third in the 2011 European Formula Renault Championship and then as runner-up in 2012, pipped to the title by Stoffel Vandoorne. In 2013, Daniil was crowned GP3 champion, with his Red Bull backing helping him into a test for Scuderia Toro Rosso.

Perhaps a year in GP2 would have been beneficial, given him a more solid grounding, but his first season with Toro Rosso included a ninth-place finish on his debut, with two more ninth places added through the year, and this earned him promotion to Red Bull Racing for 2015 after Sebastian Vettel left for Ferrari. Yet, despite a surprise second place in the Hungarian GP that helped him to rank seventh at year's end, the results didn't really come and after just four races

Daniil is hopefully more mature now he has been brought back into the F1 fold for 2019.

of the 2016 season, he was demoted to Toro Rosso again in a driver swap deal that took Max Verstappen the other way. When the Dutch teenager won first time out for Red Bull, it was a massive knock for Daniil.

Then, towards the end of the 2017 season, his career took another hit when he was dropped by Scuderia Toro Rosso as well after crashing in the Singapore GP. Although reinstated for one more outing later that year, in the United States GP, Red Bull talent spotter Helmut Marko thought that he had seen enough, and it seemed that Daniil had been dropped for good.

Surprisingly, after a year in which Daniil had no involvement with F1, even in a testing capacity, his F1 hopes were rekindled with an unexpected twist as a result of Daniel Ricciardo's decision to leave Red Bull Racing, and he was signed to drive for Scuderia Toro Rosso again.

WATCHING AND WAITING

Racing drivers tend to want to do only one thing: to race. Leave them on the sidelines, and they are far from happy. For a driver who has made it to F1, exclusion from the only activity that they have known since their childhood racing karts, watching with no involvement must be unimaginably painful. So it was for Daniil last year. He was 24 years old, without a drive, left to field endless questions about why not. Fortunately, Daniil was chosen as a Ferrari development driver, but that amounted to little meaningful track action and it was only really because Honda didn't consider that either of its F2 racers Nirei Fukuzumi and Tadasuke Makino were ready to be placed with Toro Rosso for 2019 that Daniil was given this unexpected call back to within the F1 ranks. If the time he must have spent soul searching will have added a little caution to Daniil's undoubted natural speed, then he will be able to eliminate some of the incidents that have marred his F1 career so far.

TRACK NOTES

Nationality:	RUSSIAN
Born:	26 APRIL 1994, UFA, RUSSIA
Website:	www.daniilkvyat.com
Teams:	TORO ROSSO 2014, 2016-2017 & 2019, RED BULL RACING 2015-2016

CAREER RECORD

First Grand Prix:	2014 AUSTRALIAN GP
Grand Prix starts:	74
Grand Prix wins:	0 (best result: 2nd, 2015 Hungarian GP)
Poles:	0
Fastest laps:	1
Points:	133
Honours:	2013 GP3 CHAMPION, 2012 EUROPEAN FORMULA RENAULT RUNNER-UP & ALPS FORMULA RENAULT CHAMPION, 2009 WSK KART RUNNER-UP

ALEX ALBON

After an excellent season in F2, Alex took the final opening in F1 for 2019 when he extricated himself from a contract to race in Formula E for Nissan to become reunited with the Red Bull programme by joining Scuderia Toro Rosso.

This driver, of joint British and Thai nationality, is a rarity in that he was given a second chance by Red Bull's notorious hire-them-and-fire-them scholarship programme. Ironically, he replaces Brendon Hartley, who has now been dropped by Red Bull for a second time, and will race alongside Daniil Kvyat, who is also being given a second chance.

Alex will be aware that Red Bull talent spotter Helmut Marko only offers drives with Toro Rosso to drivers who he thinks have the right sort of talent to develop into drivers capable of being promoted to Red Bull Racing in the years ahead.

Alex's father Nigel raced in the British Touring Car Championship in the 1990s, so it's not surprising that Alex took to karts. After a great season in 2011 when he ranked second in the KF1 series, at the age of 15, he was signed up as one of Red Bull's young drivers and stepped up to cars to race in Formula Renault in 2012. Unfortunately, his results were disappointing and so, at the end of the year, Red Bull dropped him.

Disheartened, but determined to press

Alex is sure to give the sport a boost in his home country as Thailand's first F1 driver.

on, Alex ranked third in his third season in the European championship. F3 came next, and he was seventh in the 2015 European series before trying GP3 in 2016 and four wins helped him to second

place behind Charles Leclerc. Then, in 2017, Alex advanced to F2 and ranked 10th in that.

At the end of last year, Alex was all set to move to Formula E, signed by Nissan, but then a door opened at Toro Rosso and he went for it. On the evidence of what happened to Hartley, though, Alex will be aware that he will have to produce consistently good results, or at least good performances, if his second chance doesn't end in the same way as his first opportunity.

Some will point to Red Bull being a company that was founded in Thailand and Alex racing as a Thai, but that is to ignore his strong years as a front runner in GP3 then F2.

ALEX FINDS FORM IN BEST YEAR YET

Last year was Alex's best in racing, topping his best year in karting, when he finished second in the KF1 series back in 2011. Racing in F2 for DAMS, he showed almost straight away that his second year in F1's immediate feeder category was going to be better than his first by taking pole position for the first race of the second round, on Baku's street circuit. Then, keeping a calm head, Alex romped off to take his first win at this level. Alex proved this was no fluke by taking pole position for each of the next two rounds, at Barcelona and Monaco. However, Alex's second win didn't come until the seventh round, at Silverstone. A third victory was added in the second race at the Hungaroring, before adding a fourth win in the first of each meeting's two races at Sochi, with the opening race always being more prestigious as it's longer. This put Alex in with a shot of ending the year as runner-up to George Russell, but a poor result in Abu Dhabi meant he ended up just short of toppling Lando Norris.

TRACK NOTES

Nationality:	THAI
Born:	23 MARCH 1996, LONDON, ENGLAND
Website:	www.alexalbon.com
Teams:	TORO ROSSO 2019

CAREER RECORD	
First Grand Prix:	2019 AUSTRALIAN GP
Grand Prix starts:	0
Grand Prix wins:	0
Poles:	0
Fastest laps:	0
Points:	0
Honours:	2016 GP3 RUNNER-UP,
	2011 WORLD KF1 KART RUNNER-UP,
	2010 EUROPEAN KF3 KART CHAMPION,
	2009 SUPER 1 HONDA KART CHAMPION

WILLIAMS

Ranked fifth in 2017 and then bottom of the table in 10th last year, Williams is in freefall, but it's encouraging to see that this once great team has, in George Russell, opted for a quick young driver rather than simply another rich one.

Williams' drivers tried hard through 2018 but couldn't find the pace in a difficult car. This year's duo look better equipped for the job.

Williams is a team that can still be identified with one man: the indefatigable Sir Frank Williams. However, it should really always be associated with two men, as his co-founder Sir Patrick Head played an equal part on its passage from also-rans in 1977 to dominant World Champions. Sadly, over the past year, the team returned to being an also-ran.

Although former racers Williams and Head didn't join forces until 1977, Williams's involvement with F1 goes back to 1969, when he entered a Brabham for Piers Courage and they took a pair of second-place finishes. Courage was then killed in 1970 and the middle part of the decade was a struggle for Williams.

Then along came Head and his excellence as a designer started to bear fruit from his first F1 Williams in 1978, something helped enormously by the team landing its first worthwhile sponsor: Saudia. This was the first time that Frank's F1 existence hadn't been hand-to-mouth,

and his rivals were uniformly stunned by the team's progress.

First came the shots at victory, achieved by Clay Regazzoni in the 1979 British GP, a

result that delighted this most patriotic of team chiefs. Then, having dominated the tail end of the 1979 season with its ground effect FW07, the team flew through 1980,

THE POWER AND THE GLORY

SIR FRANK WILLIAMS

Frank raced, but realised that he had neither the money nor enough talent to go beyond F3, so he changed direction and ran cars for others. Running his own team, Frank did everything bar design the cars, and the skills he was forced to learn have been built on ever since, with knowing when and how to delegate being one of these as the team has grown from probably 20 employees to 500 or more. Tragically, returning from a test in early 1986, Frank was paralysed in a car crash. A lesser man would have folded.

LOSING GROUND AT A RAPID RATE

By round 13 last year, the team had scored points at only one grand prix. Fortunately, the next race at Monza produced a ninth and a 10th, but this wasn't a shining record and, with the FW40 struggling for corner entry balance, Ed Wood moved on from being chief designer. Other changes included Doug McKiernan being appointed as chief engineer. So poor was the FW40 that the team turned its attention early to working on the design of its 2019 challenger, and that said it all.

2018 DRIVERS & RESULTS

Driver	Nationality	Races	Wins	Pts	Pos
Sergey Sirotkin	Russian	21	0	1	20th
Lance Stroll	Canadian	21	0	6	18th

FOR THE RECORD

Country of origin:	England
Team base:	Grove, England
Telephone:	(44) 01235 777700
Website:	www.williamsf1.com
Active in Formula One:	From 1972
Grands Prix contested:	762
Wins:	114
Pole positions:	128
Fastest laps:	133

THE TEAM

Team principal:	Sir Frank Williams
Co-founder:	Sir Patrick Head
Deputy team principal:	Claire Williams
Chief executive officer:	Mike O'Driscoll
Chief technical officer:	Paddy Lowe
Head of performance engineering:	tba
Chief engineer:	Doug McKiernan
Head of aerodynamics:	Dave Wheater
Race engineers:	Luca Baldisserri, Andrew Murdoch, James Urwin & Paul Williams
Team manager:	David Redding
Test driver:	Nicholas Latifi
Chassis:	Williams FW41
Engine:	Mercedes V8
Tyres:	Pirelli

with Alan Jones becoming its first world champion after taking five wins.

It might have been two titles in a row but, famously, Carlos Reutemann crumbled under the pressure of the 1981 decider in Las Vegas, although the drivers' tally of points were enough for a second straight constructors' title. Perhaps because he was a greater scrapper, Keke Rosberg triumphed in 1982's ultra-close battle.

Racing was still relatively simple then, as the ubiquitous Ford DFV engine was still competitive, but it was clear that a turbocharged engine would soon be needed and a deal was done with Honda.

With Jones having moved on, the team needed a bulldog of a driver and signed the fearless Nigel Mansell. He was rapid, but Williams and Head grew tired of his complaints when things went wrong, although they had sympathy when a blown tyre cost him the 1986 title at the final round. The team bounced back for Nelson Piquet to be champion in 1987.

In time, Honda lost its way and it was Renault that moved to the forefront of F1 engine development and Williams joined forces with the French manufacturer in 1989 and went on to have a fabulous run with their units, just being pipped in 1991 by Ayrton Senna's brilliance at McLaren, before delivering in spectacular style the following year when Mansell grabbed nine wins to dominate the season.

Williams and Head always liked to keep their drivers in check, so Mansell wasn't required for 1993, being replaced by Alain Prost, who promptly took control. It could have been three titles in a row, but Michael Schumacher played dirty at the 1994 finale in Adelaide and, once he knew his Benetton was damaged, drove it into Damon Hill's Williams, thus preventing Hill from becoming champion.

Williams got revenge when Hill was crowned in 1996, followed by Jacques Villeneuve in 1997, but more rule changes for 1998 left Williams marginally off the pace and it took until 2001 before it was

back in the swing, this time with BMW power. But this revival wasn't to last past 2004, since when Williams has been in the doldrums. There was a flash-in-the-pan win for Pastor Maldonado in Spain in 2012, but little else to smile about as the team has had to get by on a limited budget.

Last year, Williams looked into the possibility of becoming a B team for Mercedes, but decided not to do that as it wanted to preserve its independence.

Frank Williams and Alain Prost check the screens during Prost's fourth title-winning year, 1993.

"In the time that we have spent with George [Russell] so far, we believe that he will be a great fit for our team as his commitment, passion and dedication are exactly what we need to drive the positive momentum building at Grove." **Claire Williams**

ROBERT KUBICA

Williams was accused in 2018 of selecting its drivers primarily for their money. This has changed for 2019 and the return of this popular Pole shows how the team is now putting talent first, hoping that his injuries don't hold him back.

You know that a driver is something special if Lewis Hamilton sings their praise, and the five-time World Champion has always considered Robert an equal.

Robert travelled far and wide from his native Poland to go kart racing and took home a fair collection of trophies, including the Monaco Kart Cup twice plus the German and Italian titles.

Once he moved to car racing, he settled into Formula Renault and was second in the Italian series in 2002 but, more importantly, was selected for Renault's driver development programme. Thanks to missing much of the 2003 season because he broke an arm in a road accident, Formula Three was also a two-year project, in which he finished as runner-up in the Macau GP in 2004. However, it was when he stepped up to the more powerful Formula Renault 3.5 category that Robert really shone, racing for the Epsilon Euskadi team, taking four wins en route to the title.

His big break came when he was signed by the BMW Sauber team as its test driver for 2006. However, the year yielded more than that as he got to make his F1 debut midway through the season when Jacques

Robert will make a hugely popular return and bring much needed determination.

Villeneuve was dropped. Amazingly, he finished third at Monza on his third outing, cementing his ride for 2007.

Robert stayed with BMW Sauber for the next three seasons, peaking with fourth place overall in 2008, the year in which he became a grand prix winner. This momentous day came in Canada when he gave the team its first win in a one-two result ahead of Nick Heidfeld.

After a disappointing 2009 campaign in which he ranked 16th, Robert bounced back to rank eighth for Renault in 2010, helped by coming second in Australia plus taking third places in both Monaco and Belgium.

Robert was all set to build on that in 2011 when his love of rallying cost him dear, as he crashed on a rally and came close to losing his right forearm.

Between 2012 and 2016, Robert contested assorted rallies, but circuit racing has always been his goal.

TRACK NOTES

Nationality:	POLISH
Born:	7 DECEMBER 1984, KRAKOW, POLAND
Website:	www.kubica.pl
Teams:	BMW SAUBER 2006-2009, RENAULT 2010, WILLIAMS 2019

CAREER RECORD	
First Grand Prix:	2006 HUNGARIAN GP
Grand Prix starts:	76
Grand Prix wins:	1 (2008 Canadian GP)
Poles:	1
Fastest laps:	1
Points:	273
Honours:	2005 WORLD SERIES BY RENAULT CHAMPION, 1999 GERMAN & ITALIAN KART CHAMPION & MONACO KART CUP WINNER, 1998 ITALIAN KART CHAMPION & MONACO KART CUP WINNER, 1997 POLISH KART CHAMPION

ROBERT GETS THE MILES IN

Robert did assorted races in 2016 and 2017, including the Dubai 24 Hours for GT cars, but more importantly he got back into an F1 car for the first time since 2011. It was a daunting task to discover whether he was physically able to cope with this extreme challenge, but he coped well enough to cover 850 miles across three days with Renault and Williams, lapping near the pace. Strengthened by what he found, Robert did more F1 testing last year, covering 1,000 miles across five days with Williams, including the first practice session at the Abu Dhabi GP. By that final race, however, he knew that he had the Williams contract for a drive in 2019 in his pocket and the outpouring of affection and respect for Robert was clear for all to see in the F1 paddock when the news broke. Of course, question marks remain over his physical capabilities following the dreadful hand injuries he suffered in a rallying accident in 2011, but the team wouldn't have taken a risk if it wasn't confident that Robert can deliver again at the sport's highest level.

GEORGE RUSSELL

Last year was a wonderful time for George. Not only did he win the Formula 2 title and test for the Mercedes F1 team, but he got on the telephone and convinced technical supremo Paddy Lowe that he was worthy of a Williams seat.

With just 20 race seats on the F1 grid to aim for, the F2 championship is an extremely crowded waiting room. That George was able to arrive, win and grab an F1 seat is extremely impressive, but a look at his sparkling career record suggests that few should be surprised at this feat.

George showed his pedigree by winning the European KF3 karting title in 2012. Then, when he turned 16 in 2014, it was straight into car racing, starting with the British F4 Championship in which he just came out on top of a four-way title battle. George was busy that year, as he also raced in Formula Renault, winning a race in the European championship. Then, at year's end, he was selected as the McLaren Autosport BRDC young driver award winner.

Doors started to open for George as he became a member of the BRDC SuperStars scheme and Carlin chose him as one of its drivers for the 2015 European F3 Championship. He won the second race of the season, at Silverstone and would go on to rank sixth as the very experienced Felix Rosenqvist took the title, with another highlight being second place in the F3

George displayed remarkable form in becoming F2 champion and could star in F1.

Masters invitation race at Zandvoort.

George's second shot at the European F3 title didn't yield the title he wanted, as he finished only third overall for Hitech GP as Lance Stroll stormed the series, but he

used the experience gained very well when he moved to GP3 in 2017 and won that title with ease, taking four wins for ART Grand Prix. F1 teams were beginning to show an interest and he had test runs with both Force India and Mercedes, going well.

Then, staying on with ART Grand Prix, George stepped up to F2 last year and sailed through in what was an unusually competitive year at the final level before F1. Just as importantly, George continued to have F1 test runs with both Force India and Mercedes, going well enough to show that he was ready for an F1 break.

TRACK NOTES

Nationality:	BRITISH
Born:	15 FEBRUARY 1998, KING'S LYNN, ENGLAND
Website:	www.gerogerussellracing.com
Teams:	WILLIAMS 2019

CAREER RECORD	
First Grand Prix:	2019 Australian GP
Grand Prix starts:	0
Grand Prix wins:	0
Poles:	0
Fastest laps:	0
Points:	0
Honours:	2018 Formula 2 champion, 2017 GP3 champion, 2015 Formula 3 Masters runner-up, 2014 British Formula 4 champion & McLaren Autosport Young Driver Award winner, 2012 European KF3 kart champion

WAVING THE FLAG FOR BRITAIN

British drivers were very much at the forefront of the international junior single-seater championships last year, and George became the vanguard of the vanguard as he raced to the F2 title in dominant style. To win this title any year is special, but to do it in your first year at this level is extra special. Certainly, George was with one of the top teams, ART Grand Prix, but it was the way that he started winning as early as the second round, at Baku, that impressed. There was extra pressure as there was a stern battle between the British drivers to be top and both Lando Norris and Alexander Albon kept George on his toes. However, by season's end, not only had George landed the F2 title with seven wins, but he had a contract for a Williams race seat for 2019 in his pocket. When looking at F2, look for the drivers who win the opening race of the two at each meeting, as the second one starts with the top eight finishers from race one in reversed order on the grid. Impressively, George collected three of the more notable first race wins.

vive.com/McLaren

Hopefully life in a McLaren cockpit will be better this year, as a lack of results made Fernando Alonso choose to take time out from F1.

TALKING POINT:
THE SAVIOURS OF FORCE INDIA

There had been a dark cloud hanging over Force India for years, with court cases lining up for owner Vijay Mallya. Never a rich team, it simply got on with its racing, and did well, which is why Lawrence Stroll and his fellow investors have taken it over.

With a sensible amount of money in the bank for the first time in the team's 28-year existence, the team that started life as Jordan back in 1991 may finally be able to start spreading its wings now that it's under new ownership and set to race under its new name, Racing Point.

Based across the road from the main gate at Silverstone, Force India has always been the epitome of a proper racing team, existing solely for racing, without a focus elsewhere on, say, building supercars. It has stayed mean and lean, although this has been of necessity rather than choice, as its budget has never been up there with the top teams.

For the past handful of years, however, team principal Vijay Mallya had his mind on other matters. To be specific, the courts and his avoidance of them, and this certainly was not conducive to the team's advancement.

That all came to a close at around the time of the Hungarian GP last summer when Force India was put into administration following a court action from driver Sergio Perez for £3m of unpaid wages. As this was of little surprise, there were already several consortia in the wings, looking to buy the assets.

The winning consortium was the one led by Lawrence Stroll, a Canadian fashion industry billionaire, beating, among others, one from Michael Andretti and colleagues. Each of the groups would have brought something new and fresh to the F1 mix, perhaps giving another part of the world a team or driver of their own to cheer on.

Stroll's bid-winning consortium included his business partner Silas Chou, investment specialists Andre Desmarais and Michael de Picciotto, Monaco Sport & Management's Jonathan Dudman, fellow fashion industry leader John Idol and telecommunications industry frontman John McCaw Jr.

With chief operations officer Otmar Szafnauer keeping his hands on the reins at the time of the purchase (deputy team principal Bob Fernley moved on), the jobs of the team's 405 employees were made safe and the team's creditors were all paid. For 2019, it will be known as Racing Point, having ended last season under the cumbersome title of Racing Point Force India.

"The strength of any company is the people that make it up," said Stroll on the day of the announcement of the deal, "and it's a huge privilege to begin this exciting new journey with such a talented group.

"I've been fortunate to establish and grow a number of successful businesses, but the opportunity to take this business forward to the next level is perhaps the most exciting challenge yet. We will invest in new resources and bring fresh energy to empower the workforce to continue operating at the very highest level."

Yet, for all of Stroll's positive words, the transition wasn't entirely smooth, as Russian industrialist Dmitry Mazepin, father of GP3 racer and occasional Force India test driver Nikita Mazepin, made some waves last autumn when he announced a few weeks after Stroll's bid that he felt that his own bid had been ignored by the administrators. He claimed they had chosen not to engage with his consortium. By the end of September, his Uralkali company announced that it was suing the administrators, showing that a change of ownership hadn't stopped the team from operating under the threat of legal action.

What has emerged for 2019 is a team that will run Lance Stroll, naturally, plus Perez. Judging by the way that the team coped with the loss of all its points scored in the 12 races before the Belgian GP – 59, which had it sixth in the constructors' championship – and was still able to rank seventh at season's end with 52 points shows how competitive it might be. In fact, with the extra money in the pot, the team should do better than its "before and after" combined tally of points that would have left it fifth at year's end.

Opposite top: Rubens Barrichello gave Jordan its breakthrough podium at the 1994 Pacific GP as the team found a second wind and cemented its place in F1's midfield

Opposite middle left: Team founder Eddie Jordan offers Andrea de Cesaris advice.
Opposite middle right: Sergio Perez heading for third in Monaco in 2016

Opposite bottom: Esteban Ocon put in some impressive drives in 2018, the last year of the team competing as Force India, but he has not been kept on after the name change

TALKING POINT:
THE DECLINE OF HELMET LIVERIES

Making overtaking easier to do is on the wish list of most F1 fans. Another matter that almost everyone would love to see is drivers' helmets reverting to being identifiable from a distance, a return to when a driver's helmet design was their trademark.

When the Formula One World Championship had its inaugural race at Silverstone in 1950, it wasn't even mandatory to wear a helmet, with many simply wearing what was a brimless canvas hat. Basic, pudding-basin helmets followed in a range of single colours. It was only really when Graham Hill arrived in 1958 and had a band of white vertical stripes painted around his dark blue helmet – in tribute to his old rowing club – that identifiable differences began to occur. Some drivers simply added a bit of coloured tape so that their pit-crew could identify them from a team-mate who might also be wearing a white helmet. Others, like aristocratic German Wolfgang von Trips, augmented their helmet with the family crest.

As open-face helmets gave way to full-face helmets in the late 1960s, offering more scope for difference, so drivers wrought their identity, something that was especially useful when teams like BRM had multiple entries. Certainly, the racing numbers on the cars were larger then and easier to pick out on largely single-colour backgrounds, but identifying the difference between, say, Emerson Fittipaldi and Ronnie Peterson in their black and gold Lotuses was easy. Every F1 fan knew that Emmo's helmet was dark blue with a red stripe over

the top and Ronnie's was a lighter blue with yellow edging. Jackie Stewart had a white helmet banded with Stewart tartan.

Even into the 1990s, you could be sure that any F1 fan would be able to describe the helmet livery of every driver on the grid. They were a trademark, and not just for one season, but for their entire career, even being seen as an extension of their character. John Watson? Silver with an orange stripe over the top and around its base. Nelson Piquet? White with red stripes and a red teardrop on each side. One livery that continues to be copied by drivers in all categories is Ayrton Senna's. The three-time World Champion had a simple design incorporating Brazil's national colours, with a yellow base augmented by a blue band and a green band. It was simple, clear and, on his head, very fast indeed.

The beauty of the modern F1 helmet is that the outside, the part that can carry a livery, remains very much the same clean shape as it has been since full-face helmets were introduced, with the modern fittings inside, from radio to drinks bottle to emergency oxygen supply, all being hidden inside.

David Coulthard was being a patriotic Scotsman when he decided to race his kart in a simple blue helmet topped with

the diagonal stripes of the Scottish flag, the saltire. It was so good, though, so definable, that he kept it through his entire career and could always be identified by this classical design.

Being obliged contractually to carry sponsors' logos has made having a clear, clean livery harder to do, especially for any driver allied to the two Red Bull-funded teams. Red Bull insists on taking the entire middle of its drivers' helmets for its leaping bull logo, leaving the drivers just the top and the strip around the bottom to show off their chosen colours.

There is a simple rule that the more elaborate a helmet livery, the harder it is to identify, especially at speed. Some drivers make life harder still for fans in the grandstands and those watching on TV: they change their helmet several times a season. It might make a news story as they dedicate the new livery to a cause, an event or a simple whim, but it all chips away from their identity, even their brand.

An added complication since last year has been the halo fitted to F1 cars, to protect the driver's head, as this all but screens the drivers within. Nobody wishes to go back on safety measures by removing the halo, but wouldn't it be great if helmet liveries were made distinctive again?

TALKING POINT: DRIVERS WHO CHOSE BADLY

When Fernando Alonso announced last August that he would skip F1 in 2019, his move borne of frustration, he wasn't the first former World Champion who was left to rue quitting or ending up with a team that wasn't competitive enough to help him shoot for further titles.

It's hard to refute the fact that however great a driver is they will never win a world title with a team that isn't at or near the top of the competitive pile. Some drivers have picked well, or been guided to the teams most likely to provide them with a competitive ride by an agent. Others seem to get it more wrong than right, which is why a driver as supremely talented as Fernando Alonso has a mere two F1 drivers' titles to his name, as far back as 2005 and 2006 for Renault, when his talent was more than sufficient to have landed him at least double that title tally over the past decade and more.

Alonso's shortfall can't be laid solely at the door of the McLaren team which let him down so badly between 2015 and last year. Its Honda engines were seen as the main reason why its car wasn't competitive for the first three of those campaigns and then its chassis shortfall was clear for all to see in 2018. No, in the Spaniard's case in 2007 having jumped from Renault to McLaren, his impetuosity caused by the pace of rookie team-mate Lewis Hamilton probably cost him the title which Ferrari's Kimi Raikkonen took by a single point and his decision to quit at the end of that year to return to less competitive Renault was impetuous at best.

Moving to Ferrari in 2010 for what would be a five-year stay could have taken Fernando back to the top, and he was runner-up three times as Red Bull Racing then Mercedes moved to the front. Then came those wasted years with McLaren where he always outstripped his team-mates to work miracles, albeit ones that might yield only an eighth place rather than a win. No wonder he looked to Indycars and the Le Mans 24 Hours to satisfy his craving to win races.

Yet, Alonso isn't alone in jumping the wrong way, as Phil Hill moved from Ferrari to a new team, ATS, just two seasons after he landed the F1 title in 1961. Although manned by a swathe of ex-Ferrari staff, he scored not one point.

Family ties can lead to heart really ruling head. Take Emerson Fittipaldi, with F1 titles in 1972 and 1974 for Lotus and McLaren. Then, after finishing second in 1975, he opted at the 11th hour to join the family team, leaving the way clear for James Hunt to take his place at McLaren and land the 1976 title. That year, Emerson ranked only 17th in his Copersucar Fittipaldi.

When Williams was at the top of its game in the early 1990s, it played hardball with its drivers. After all, it didn't welcome Nigel Mansell back after he made the most of its dominant car to wn the 1992 title. Snubbed, he headed off to race Indycars and took his second title in two years. Instead, Williams welcomed Alain Prost, who duly took the 1993 F1 crown. But he too sought more money than Frank Williams and Patrick Head wanted to offer, so Prost's nemesis Ayrton Senna was brought in as he was prepared to race for less than Prost simply in order to have the best car. On top of this, Williams had long wanted him. Sadly, Senna was killed on his third outing.

F3000 racer David Coulthard was promoted to fill Senna's seat. Like Stirling Moss in the 1950s, though, Coulthard never landed a title despite winning grands prix galore. What will still grate for the Scot is that during his first full season with Williams he was advised to join McLaren for 1996. This meant an appreciably larger pay cheque, but it took him away from a team that helped Damon Hill and Jacques Villeneuve to the title in the next two years, while he ranked seventh and then equal third.

After a few years of F1, drivers should have a nose for a team's potential, but some plump for the wrong choice and their reputation takes the hit. Only this year's 21-race World Championship will tell whether Daniel Ricciardo has been the latest to do so in leaving Red Bull Racing for Renault.

KNOW THE TRACKS 2019

The calendar was a long time coming for 2019 as F1 owners Liberty Media worked hard on zoning the grands prix, to reorganize them into more sensible clusters to streamline the logistics. F1's new owners still want to push the number of grands prix out to 25 to expand their product, but the teams are resisting as they fear burn-out of their staff plus the additional expense.

There was a time in the 1970s and 1980s that a standard World Championship season consisted of 16 grands prix. Almost all of the races were held in Europe and they ran to a time-honoured pattern. Then the number of races beyond Europe began to grow, with these "flyaways" ever further from F1's heartland. Not all were successes, but the push was relentless: the F1 message must be spread.

Inexorably, though, the number of grands prix crept up every year. Hitting 20 grands prix for the first time in 2012 was a milestone, then 21 races became a reality in 2016. Fortunately for the teams, Liberty Media has stuck with 21 races for 2019, run to a very similar pattern to last year.

Teams talked of burn-out, so a summer break in August was implemented, to give the personnel time to recharge their batteries. Albeit this came at the "cost" of shunting grands prix onto consecutive weekends, with last year's run of five grands prix in six weeks from the French GP in June to the Hungarian GP at the end of July leaving the crews feeling out on their feet. For this year, though, the three races on consecutive weekends in the run-up to the summer break has been lost, making things that shade less brutal.

As it has for years, the season will kick off with the Australian GP in Melbourne. To provide a little more time between later races, it will be on 17 March, a week earlier than last year's

opener there and the season's final round has been moved back a week. A fortnight after Australia, it's Bahrain's turn, with the Chinese GP coming two weeks later.

The pattern of having grands prix every two weeks will continue through the sequence of Azerbaijan, Spain, Monaco, Canada and France. Then, hopefully with a fantastic battle at the top of the championship table, there will be the first shorter turnaround, with just a week between the race at Paul Ricard and the Austrian GP on the last weekend in June.

The British GP at Silverstone comes next before the race that had a question mark against it through most of 2018. This is the German GP. Indeed, this longstanding race was in doubt until news broke late last summer that it had been reinstated, for 2019 at least. The other option was the German GP falling into a pattern of one year on, one year off, alternating with a venue in another country that would have been unsatisfactory for a country with such a rich F1 history.

A week after the race at Hockenheim comes the final round before the four-week summer break, with the Hungaroring no doubt providing a hot and humid venue for the teams to try to maximize any performance advantages they may be enjoying.

From the middle of August to the first weekend in September, the idea is that the teams take a well-earned break, but you can be absolutely certain that any team that is struggling to get up to speed might just keep some of its engineers away from their families and the beach.

The Belgian GP is the best venue for F1 to mark that it is bursting back into life, as Spa-Francorchamps remains a brilliant place to go racing. Ancient Monza follows, with even more history seeping through it, but less of a challenging track layout.

Then it's time for the teams to leave their high-tech transporters back at their bases and load their equipment onto aeroplanes for the flyaway races, starting with the Singapore GP, a race made all the more spectacular as it's held after nightfall. From there, they head to the shores of the Black Sea for the Russian GP at Sochi before the global crisscrossing commences in earnest with the leap to Suzuka for the Japanese GP. Everyone then crosses half the planet to get to Mexico City. Unusually, the race will be held before the United States GP rather than after it.

The season will conclude with two of F1's most contrasting venues: organic, passion-filled Interlagos for the Brazilian GP and then ultra-modern, tailor-made Yas Marina for the finale at the Abu Dhabi GP.

So, the format is all but identical to last year's World Championship, but there is a strong feeling that this won't be the case for long, as Liberty Media is anxious to give F1 a shake-up, perhaps starting in 2020, as it looks to boost F1's appeal, expand its global spread and of course put more money into its coffers.

This shot across the Albert Park lake shows the Melbourne skyline to good effect, with the run from Turn 8 to Turn 10 in the foreground.

MELBOURNE

Built around a lake in a park in suburban Melbourne, Albert Park doesn't offer the flow of the great tracks, but the fans' enthusiasm makes it a popular place to start the season.

You need to attend a sporting event in Australia to understand just how much this most sports-mad of nations embraces anything that involves bat, ball or steering wheel. The Australian GP is not only the season-opener but also the one blessed with the best support programme of any on the World Championship calendar, with something on the track seemingly at all points across three days. That the Albert Park circuit is just a short tram ride from the city centre ensures that there is always a good crowd. Many of these might be there principally for the corporate entertainment, but their enthusiasm for a good party means that even those not born into motor racing have a good time, adding to the atmosphere.

The circuit runs in a clockwise direction around a lake in suburban Albert Park, with Turn 1 all too often a point of collision on the opening lap. If not there, then it may come at the even tighter right at Turn 3.

After running down an avenue of trees, the track finally gets to open out after Turn 6 as it runs between the edge of a golf course and the far side of the lake, with a wonderful esses at Turns 11 and 12. After Turn 13, though, the remainder of the lap falls back to the point-and-squirt format of the opening five turns.

What marks the Albert Park circuit out though, is that it sometimes produces an odd result for a minor team that just happens to get any new regulations right and manages to stay clear of trouble. Mark Webber's fifth place for tailenders Minardi in 2002 is one such result and more recently Romain Grosjean's sixth place on little-fancied Haas F1's debut in 2016.

INSIDE TRACK
AUSTRALIAN GRAND PRIX

Date:	**17 March**
Circuit name:	**Albert Park**
Circuit length:	**3.295 miles/5.300km**
Number of laps:	**58**
Email:	**enquiries@grandprix.com.au**
Website:	**www.grandprix.com.au**

PREVIOUS WINNERS

2009	**Jenson Button** BRAWN
2010	**Jenson Button** McLAREN
2011	**Sebastian Vettel** RED BULL
2012	**Jenson Button** McLAREN
2013	**Kimi Raikkonen** LOTUS
2014	**Nico Rosberg** MERCEDES
2015	**Lewis Hamilton** MERCEDES
2016	**Nico Rosberg** MERCEDES
2017	**Sebastian Vettel** FERRARI
2018	**Sebastian Vettel** FERRARI

Location: Albert Park is a mile or so from Melbourne's central business district, on the south side of the River Yarra.

How it started: Australian GPs have been held since 1928, when the race was run on Phillip Island. However, the race didn't gain World Championship status until 1985 when Adelaide hosted a street race. By 1996, Melbourne's greater financial clout had brought the race to Albert Park.

Most memorable race: As extravagant accidents tend to stick in the mind more than efficient victories, Ralf Schumacher getting airborne in his Williams into Turn 1 after hitting Rubens Barrichello's Ferrari in 2002 will always be connected with the venue.

Greatest local driver: Mark Webber and Daniel Ricciardo have been the top Aussies in recent years, and Alan Jones was champion in 1980, but Jack Brabham is the best of all. He was a three-time World Champion – in 1959, 1960 and 1966 – and the third of these was in a car bearing his name.

Rising star: Aussie Grit is the brand founded by Mark Webber and it sums up the attitude Australian racers require to head to Europe to further their nascent careers. Leading the way is Alex Peroni and Oscar Piastri shining in European Formula Renault.

2018 POLE TIME: **HAMILTON (MERCEDES),** 1M21.164S, 146.154MPH/235.212KPH
2018 WINNER'S AVERAGE SPEED: **128.044MPH/206.068KPH**

2018 FASTEST LAP: **RICCIARDO (RED BULL),** 1M25.945S, 138.024MPH/222.128KPH
LAP RECORD: **M SCHUMACHER (FERRARI),** 1M24.125S 141.016MPH/226.944KPH, 2004

SAKHIR

Formula One is making its 15th visit to Bahrain's purpose-built circuit, a venue that broke new ground on its debut in 2004 as it was split into distinct areas of desert and oasis.

An overriding feature of all of the racing circuits which have been built in the Middle East is that none have been held back by a lack of investment. Abu Dhabi's Yas Marina Circuit may be the most resplendent of all, but there was ample money available half a decade earlier when Bahrain beat the other Arab states to host a grand prix.

The people behind this circuit, built on scrubby land at Sakhir, wanted to present an image that wasn't just sand and rock, so paid for irrigation to keep the grass verges around its hub - the pits and main grandstands - green. This was done to suggest an oasis, with the track beyond Turn 3 kept in natural form, to represent the natural landscape: desert. In fact, it isn't entirely natural as the all too regular problem of sand blowing

onto the circuit is limited by spraying the verges with glue. It keeps the sand largely in check.

The lap kicks off with a tight right feeding into a tight left, like at Sepang, which is something of a signature of circuit architect Hermann Tilke. Then, a long straight gives the drivers a chance to settle down before turning sharp right at Turn 4. Coming back down a gentle slope offers the trickiest part of the lap, with a fabulous esse that can be made trickier still if a layer of sand blows in... Get it right, though, and a driver can gain enough of an advantage over a rival to have a go at overtaking into Turn 8.

Other potential passing points come at the top of the second country loop, Turn 13 or, as with all Tilke circuits, after a blast down the main straight in to Turn 1.

INSIDE TRACK
BAHRAIN GRAND PRIX

Date:	**31 March**
Circuit name:	**Bahrain International Circuit**
Circuit length:	**3.363 miles/5.412km**
Number of laps:	**57**
Email:	**info@bic.com.bh**
Website:	**www.bahraingp.com.bh**

PREVIOUS WINNERS

2008	**Felipe Massa** FERRARI
2009	**Jenson Button** BRAWN
2010	**Fernando Alonso** FERRARI
2012	**Sebastian Vettel** RED BULL
2013	**Sebastian Vettel** RED BULL
2014	**Lewis Hamilton** MERCEDES
2015	**Lewis Hamilton** MERCEDES
2016	**Nico Rosberg** MERCEDES
2017	**Sebastian Vettel** FERRARI
2018	**Sebastian Vettel** FERRARI

Location: Not much of the land in Bahrain has been developed, as industry is still limited and farming most certainly is not an option. On the other hand, this is why the circuit was able to find the space it needed in rocky and inhospitable open ground to the south of the capital, Manama.

How it started: The oil-rich Arab states all decided at the start of the millennium that they needed to build an image, to help make them look like appealing places to visit or even to live. This was why several looked to motor racing. Dubai was the first to build a track, but Bahrain did it better and landed a round of the World Championship in 2004.

Most memorable race: The racing hasn't been bad here, however, the drama has grown since 2014 when the actual time of the race was moved to later in the day - thus making it a night race. The best of these came in 2016, when Lewis Hamilton was left hanging on for the victory in a Mercedes which was fading more quickly than the daylight earlier in the evening.

Greatest local driver: Despite having plenty of oil money to promote a rising talent, the list of Bahraini racing stars is, well, short. In fact, not one Bahraini national even contested the recent Middle Eastern F4 series.

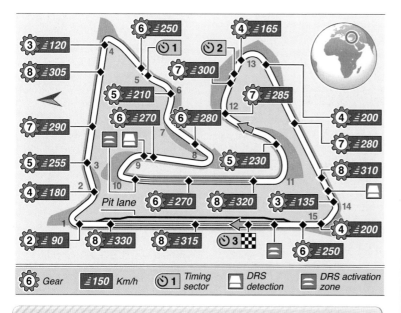

6 ≣ 250	**4** ≣ 165	
3 ≣ 120	**1**	**2**
8 ≣ 305	**7** ≣ 300	
5 ≣ 210	**7** ≣ 285	
7 ≣ 290	**6** ≣ 270	**6** ≣ 280	**4** ≣ 200
5 ≣ 255		**7** ≣ 280
4 ≣ 180	**5** ≣ 230	
Pit lane	**8** ≣ 310
6 ≣ 270	**8** ≣ 320	**3** ≣ 135
2 ≣ 90	**8** ≣ 330	**8** ≣ 315	**3**	**4** ≣ 200
	6 ≣ 250

6 Gear	≣ **150** Km/h	**1** Timing sector	DRS detection	DRS activation zone

2018 POLE TIME: VETTEL (FERRARI), 1M27.958S, 137.637MPH/221.505KPH
2018 WINNER'S AVERAGE SPEED: 124.867MPH/200.954KPH

2018 FASTEST LAP: BOTTAS (MERCEDES), 1M33.740S, 129.147MPH/207.842KPH
LAP RECORD: M SCHUMACHER (FERRARI), 1M30.252S 134.262MPH/216.074KPH, 2004

SHANGHAI

This modern circuit outside the burgeoning metropolis of Shanghai is built on a truly giant scale, from its towering grandstands to its lengthy back straight and huge paddock.

One of the remarkable elements of China's development over the past two decades has been the transformation of once minor towns into modern cities seemingly almost overnight, and similarly local roads turned into major motorways. The Shanghai International Circuit is one such example, as it was just a patch of marshy land before it was chosen for its new purpose. It took considerable engineering know-how, with huge polystyrene blocks sunk into the ground to stabilize it. Then a circuit was built upon it with infrastructure so large that it took the F1 teams' breath away when they saw it for the first time in 2004. Everything from the pit building to the grandstands was oversized. The team offices were larger than most people's houses.

The track also exudes space, with plenty of width for overtaking at several points around its lap. The first three corners are unusual in that Turn 1 leads directly into a short climb to Turn 2, where it crests the rise before plunging the pack down into the even sharper left of Turn 3. It's worth a shot around the outside, which becomes the inside of Turn 3, but success is far from guaranteed.

A more likely place to pass a rival is after the run to Turn 6, a righthand hairpin. The cornering then becomes more challenging, with the sweep through Turns 7 and 8 before another hairpin. Turns 11 to 13 are a reverse of Turns 1 to 3, albeit on the level, and the exit to 13 is key as it feeds onto the longest straight. Drivers can hit 210mph before they break from the tow of a rival to try to pass into the Turn 14 hairpin.

70

INSIDE TRACK
CHINESE GRAND PRIX

Date:	**14 April**
Circuit name:	**Shanghai International Circuit**
Circuit length:	**3.390 miles/5.450km**
Number of laps:	**56**
Email:	**f1@china-sss.com**
Website:	**www.f1china.com.cn**

PREVIOUS WINNERS

2009	**Sebastian Vettel** RED BULL
2010	**Jenson Button** McLAREN
2011	**Lewis Hamilton** McLAREN
2012	**Nico Rosberg** MERCEDES
2013	**Fernando Alonso** FERRARI
2014	**Lewis Hamilton** MERCEDES
2015	**Lewis Hamilton** MERCEDES
2016	**Nico Rosberg** MERCEDES
2017	**Lewis Hamilton** MERCEDES
2018	**Daniel Ricciardo** RED BULL

Location: Head out of Shanghai and a different backdrop will greet you each year as more and more of the surrounding countryside is built over. The circuit is 20 miles north of the city centre.

How it started: The Chinese government put up all the necessary money to ensure a patch of marshy land was made firm and a circuit was built – with gargantuan infrastructure – in time for the first Chinese GP in 2004.

Most memorable race: Although Lewis Hamilton's fumble makes 2007 the best known, Hamilton was also is a tense situation in 2015 when he beat Mercedes team-mate Nico Rosberg, who accused him of "backing him up" into the reach of Sebastian Vettel.

Greatest local driver: With no F1 racer yet, bar the dabbling of Ma Qing Hua in 2012 and 2013, China's most successful driver is Dutch-born (to Chinese parents) Ho Pin Tung who was second in the 2017 World Endurance Championship P2 category, including second place outright in the Le Mans 24 Hours.

Rising star: There are a number of upcoming Chinese single-seater racers, and Guan Yu Zhou is the pick, having spent 2018 as a frontrunner in the European F3 series for leading team Prema Theodore Racing.

2018 POLE TIME: RICCIARDO (RED BULL), 1M31.095S, 133.855MPH/215.419KPH
2018 WINNER'S AVERAGE SPEED: 118.962MPH/191.451KPH

2018 FASTEST LAP: RICCIARDO (RED BULL) 1M35.785S, 127.301MPH/204.871KPH
LAP RECORD: M SCHUMACHER (FERRARI), 1M32.238S 132.202MPH/212.759KPH, 2004

BAKU

Azerbaijan's capital provides the backdrop for a circuit that comes in two distinct parts, starting with open spaces before entering the confines around the citadel's ancient walls.

Formula One purists threw up their hands in horror when Azerbaijan was bidding to host a grand prix. This surely, they cried, was not on, a country with close to zero motorsport history trying to land a round of the World Championship when France – the home of the first ever grand prix in 1906 – was on the sidelines and Germany was struggling to keep its place on the calendar. This was simply chasing the money rather than staying true to its roots. Indeed it was, with oil-rich Azerbaijan keen to use F1 to promote its capital, Baku.

With its place guaranteed for 2016, it impressed all who visited by its temporary circuit offering a distinctive backdrop to further counterbalance the series of not always distinctive modern autodromes favoured in the previous decade.

With a lap starting with a blast along the seafront, the early part of the lap was kept interesting by longish straights between its run of four 90-degree corners, with the buildings behind adding character.

However, where the track really shows its difference is the tighter environment after Turn 8, where it skirts the outside of the citadel, huge stone walls making the circuit feel very enclosed. Opening out at Turn 11, it then offers a series of quick kinks past the city's grandest buildings along to Turn 16 before plunging downhill back to sea level and another run of quick flicks past a park.

Top speed is achieved towards the end of the start/finish straight, before drivers brake hard for the start of that run of 90-degree bends.

INSIDE TRACK
AZERBAIJAN GRAND PRIX

Date:	28 April
Circuit name:	Baku City Circuit
Circuit length:	3.753 miles/6.006km
Number of laps:	51
Email:	info@bakugp.az
Website:	www.bakugp.az

PREVIOUS WINNERS

2016	**Nico Rosberg** MERCEDES
2017	**Daniel Ricciardo** RED BULL
2017	**Lewis Hamilton** MERCEDES

Location: Tourists to the capital of this oil-rich former Soviet state won't have far to travel to see the action. The pit and paddock area is located on Baku Boulevard, the city's smartest street with its views out onto the Caspian Sea.

How it started: A few years before the Baku City Circuit was prepared for the country's F1 debut, Azerbaijan's capital put up the money for an international GT race in 2013, at a temporary venue nearby. This went well enough as the country pushed to raise its international profile and another was held the following year. After signing the contract with FOM, a race date was chosen for 2016. Strangely, it was allowed in by racing under the convenience title of the European GP despite the, ahem, small matter of not being in Europe... Commonsense - or reality - prevailed thereafter and, since 2017, it has hosted the event as the Azerbaijan GP. Held in June in 2016 and 2017, the race is now held at the start of the season, in late April.

Most memorable race: The 2017 grand prix will be remembered for reasons that didn't show Sebastian Vettel in a good light. Ferrari's team leader became frustrated and drove into Lewis Hamilton as they ran behind the safety car. He collected a 10s penalty and Hamilton was delayed in the pits having a loose headrest reaffixed, so Daniel Ricciardo came through to win for Red Bull Racing.

Rising star: The world is still waiting for one... and the same can be said for the category of Greatest local driver!

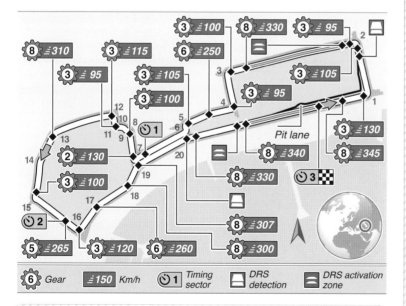

6 Gear	≣150 Km/h	🕐1 Timing sector	▱ DRS detection	▱ DRS activation zone

2018 POLE TIME: **VETTEL (FERRARI)**, 1M41.498S, 132.301MPH/212.918KPH

2018 WINNER'S AVERAGE SPEED: **109.990MPH/177.012KPH**

2018 FASTEST LAP: **BOTTAS (MERCEDES)**, 1M45.149S, 127.707MPH/205.525KPH

LAP RECORD: **VETTEL (FERRARI)**, 1M43.441S 129.816MPH/208.919KPH, 2017

The Circuit de Catalunya would come to life if now retired national hero Fernando Alonso was driving a competitive car in 2019 and pitching for a home win for the first time since 2013.

This circuit used to be home from home for the F1 teams back in the days when testing was all but unlimited. Teams spent much of the winter and many of the weeks between grands prix here. This was because the weather was generally better than at more northerly circuits, especially Silverstone, the track closest to the bases of the majority of the teams. Furthermore, its lap offered a wide range of corners that echoed everything from fast sweeps through mid-speed corners to hairpins.

Since then, the Circuit de Catalunya has been shorn of its finest feature, its magnificent final sweep onto the start/finish straight. This was neutered in 2007 by a new turn at Turn 13 leading to a chicane to slow the cars' entry to the start/finish straight and, in turn, also

slow their arrival into Turn 1. Nonetheless, the cars can still exceed 205mph as they make the downhill approach to that tight right corner.

The first two turns have to be considered as a pair on lap 1 as they are so close together, with it not being unknown for cars to end up in the gravel trap. From there, the track rises gently through a long right and a short straight, before rising some more out to Turn 4, plunging down out of Turn 5, then flicking up the slope at Turn 7. Turn 9, Campsa, remains the trickiest of all, as the entry is blind, being on the crest of the hill, and a good exit is vital as it feeds on to the infield straight.

Out of the Turn 10 hairpin, it's uphill again, until dropping all the way to the start line from Turn 12.

INSIDE TRACK
SPANISH GRAND PRIX

Date:	**12 May**
Circuit name:	**Circuit de Barcelona-Catalunya**
Circuit length:	**2.892 miles/4.654km**
Number of laps:	**66**
Email:	**info@circuitcat.com**
Website:	**www.circuitcat.com**

PREVIOUS WINNERS

2009	**Jenson Button** BRAWN
2010	**Mark Webber** RED BULL
2011	**Sebastian Vettel** RED BULL
2012	**Pastor Maldonado** WILLIAMS
2013	**Fernando Alonso** FERRARI
2014	**Lewis Hamilton** MERCEDES
2015	**Nico Rosberg** MERCEDES
2016	**Max Verstappen** RED BULL
2017	**Lewis Hamilton** MERCEDES
2018	**Lewis Hamilton** MERCEDES

Location: The circuit can be found in an increasingly industrialized hilly area at Montmelo, some 15 miles to the north of Barcelona's city centre.

How it started: Spain has had a round of the World Championship since 1951, but it has moved between five circuits - Pedralbes, Jarama, Montjuich Park and Jerez - before finding its home here in 1991.

Most memorable race: The 2001 encounter was one that got away from Mika Hakkinen, as he retired his McLaren with clutch failure when leading on the final lap, thus handing victory to Ferrari's Michael Schumacher.

Greatest local driver: Spain had to wait 52 years from hosting its first grand prix to having a grand prix winner of its own, when Fernando Alonso triumphed in Hungary in 2003. He won the world title in both 2005 and 2006 for Renault, then lost out by a point in 2008, when racing for McLaren. Had he chosen his teams better, he'd probably have a couple more titles to his name.

Rising star: Carlos Sainz Jr has showed great speed for Renault, while Roberto Mehri races well in F2 but has had his shot at F1. This leaves F3 racer Alex Palou as Spain's next big hope.

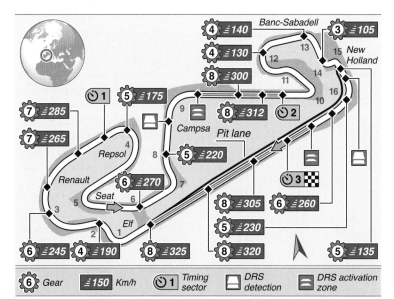

Banc-Sabadell · New Holland · Campsa · Pit lane · Repsol · Renault · Seat · Elf

| 6 Gear | 150 Km/h | ⏱1 Timing sector | DRS detection | DRS activation zone |

2018 POLE TIME: HAMILTON (MERCEDES), 1M16.173S, 136.701MPH/219.999KPH
2018 WINNER'S AVERAGE SPEED: 119.890MPH/192.945KPH

2018 FASTEST LAP: RICCIARDO (RED BULL), 1M18.441S, 132.748MPH/213.638KPH
LAP RECORD: RICCIARDO (RED BULL), 1M18.441S, 132.748MPH/213.638KPH, 2018

MONACO

There is no circuit like Monaco. A fixture since the 1920s, it is glamour and backdrop rather than a real driving challenge, but it remains an essential ingredient in every World Championship.

Every F1 fan will have a different view of the world famous circuit around the streets of Monte Carlo, and not all of them favourable, but it remains an integral and key element of the World Championship due to its fame, perceived glamour and globally recognized identity.

Any circuit that has hosted a grand prix since 1929 is due respect, but it's safe to say that the streets and harbourfront in this principality on the Riviera had more space to play with in those simpler days. Remarkably, though, as the price of Monaco's residential property has soared, there is still space made for this annual invasion by the teams with their ever-growing amount of kit and personnel.

While there have certainly been nips and tucks to the track across the decades, not unlike those done to many of the residents,

it is intrinsically the lap of old as it starts low down just back from the harbourfront before angling both right and uphill from the first corner and best passing spot, Sainte Devote. The twisting rise reaches its crest at Massenet, a tricky corner with a blind entry between the all-enclosing barriers. Casino Square is a quick flick across a rare open space before the track dips down again to Mirabeau, doubles back to a lefthand hairpin and then a sharp right to reach the seafront at Portier.

Drivers then race through a long tunnel under a hotel before bursting back into daylight. After a gentle decline, albeit at 190mph, they're back at harbour level, with a point-and-squirt past the billionaires' yachts, around the swimming pool and then through the La Rascasse hairpin and back onto the curving start/finish straight.

INSIDE TRACK
MONACO GRAND PRIX

Date:	**26 May**
Circuit name:	**Circuit de Monaco**
Circuit length:	**2.075 miles/3.339km**
Number of laps:	**78**
Email:	**info@acm.mc**
Website:	**www.acm.mc**

PREVIOUS WINNERS

2009	**Jenson Button** BRAWN
2010	**Mark Webber** RED BULL
2011	**Sebastian Vettel** RED BULL
2012	**Mark Webber** RED BULL
2013	**Nico Rosberg** MERCEDES
2014	**Nico Rosberg** MERCEDES
2015	**Nico Rosberg** MERCEDES
2016	**Lewis Hamilton** MERCEDES
2017	**Sebastian Vettel** FERRARI
2018	**Daniel Ricciardo** RED BULL

Location: Monte Carlo is the heart of Monaco, and this is where the track is formed every year, laid out on public roads beneath the Grimaldis' (Monaco royal family) castle before bucking up a slope to Casino Square and then descending again to the harbourside.

How it started: Monaco's royal family was convinced in 1929 that a race around the streets would be a great way to give the principality some allure. It worked.

Most memorable race: The 1968 Monaco GP looked all set to provide a massive shock result, with French novice Johnny Servoz-Gavin streaking into the lead in his Matra. But he went too hard as he revelled in the glory, clouted a barrier and was out, hero to zero. This left Graham Hill to win for Lotus, this his fifth and final victory there.

Greatest local driver: Droves of F1 drivers have based themselves in Monaco, attracted by its lenient tax regime. However, after Louis Chiron in the 1950s, there were no Monegasque frontrunners, until Charles Leclerc, who looks set to put that record straight, especially having joined Ferrari for 2019.

Rising star: The next crop of Monaco-born racing drivers is being led by Louis Prette Jr, who has been learning the ropes in Asia, first in Formula Renault and more recently in F3.

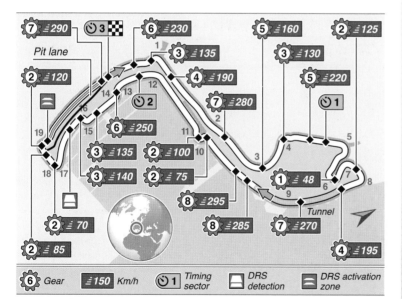

⚙ Gear	≡150 Km/h	⏱1 Timing sector	▭ DRS detection	▱ DRS activation zone

2018 POLE TIME: RICCIARDO (RED BULL), 1M10.810S, 105.418MPH/169.654KPH
2018 WINNER'S AVERAGE SPEED: 94.293MPH/151.750KPH

2018 FASTEST LAP: VERSTAPPEN (RED BULL), 1M14.260S, 100.520MPH/161.772KPH
LAP RECORD: VERSTAPPEN (RED BULL), 1M14.260S 100.520MPH/161.722KPH, 2018

There's no time to admire the yachts or the cast of celebrities on them in the Monaco harbour as the drivers power out of the chicane and head to Tabac.

MONTREAL

With water on either side, this island circuit across the river from downtown Montreal, always feels constrained. It's brutal on cars, with several points where heavy braking is required.

It seems a very, very long time ago that Canada's grand prix was held in the woods outside Toronto when Mosport Park was its home in the 1970s. Yet the rise of Canada's first great driver, Gilles Villeneuve, encouraged his home province of Quebec to bring their French-speaking hero to play closer to home in its largest city, Montreal. This was when its grand prix became cosmopolitan. That was in 1978, and it has never looked back.

The venue chosen for this was on an island in the broad St Lawrence River, an area previously developed first for the EXPO world fair in 1967 and then as the home of the Olympic rowing lake in 1976. The island is narrow, and this meant that the track had to be packed tightly into the space available, although a new pit and paddock area this year should help. The resulting layout is one that allows for an unusual amount of full throttle acceleration matched by many points of heavy braking, making life tough for the cars.

The first corner is approached via a right flick and it's a tight left where many a driver gets into trouble on the opening lap. It's followed immediately by Coin Senna, a righthand hairpin that feeds the cars into a twisting run of esses that has trees on one side and the river on the other. Heavy braking into Turn 6 is followed by a longer run down to an esse then another blast to the Epingle hairpin.

From here it's flat-out all the way to the final twist onto the start/finish straight where 210mph can be topped before drivers brake hard and some attempt a passing move as they dive into the right/left chicane.

INSIDE TRACK
CANADIAN GRAND PRIX

Date:	**9 June**
Circuit name:	**Circuit Gilles Villeneuve**
Circuit length:	**2.710 miles/4.361km**
Number of laps:	**70**
Email:	**info@circuitgillesvilleneuve.ca**
Website:	**www.circuitgillesvilleneuve.ca**

PREVIOUS WINNERS

2008	**Robert Kubica** BMW SAUBER
2010	**Lewis Hamilton** McLAREN
2011	**Jenson Button** McLAREN
2012	**Lewis Hamilton** McLAREN
2013	**Sebastian Vettel** RED BULL
2014	**Daniel Ricciardo** RED BULL
2015	**Lewis Hamilton** MERCEDES
2016	**Lewis Hamilton** MERCEDES
2017	**Lewis Hamilton** MERCEDES
2018	**Sebastian Vettel** FERRARI

Location: This is a city circuit that isn't in downtown; the Circuit Gilles Villeneuve is actually located across the St Lawrence River on the Ile de Notre Dame.

How it started: Gilles Villeneuve's ascent to F1 stardom encouraged Montreal to build a circuit where he could shine. That was in 1978 and he rewarded them by winning the first race there.

Most memorable race: Jenson Button's win in 2011 is the most impressive, as he achieved it in adverse conditions. The race lasted four hours because of a rain stoppage, and he came through to win for McLaren by passing Sebastian Vettel with half a lap to go when the Red Bull driver slipped wide.

Greatest local driver: Jacques Villeneuve landed Canada's only world title in 1997 when he starred for Williams in his second year of F1. However, his father Gilles was better, showing almost unnatural speed, but he was killed in 1982 before he could be crowned.

Rising star: Lance Stroll has two years of F1 behind him, but questions remain whether this son of a billionaire will be the next Canadian to win. He has talent but, as is the modern way, won't win a grand prix unless he joins a top team. Before injury, Indycar racer Robert Wickens showed greater potential.

Droit du Casino

Pit lane

Virage Senna

Gear | 150 Km/h | Timing sector | DRS detection | DRS activation zone

2018 POLE TIME: VETTEL (FERRARI), 1M10.764S, 137.856MPH/221.858KPH
2018 WINNER'S AVERAGE SPEED: 124.894MPH/200.997KPH

2018 FASTEST LAP: VERSTAPPEN (RED BULL), 1M13.864S, 132.070MPH/212.547KPH
LAP RECORD: BARRICHELLO (FERRARI), 1M13.622S 132.511MPH/213.256KPH, 2004

PAUL RICARD

Back in harness as the home of the French Grand Prix, this completely modernized 1970s circuit has sweeping turns, colour-striped outfields and, sadly, serious access problems.

When a circuit is brought back to the World Championship after a lengthy break, it's hard to tell how it will be received. The passing of decades have meant, inevitably, that health and safety concerns – scarcely aired in its former life – would have to be considered, invariably changing the nature of the venue.

Paul Ricard had already been changed from the high-speed circuit on a windy plateau inland from Toulon. Major modernization had been completed a decade before, when it was given run-off galore and modern facilities to make it attractive as an F1 test venue. However, a lot of its original nature still remains, as, thankfully, does its generally sunny weather.

The lap had been tweaked remarkably little from its previous French GP era, back in the days of Alain Prost's pomp in 1989. However, the insertion of one small feature, the chicane midway along the Mistral Straight, has made a large difference to its flow. It is approached at more than 200mph and so quite how high terminal speed would be for the cars in the seventh-gear right at its end, Signes, remains a tantalizing and frankly frightening thought.

Like the start of the lap, the final sector offers a series of twisting curves; none are fast and the final turn is tricky. There are wide expanses of coloured banding out beyond the tarmac, becoming ever coarser in surface texture to slow errant cars.

One issue the circuit doesn't want to be known for is traffic trouble. The horrendous tailbacks endured by teams, drivers and fans alike in 2018 will need to be eradicated if the race is to continue here.

INSIDE TRACK
FRENCH GRAND PRIX

Date:	23 June
Circuit name:	Circuit Paul Ricard
Circuit length:	3.630 miles/5.842km
Number of laps:	53
Email:	circuit@circuitpaulricard.com
Website:	www.circuitpaulricard.com

PREVIOUS WINNERS

1980	**Alan Jones** WILLIAMS
1982	**Rene Arnoux** RENAULT
1983	**Alain Prost** RENAULT
1985	**Nelson Piquet** BRABHAM
1986	**Nigel Mansell** WILLIAMS
1987	**Nigel Mansell** WILLIAMS
1988	**Alain Prost** McLAREN
1989	**Alain Prost** McLAREN
1990	**Alain Prost** FERRARI
2018	**Lewis Hamilton** MERCEDES

Location: Up on a plateau 20 miles to the north-west of Toulon, the circuit is built on an arid patch of land surrounded by pine forests.

How it started: The first French GP was held at Le Mans in 1906 and then moved to various locations, including Dieppe and Montlhery. When the World Championship began in 1950, it was Reims that had the honour, but all-new Paul Ricard took it over from Clermont-Ferrand in 1971, with new levels of safety.

Most memorable race: The last grand prix before F1 turned its back on Paul Ricard was in 1990 and there was nearly a shock result as Ivan Capelli led half the race until, with just three laps to go, his Leyton House faltered and Alain Prost came through to win for Ferrari.

Greatest local driver: With four F1 world titles to his name – in 1985, 1986, 1989 and 1993 – Alain Prost is by far the most garlanded French racer of all time, and he shared those between two teams, with three for McLaren and the last for Williams.

Rising star: France has a number of young stars doing well on the nursery slopes, with Sacha Fenestraz, a winner in European F3, and Anthoine Hubert leading the way in GP3.

77

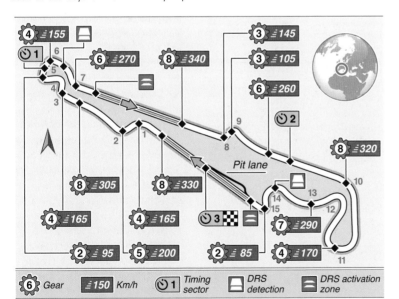

6 Gear	
150 Km/h	
⟳1	Timing sector
▢	DRS detection
▱	DRS activation zone

2018 POLE TIME: HAMILTON (MERCEDES), 1M30.029S, 145.155MPH/233.604KPH
2018 WINNER'S AVERAGE SPEED: 128.018MPH/206.025KPH

2018 FASTEST LAP: BOTTAS (MERCEDES), 1M34.225S, 138.690MPH/223.201KPH
LAP RECORD: BOTTAS (MERCEDES), 1M34.225S, 138.690MPH/223.201KPH, 2018

RED BULL RING

No circuit visited by Formula One is more picturesque, with the Red Bull Ring being blessed with a mountainside location that offers gradient changes galore and a stunning backdrop too.

Austria's return to the World Championship in 2014 was something heralded not only by F1 fans but also by photographers and TV camera crews. The track looks beautiful from almost every angle, the cars can be silhouetted against the sky from the lower angles or with the broad valley beyond if shown from above.

There's more to the Red Bull Ring than just spectacle, though, as it has history behind it too. Indeed, it has been raced on under two previous names, starting life as the Osterreichring and then returning in truncated form as the A1 Ring up until 2003. It was then renamed, but not changed when it became the Red Bull Ring, although the facilities were spruced up.

The essence of the lap is that it starts low then rears up sharply to the first corner, flattens out with a crest just before the apex and then climbs all the way to just after Remus before snaking its way back down again.

From that first turn, drivers hunt for a tow on the ascent to Remus as it's undoubtedly the best passing spot. This tight second-gear right is also the scene of much contact when moves go wrong...

Schlossgold is a tricky corner and another potential passing spot as the track folds back on itself, with width for a move on the exit. The downhill return through Turns 4 to 6 has a good flow, but after the right flick at Turn 7, the track runs along the level until reaching the next possible place to pass at what is also the circuit's most challenging corner. This is the penultimate corner, the Rindtkurve, out of which the track drops sharply to the final corner.

INSIDE TRACK
AUSTRIAN GRAND PRIX

Date:	30 June
Circuit name:	Red Bull Ring
Circuit length:	2.688 miles/4.326km
Number of laps:	71
Email:	information@projekt-spielberg.at
Website:	www.projekt-spielberg.at

PREVIOUS WINNERS

Year	Winner	Team
1999	Eddie Irvine	FERRARI
2000	Mika Hakkinen	McLAREN
2001	David Coulthard	McLAREN
2002	Michael Schumacher	FERRARI
2003	Michael Schumacher	FERRARI
2014	Nico Rosberg	MERCEDES
2015	Nico Rosberg	MERCEDES
2016	Lewis Hamilton	MERCEDES
2017	Valtteri Bottas	MERCEDES
2018	Max Verstappen	RED BULL

Location: Far from any city of note, the Red Bull Ring is in the mountainous Styrian region, some 45 miles to the north-west of Graz, near the village of Zeltweg.

How it started: Austria hosted its first grand prix on an airfield circuit at Zeltweg in 1963, then had one with World Championship status in 1964. However, the Osterriechring was built on the valleyside above it in 1969. This was the circuit on which the Red Bull Ring is based.

Most memorable race: If you like your finishes close, the 1982 Austrian GP is the race for you, as Elio de Angelis kept the nose of his Lotus ahead of Keke Rosberg's charging Williams by just 0.05s to give the Ford Cosworth DFV its 150th win.

Greatest local driver: Austria has a strong representation among the ranks of world champions, with Jochen Rindt leading the way, albeit posthumously, in 1970. Then Niki Lauda won the title with Ferrari in 1975 and 1977 before coming back to F1 and being crowned with McLaren in 1984.

Rising star: Ferdinand Habsburg of Austria's royal dynasty could well be the country's top racer, although his 2018 form in European F3 was a step down from his great late-season races in 2017.

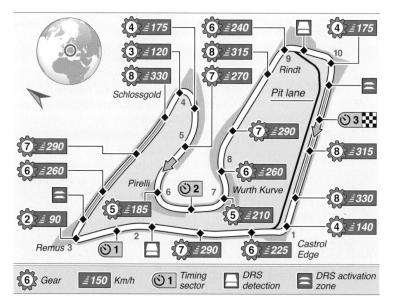

6 Gear	
150 Km/h	
1	Timing sector
DRS	detection
DRS activation	zone

2018 POLE TIME: **BOTTAS (MERCEDES),** 1M03.130S, 153.002MPH/246.234KPH
2018 WINNER'S AVERAGE SPEED: **139.444MPH/224.414KPH**

2018 FASTEST LAP: **RAIKKONEN (FERRARI),** 1M06.957S, 144.257MPH/232.160KPH
LAP RECORD: **RAIKKONEN (FERRARI),** 1M06.957S, 144.257MPH/232.160KPH, 2018

SILVERSTONE

It is more than 70 years since this former World War Two airfield circuit hosted its first grand prix but, unless a change occurs in its relationship with F1, this could be its last.

Visit Silverstone in spring or autumn, when the wind is blowing across the flat terrain and rain is strafing the circuit, and it's hard to find any charm. Be there on a summer day, though, when the sun is blazing down and every inch of the spectator banking is packed with fanatical spectators for the British GP and the place is transformed. It's beer, barbecues and shared passion. On days like these, when it's doing what it does best – showing cars being driven on the edge through fast corners – it's easy to understand why Silverstone is still one of the temples of world motorsport.

Fast and open has always been the essence of the track, as you'd expect of a track built on and around an old airfield. It matters not that the startline moved in recent years to the straight between Club and Abbey following the construction of the Wing pits complex rather than being located, as it was for decades, between Woodcote and Copse, as the nature of the lap remains.

Village provides an early passing opportunity, with several moves started here carrying on through the next twist or two through The Loop. A good run out of here onto the Wellington Straight offers another chance into Brooklands. Copse is still a mighty test, taken in sixth. However, the pick of the turns of not just this circuit but also of the whole season is Becketts. This right/left/right complex is awesome, taken at considerable speed with cars right on the edge of adhesion. A top speed of 210mph is achieved before braking into Stowe, then diving into the Vale, with a clear passing chance coming at the tight left that feeds into the long final corner: Club.

INSIDE TRACK
BRITISH GRAND PRIX

Date:	**14 July**
Circuit name:	**Silverstone**
Circuit length:	**3.659 miles/5.900km**
Number of laps:	**52**
Email:	**sales@silverstone-circuit.co.uk**
Website:	**www.silverstone-circuit.co.uk**

PREVIOUS WINNERS

2009	**Sebastian Vettel** RED BULL
2010	**Mark Webber** RED BULL
2011	**Fernando Alonso** FERRARI
2012	**Mark Webber** RED BULL
2013	**Nico Rosberg** MERCEDES
2014	**Lewis Hamilton** MERCEDES
2015	**Lewis Hamilton** MERCEDES
2016	**Lewis Hamilton** MERCEDES
2017	**Lewis Hamilton** MERCEDES
2018	**Sebastian Vettel** FERRARI

Location: Silverstone is a few miles to the west of Towcester and 40 miles north-east of Oxford.

How it started: There were many airfields after World War Two that had lost their purpose, and Silverstone gained a new life when a circuit was laid out around its perimeter roads in 1948, also taking in stretches of the runways.

Most memorable race: The 1969 British GP enjoyed a spectacular battle between Matra's Jackie Stewart and Jochen Rindt, in which they dropped their rivals, and chopped and changed positions until Rindt's Lotus pitted when a wing endplate was snagging a tyre.

Greatest local driver: Graham Hill has two F1 titles, Jackie Stewart three and Lewis Hamilton five, but there can be few protests if Jim Clark, F1 champion in 1963 and 1965, is selected ahead of them. He made winning look simple, a great stylist who was not only unbelievably smooth but had the good fortune to be under the wing of Colin Chapman when Lotus was building the fastest cars.

Rising stars: Britain has an impressive number of drivers dominating the junior categories, with George Russell and Lando Norris doing enough in F2 to earn F1 seats for 2019 and Callum Ilott a pacesetter in GP3.

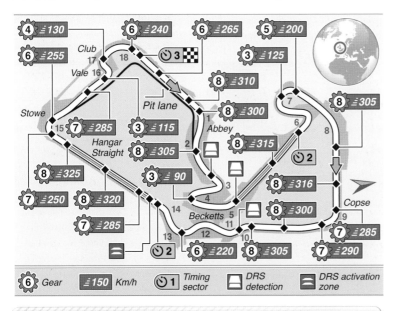

6 Gear	150 Km/h	⏱1 Timing sector	▱ DRS detection	▱ DRS activation zone

2018 POLE TIME: HAMILTON (MERCEDES), 1M25.892S, 153.422MPH/246.910KPH
2018 WINNER'S AVERAGE SPEED: 130.470MPH/209.972KPH

2018 FASTEST LAP: VETTEL (FERRARI), 1M30.696S, 145.296MPH/233.831KPH
LAP RECORD: HAMILTON (MERCEDES), 1M30.621S 145.416MPH/234.025KPH, 2017

HOCKENHEIM

There was much doubt that the German GP would happen in 2019 as Hockenheim's poor financial state meant it wanted another European venue with which to share this grand prix.

However, a deal was done thanks to the commitment of sponsors, including Mercedes. The thought of a World Championship without a round in Germany simply feels wrong and F1 owners Liberty Media get that. For now at least...

In fact, 2018-19 will be the first time Hockenheim has hosted a round of the World Championship in consecutive years since 2005-06, though there was a time that it shared the German GP with the Nurburgring.

The circuit has been changed radically over the years. Anyone visiting would be surprised to know that it opened in 1929, for there's no real sign of the original circuit. However, anyone who hadn't visited since 2001 would also be surprised, as the "forest loop" has gone. The lengthy blast away from the first corner into the forest

before braking heavily for the first of three chicanes has been transformed. Instead, a third of the way along its original length, there's a hairpin right that feeds into a left onto the lap's longest straight, Actually, it's a long arc to the left up to a second hairpin, a key spot for overtaking as the drivers brake from just over 200mph.

The lap then changes nature and a fast kink to the right is followed by a tighter left and then a right. Flowing it's not.

What follows is a section that wasn't affected by the 2001 shortening of the lap, as that right feeds onto what was the original return leg from the forest loop and it fires the cars into the stadium section. This is where the track turns hard right to put the cars into a loop in front of the grandstands, with the drivers being greeted by a gladiatorial atmosphere.

INSIDE TRACK
GERMAN GRAND PRIX

Date:	28 July
Circuit name:	Hockenheimring
Circuit length:	2.842 miles/4.574km
Number of laps:	67
Email:	info@hockenheimring.de
Website:	www.hockenheimring.de

PREVIOUS WINNERS

2003	Juan Pablo Montoya WILLIAMS
2004	Michael Schumacher FERRARI
2005	Fernando Alonso RENAULT
2006	Michael Schumacher FERRARI
2008	Lewis Hamilton McLAREN
2010	Fernando Alonso FERRARI
2012	Fernando Alonso FERRARI
2014	Nico Rosberg MERCEDES
2016	Lewis Hamilton MERCEDES
2018	Lewis Hamilton MERCEDES

Location: Hockenheim lies 55 miles south of Frankfurt, with the circuit tucked into an area of woodland on the north side of town, hemmed in by an autobahn.

How it started: Mercedes created Hockenheim as a test facility in 1929. As the Nurburgring was the chosen home of the German GP, Hockenheim remained Germany's second circuit, until it was given the 1970 grand prix while the Nurburgring was modernized. Jochen Rindt won that for Lotus.

Most memorable race: There have been some great races at Hockenheim, but 1987 stands out for its surprise result. Alain Prost was cruising to victory for McLaren, but an alternator belt snapped with four laps to go and handed the win to Williams's Nelson Piquet.

Greatest local driver: Michael Schumacher would top any country's list, with his record seven F1 titles and he remains at the top of the pile. Behind him is Sebastian Vettel, the winner of four World Championships.

Rising star: Nico Hulkenberg deserves to be Germany's next World Champion, but he has yet to be chosen by a top team. On the way up to F1, Maximilian Gunther looks to be carrying the most speed. Last year, he won a round in F2, but was inconsistent.

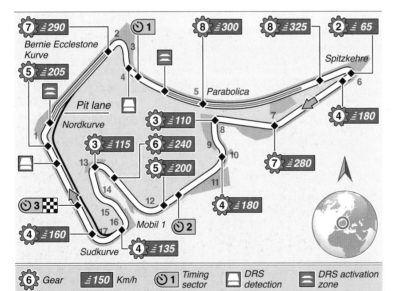

7 ≡ 290 — Bernie Ecclestone Kurve
5 ≡ 205
Pit lane
Nordkurve
3 ≡ 115
13
14
15
16
3 ≡ 3
4 ≡ 160
Sudkurve
4 ≡ 135
Mobil 1 ⏱ 2
12
5 ≡ 200
6 ≡ 240
3 ≡ 110
⏱ 1
5 Parabolica
8
9
10
11
4 ≡ 180
7 ≡ 280
8 ≡ 300
8 ≡ 325
2 ≡ 65 — Spitzkehre
6
4 ≡ 180
7

6 Gear | ≡ 150 Km/h | ⏱ 1 Timing sector | DRS detection | DRS activation zone

2018 POLE TIME: **VETTEL (FERRARI)**, 1M11.212S, 143.679MPH/231.230KPH
2018 WINNER'S AVERAGE SPEED: **123.522MPH/198.789KPH**

2018 FASTEST LAP: **HAMILTON (MERCEDES)**, 1M15.545S, 135.439MPH/217.968KPH
LAP RECORD: **RAIKKONEN (MCLAREN)**, 1M14.917S, 136.567MPH/219.784KPH, 2004

HUNGARORING

Almost inevitably run in searing temperatures, the Hungarian GP is a test more of patience and race strategy rather than outright performance around the twisty Hungaroring.

Any first-time visitor will be impressed with the Hungaroring as it is far more scenic than it appears on television, offering fantastic views from one side of the valley to the other, picking out the track at several points in between.

However, the circuit's greatest flaw soon becomes apparent: there aren't many places even to attempt a passing manoeuvre. It's too tight and twisty, it's begging for more width in places and it could do with a genuine high-speed corner or two.

The first corner remains the main passing place, with its downhill approach affording drivers a chance to hug the inside line to defend against an attacking rival. However, this leaves the door open for their rival to try to go around the outside in this long, long right. Should the attacker be able to hang on and not slide into the gravel trap, this ought to put them into position to go up the inside into the lefthand hairpin that follows.

From here, the track falls away further until it reaches its lowest point midway between Turns 3 and 4. The latter, a fast flick to the left with something of a blind entry is the lap's most challenging corner. From Turn 5, the track levels out to run across the far side of the valley through a series of esses until reaching Turn 11. At this point, the track drops back downhill, levels out before Turn 12, then climbs all the way through the final three tight corners until drivers pop back onto the level to blast past the pits.

On a track as tight as the Hungaroring, there's only place for drivers to hit over 200mph, and that's at the end of the pit straight.

INSIDE TRACK
HUNGARIAN GRAND PRIX

Date:	**4 August**
Circuit name:	**Hungaroring**
Circuit length:	**2.722 miles/4.381km**
Number of laps:	**70**
Email:	**office@hungaroring.hu**
Website:	**www.hungaroring.hu**

PREVIOUS WINNERS

2009	**Lewis Hamilton** McLAREN
2010	**Mark Webber** RED BULL
2011	**Jenson Button** McLAREN
2012	**Lewis Hamilton** McLAREN
2013	**Lewis Hamilton** MERCEDES
2014	**Daniel Ricciardo** RED BULL
2015	**Sebastian Vettel** FERRARI
2016	**Lewis Hamilton** MERCEDES
2017	**Sebastian Vettel** FERRARI
2018	**Lewis Hamilton** MERCEDES

Location: Visitors to the Hungaroring need to head north-east out of Budapest, past Heroes' Square and on out into the countryside. Once the landscape starts to become hilly, the circuit can be found near the village of Mogyorod.

How it started: Back in 1986, people thought that this first Hungarian GP of the modern era was going to flop, as the country was still behind the Iron Curtain. After 200,000 turned out to watch, it was deemed a success...

Most memorable race: In 2007, the tension was as great off the track as it was on it. This was Lewis Hamilton's rookie year when he was pitched against his double world champion team-mate Fernando Alonso. In qualifying, Hamilton refused to let Alonso through, defying team instruction. Then Alonso delayed his departure from the pits long enough to ensure that Hamilton couldn't do a final flying lap. Team boss Ron Dennis was furious and the FIA penalized Alonso five places on the grid.

Greatest local driver: Hungary's one and only grand prix winner was Ferenc Szisz, but he was a little before the World Championship began in 1950. Indeed, he was the first ever grand prix winner, triumphing in the French GP of 1906 at Le Mans...

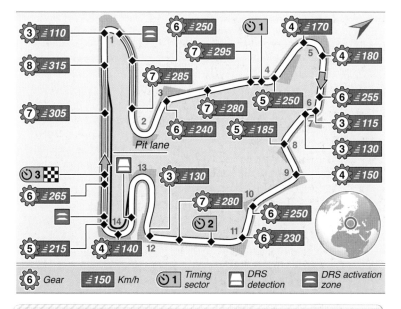

Pit lane

6 Gear	**≡150** Km/h	**⏱1** Timing sector	⬜ DRS detection	DRS activation zone

2018 POLE TIME: HAMILTON (MERCEDES), 1M35.658S, 102.448MPH/164.874KPH
2018 WINNER'S AVERAGE SPEED: 122.481MPH/189.134KPH

2018 FASTEST LAP: RICCIARDO (RED BULL), 1M20.012S, 122.481MPH/197.115KPH
LAP RECORD: M SCHUMACHER (FERRARI), 1M19.071S 123.828MPH/199.282KPH, 2004

SPA-FRANCORCHAMPS

What makes a circuit great? Fans have many answers, but gradient and scenery clearly help, augmenting the layout's best features. Spa-Francorchamps is living proof of this.

The order of the World Championship calendar throws into the spotlight the merits and demerits of some of the tracks. Indeed, the Hungaroring is left looking very limited once the drivers hit the next venue: Spa-Francorchamps. This classic Belgian circuit offers not only a more spectacular backdrop as it snakes through the wooded slopes of the Ardennes countryside, but also true high-speed corners too and plenty of scope for attempting overtaking moves.

The short blast up from the startline to La Source is followed by the steep plunge downhill past the old pits before the circuit's landmark corner: Eau Rouge. With more space around it, this rearing uphill left/right/left flick isn't as fearsome as before, but it's still a fabulous spectacle.

The track continues to climb as it cuts its way through the forest all the way to Les Combes, a definite passing opportunity as the drivers brake down from 210mph for the chicane. Twisty as it starts its descent, the track then opens out and the long, long left known as Pouhon is a great corner. Any driver with a car short on grip will struggle here, offering a rival a chance to close in and perhaps line up a passing move into Fagnes.

After a series of fairly open corners, the track then reaches the point where cars on the original track – used until the 1970s – would be long into their return leg from the neighbouring valley. This is at Curve Paul Frere and it's flat-out from here, with top gear Blanchimont a magnificent corner.

The lap is completed with heavy braking from a whisker over 200mph into a tight right and an even tighter left back onto the short start/finish straight.

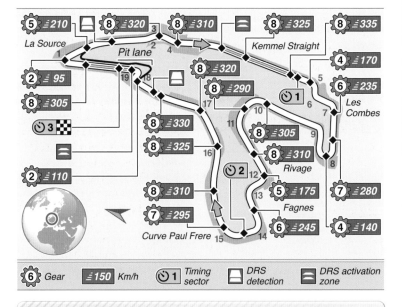

2018 POLE TIME: HAMILTON (MERCEDES),
1M58.179S, 132.572MPH/213.358KPH
2018 WINNER'S AVERAGE SPEED:
137.418MPH/221.731KPH

2018 FASTEST LAP: BOTTAS (MERCEDES),
1M46.286S, 147.422MPH/237.290KPH
LAP RECORD: BOTTAS (MERCEDES),
1M46.286S, 147.422MPH/237.290KPH, 2018

INSIDE TRACK
BELGIAN GRAND PRIX

Date:	1 September
Circuit name:	Spa-Francorchamps
Circuit length:	4.352 miles/7.004km
Number of laps:	44
Email:	secretariat@spa-francorchamps.be
Website:	www.spa-francorchamps.be

PREVIOUS WINNERS

2009	Kimi Raikkonen	FERRARI
2010	Lewis Hamilton	McLAREN
2011	Sebastian Vettel	RED BULL
2012	Jenson Button	McLAREN
2013	Sebastian Vettel	RED BULL
2014	Daniel Ricciardo	RED BULL
2015	Lewis Hamilton	MERCEDES
2016	Nico Rosberg	MERCEDES
2017	Lewis Hamilton	MERCEDES
2018	Sebastian Vettel	FERRARI

Location: The Ardennes, a popular wooded area of hills in south-east Belgium, is home to the resort town of Spa and the circuit is located some miles to the south, just below the village of Francorchamps.

How it started: When the circuit first opened in 1924, it carried on into the neighbouring valley between Malmedy and Stavelot before returning towards La Source on a course that was frighteningly fast and enclosed by trees.

Most memorable race: There have been so many classic races at Spa, but one that sticks out was the one in 1992 that resulted in Michael Schumacher's first win. Driving for Benetton, he picked the optimum moment in changing conditions to change from rain tyres and then benefitted when Nigel Mansell's Williams faltered.

Greatest local driver: Jacky Ickx was never World Champion, but he came very close in 1970, and remains Belgium's fleetest racer. He achieved greater rewards in sports-prototype racing, winning six Le Mans 24 Hours.

Rising star: While Stoffel Vandoorne continues to find his feet in F1, Belgian fans might have to wait a little longer for their next star, as Max Defourny has become mired in Formula Renault, perhaps set to be passed by F4 star Charles Weerts.

MONZA

Monza is certainly not the track that it was, as it once used a fearsome banked section, but it's still very much as it has been since a trio of chicanes were inserted in 1971.

Few circuits have stayed as true to their roots as Monza. What makes it even more amazing is the fact that it has been almost a century since it opened for racing. Indeed, bar the insertion of chicanes in the 1970s, the main change has been the inclusion of gravel traps outside the corners and the felling of trees at the Lesmos to add a degree of safety. What Monza keeps, though, and must always keep, is its core attraction: speed.

The start of the lap is a dash to the first chicane, a tight right and a curving left. Without it, Curva Biassone would be taken at magnificent velocity. The second chicane is more open and also serves the purpose of limiting speed into the first of the Lesmos. Running through the wooded area of the park, the track then turns right for the kinked straight that dips under the abandoned banked circuit that was once part of the lap.

A good exit from Variante Ascari is key to a quick lap, as there is then a good run down to Curva Parabolica, the most challenging corner. Approached at close to 220mph, this fifth-gear sweep opens up from the apex, but momentum on tiring tyres can leave drivers breathing in sharply as they skirt with ending up in the gravel trap beyond.

However, a good exit onto the start/finish straight is essential for a crack at overtaking into the first chicane, where a good tow and the latest possible moment in hitting the brakes to haul the car down from nigh on 220mph offers hope. However, moves into this tight right often require the defending driver to elect not to be overly defensive and risk damage to both cars.

INSIDE TRACK
ITALIAN GRAND PRIX

Date:	8 September
Circuit name:	Autodromo Nazionale Monza
Circuit length:	3.600 miles/5.793km
Number of laps:	53
Email:	infoautodromo@monzanet.it
Website:	www.monzanet.it

PREVIOUS WINNERS

2009	**Rubens Barrichello** BRAWN
2010	**Fernando Alonso** FERRARI
2011	**Sebastian Vettel** RED BULL
2012	**Lewis Hamilton** McLAREN
2013	**Sebastian Vettel** RED BULL
2014	**Lewis Hamilton** MERCEDES
2015	**Lewis Hamilton** MERCEDES
2016	**Nico Rosberg** MERCEDES
2017	**Lewis Hamilton** MERCEDES
2018	**Lewis Hamilton** MERCEDES

Location: The track is set beautifully into a wooded park in the town of Monza some 10 miles to the north-west of Milan.

How it started: This was a circuit made to celebrate speed when it was opened in 1922, with its long straights and a magnificent banked oval incorporated into its lap. Its essence has changed little.

Most memorable race: In 1971, the gap between first and second at the finish was just 0.01s, with the first five home covered by only 0.61s after an unbelievable slipstreaming battle that had the lead changing several times per lap and the outcome not known until the final second when Peter Gethin nosed his BRM to the front of the pack to pip Ronnie Peterson's March.

Greatest local driver: Enzo Ferrari's disinclination to run Italian drivers after a string of deaths in the 1950s limited the nation's hopes, leaving Alberto Ascari as its only two-time World Champion, after he dominated in 1952 and 1953.

Rising star: Last year, Italy's most promising Italian driver, Antonio Giovinazzi, was on the sidelines in that nether world of being an F1 test driver. Racing in F2, Antonio Fuoco and Luca Ghiotto continue to vie to be the next star after a run of podium finishes.

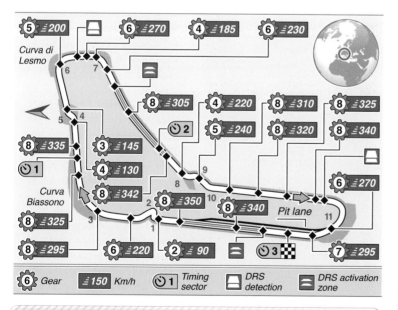

Curva di Lesmo

Curva Biassono

Pit lane

Gear		Km/h	Timing sector	DRS detection	DRS activation zone

2018 POLE TIME: RAIKKONEN (FERRARI), 1M19.119S, 163.785MPH/263.587KPH

2018 WINNER'S AVERAGE SPEED: 148.686MPH/239.288KPH

2018 FASTEST LAP: HAMILTON (MERCEDES), 1M22.497S, 157.079MPH/252.794KPH

LAP RECORD: M SCHUMACHER (FERRARI), 1M21.046S 159.909MPH/257.349KPH, 2004

MARINA BAY

Singapore offers something different in several ways, as it is unusual for a street circuit to cross a bridge or to dive under a grandstand. Also, the grand prix is run after dark.

Singapore is a nation that makes things happen. Pivotal as the centre of South-East Asia, it was encouraged to host a round of the World Championship and accepted that challenge in the first decade of the 21st century.

With typical efficiency, the organizers cleared the path of any obstacles and had the track ready for the end of the 2008 season and the backdrop of sleek office blocks and parks gave the circuit immediate appeal. What makes it yet more dramatic as a venue is that the race is held in the dark, allowing the twinkling lights of the cityscape to add to the spectacle.

The lap starts with a tricky swerve from Turn 1 through to the tight left at Turn 3. On the opening lap, this can get a little bit messy. Then the lap opens out and drivers hit their highest speed along Raffles Boulevard on their approach to Turn 7, reaching over 200mph.

Despite the sequence of 90-degree bends, there's a feeling of space from Turn 8 as the track skirts around a park dotted with playing fields. It then tightens up as it runs across the Andersen Bridge to reach the very sharp left onto a decent straight that takes it up to Turn 14 where it almost touches Turn 8.

The homeward leg gets technical when it tightens up at Turn 16 and not a little unusual at Turn 18 when it dives underneath one of the temporary grandstands.

After Turn 21, just before passing a giant ferris wheel, the lap opens out again and a good run through the pairing of Turns 22 and 23 are critical for a rapid blast along the start/finish straight to assist any passing attempt into Turn 1.

INSIDE TRACK
SINGAPORE GRAND PRIX

Date:	**22 September**
Circuit name:	**Marina Bay Circuit**
Circuit length:	**3.152 miles/5.073km**
Number of laps:	**61**
Email:	**info@singaporegp.sg**
Website:	**www.singaporegp.sg**

PREVIOUS WINNERS

2009	**Lewis Hamilton** McLAREN
2010	**Fernando Alonso** FERRARI
2011	**Sebastian Vettel** RED BULL
2012	**Sebastian Vettel** RED BULL
2013	**Sebastian Vettel** RED BULL
2014	**Lewis Hamilton** MERCEDES
2015	**Sebastian Vettel** FERRARI
2016	**Nico Rosberg** MERCEDES
2017	**Lewis Hamilton** MERCEDES
2018	**Lewis Hamilton** MERCEDES

Location: Like any city centre street course, it's right in the middle of the city, looped in a temporary lay-out around Singapore's finest buildings, including the smartest offices and hotels as well as the Singapore Cricket Club and Raffles Hotel.

How it started: Setting up a street circuit is far from easy, yet the organizers got it all done for this temporary circuit's opening and World Championship debut in 2008.

Most memorable race: The Renault F1 team felt the fallout of its controversial win here in 2008 after Fernando Alonso was assisted to victory by team-mate Nelson Piquet Jr agreeing to crash at the very point in the race at which a safety car deployment would enable the Spaniard to triumph.

Greatest local driver: The highest reached by Singaporean drivers was in the A1GP single-seater series, between 2005 and 2009. The Singapore team was represented by Christian Murchison and Denis Lian, but neither went higher in single-seaters.

Rising star: Singapore is a city/state aimed more at commerce than developing sporting stars, but Pavan Ravishankar was a winner in British F3 last year, while 16-year-old Danial Frost has gathered useful experience in South East Asian F4 and American FF2000.

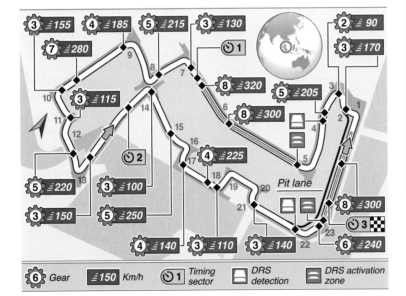

6 Gear	150 Km/h	⏱1 Timing sector	DRS detection	DRS activation zone

2018 POLE TIME: HAMILTON (MERCEDES), 1M36.015S, 117.459MPH/189.832KPH
2018 WINNER'S AVERAGE SPEED: 103.506MPH/166.577KPH

2018 FASTEST LAP: MAGNUSSEN (HAAS), 1M41.905S, 109.900MPH/178.860KPH
LAP RECORD: MAGNUSSEN (HAAS), 1M41.905S 109.900MPH/178.860KPH, 2018

SOCHI

Russia spent decades trying to entice a round of the World Championship to its shores. President Putin's pet project to make Sochi a sporting venue produced this interesting track.

In recent years, with the arrival of Singapore's Marina Bay track and the coming and going of the Valencia circuit, there has been a major change in expectations of a street circuit. They no longer have to be seen as low-speed, point-and-squirt venues. Indeed, when Sochi landed the right to host a round of the World Championship, for Russia's first-ever grand prix, it, too, was far more open and high-speed than F1 street venues of yore.

The opening stretch of the circuit gives clear evidence of this. Unlike many a circuit opened for F1 in the past few decades, this doesn't almost immediately greet the drivers with a tight corner and, without a doubt, the best place for making an overtaking move is into the lap's second corner, a 90-degree righthander that is wide on entry and has a high-speed approach, allowing slipstreaming. The track then immediately starts turning left into what is the trickiest corner of the lap, as from Turn 2 through Turn 3 to the point at which it finally changes direction by turning right at Turn 4, the corner is in reality just one long left-turning parabola.

From here, it does become a little bit easier, but slower, through a series of tightish corners, with short straights in between, until the fastest point of the lap is reached at the lefthand kink on the stretch from Turn 10 to Turn 13, where drivers can top 200mph.

Then it all slows right down for the next four corners behind the paddock before the final two rights complete the lap, with a good exit from Turn 18 vital for a good run up to Turn 2, through the top gear kink that's Turn 1.

INSIDE TRACK
RUSSIAN GRAND PRIX

Date:	29 September
Circuit name:	Sochi Autodrom
Circuit length:	3.634 miles/5.848km
Number of laps:	53
Email:	info@sochiautodrom.ru
Website:	www.sochiautodrom.ru

PREVIOUS WINNERS

2014	**Lewis Hamilton**	MERCEDES
2015	**Lewis Hamilton**	MERCEDES
2016	**Nico Rosberg**	MERCEDES
2017	**Valtteri Bottas**	MERCEDES
2018	**Lewis Hamilton**	MERCEDES

Location: Sochi is a year-round resort on the northern coast of the Black Sea, with skiing on the Caucasus Mountains behind, and many of its facilities were built for when the town hosted the Winter Olympic Games in 2014.

How it started: Russia was granted a grand prix for 2014 after earlier failed attempts to land a race for Moscow and then St Petersburg. There was a hurried push to complete the circuit on time, with many of the buildings having to be converted from their initial use as venues for the Winter Olympics.

Most memorable race: It's special whenever a driver takes their first F1 win, so the 2017 Russian GP stands out as Valtteri Bottas's moment. Drafted into the Mercedes line-up for 2017 after Nico Rosberg's shock retirement from racing, he did everything right to first out-qualify team-mate Lewis Hamilton then blast past both Ferraris to lead into Turn 2.

Greatest local driver: Vitaly Petrov and Daniil Kvyat vie to be remembered as Russia's best F1 driver, with Petrov being the country's trailblazer and achieving a best of third when racing for Renault in Australia in 2011, while Kvyat peaked with second in the 2015 Hungarian GP for Red Bull Racing. He lost his ride briefly but returns for Toro Rosso in 2019.

Rising star: Russia has a host of rising stars, with Artem Markelov leading the way by being a race-winner in F2 last year, while GP3 race-winner Nikita Mazepin is the next in line for promotion.

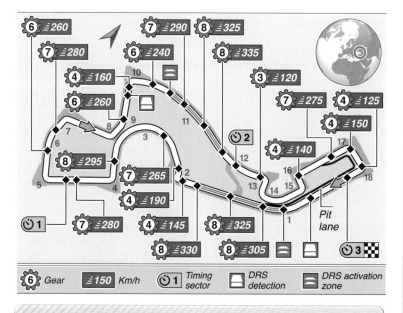

6 ≡260	7 ≡290	8 ≡325		
7 ≡280	6 ≡240	8 ≡335		
4 ≡160	10	3 ≡120		
6 ≡260		7 ≡275	4 ≡125	
	9	11	4 ≡150	17
7	8	3	2	
6		12	4 ≡140	16
8 ≡295			15	18
	7 ≡265	2	13 14	
5	4			Pit lane
4 ≡190			1	
1	7 ≡280	4 ≡145	8 ≡325	
		8 ≡330	8 ≡305	3

6 Gear	≡**150** Km/h	**1** Timing sector	DRS detection	DRS activation zone

2018 POLE TIME: **BOTTAS (MERCEDES)**, 1M31.387S, 143.144MPH/230.369KPH
2018 WINNER'S AVERAGE SPEED: 132.098MPH/212.591KPH

2018 FASTEST LAP **BOTTAS (MERCEDES)**, 1M35.861S, 136.463MPH/219.617KPH
LAP RECORD: **BOTTAS (MERCEDES)**, 1M35.861S 136.463MPH/219.617KPH, 2018

SUZUKA

This Japanese track has been transformed from a great circuit to an old-school one almost without people noticing, which makes its appeal even more alluring to longstanding F1 fans.

Stand in the paddock at Suzuka and you'll be disappointed, as it feels enclosed and the buildings have seen better days. Yet, move to the banking around the circuit, and you'll immediately see why Suzuka is so revered and why it's such a massive challenge for the drivers.

Key to the flow of the circuit is the terrain, with the sloping piece of land used to maximum effect. The startline is on a slope, with a descent down to Turns 1 and 2, where the track turns to come back up the incline. What comes next is the circuit's most challenging corner. Well, corners, as Turns 3 to 6 make a double esse in which any deviation from the racing line can have increasing ramifications in the following turns.

The track finally flattens out at Turn 7, Dunlop Curve, and then the Degner rights lead the track under the return leg. The Hairpin is a definite overtaking opportunity, the last for a while, as the track climbs again through the long, fast right to its highest point, Turn 13. After this, the track drops into the most crucial corner, Spoon Curve, out of which a quick exit is vital to carry the most speed possible down the long return straight, through top-gear 130R all the way to the best overtaking spot, into the ultra-tight Casio Triangle.

Many a scrap has come to a sticky end here, most notably in 1989, when McLaren team-mates Ayrton Senna and Alain Prost clashed at the chicane.

The final corner is a simple right onto the downhill start/finish straight and a good exit can help a driver hit up to 210mph before they have to brake and balance their car for Turn 1.

INSIDE TRACK
JAPANESE GRAND PRIX

Date:	**13 October**
Circuit name:	**Suzuka Circuit**
Circuit length:	**3.608 miles/5.806km**
Number of laps:	**53**
Email:	**info@suzukacircuit.co.jp**
Website:	**www.suzukacircuit.co.jp**

PREVIOUS WINNERS

2009	**Sebastian Vettel**	RED BULL
2010	**Sebastian Vettel**	RED BULL
2011	**Jenson Button**	McLAREN
2012	**Sebastian Vettel**	RED BULL
2013	**Sebastian Vettel**	RED BULL
2014	**Lewis Hamilton**	MERCEDES
2015	**Lewis Hamilton**	MERCEDES
2016	**Nico Rosberg**	MERCEDES
2017	**Lewis Hamilton**	MERCEDES
2018	**Lewis Hamilton**	MERCEDES

Location: You might have thought that the grand prix would be held on a circuit near Tokyo, but this circuit – 240 miles west of the capital – is Japan's premier venue and about 30 miles south-west of Nagoya.

How it started: Built as a test venue for Honda, the circuit was designed by John Hugenholtz, who created Zandvoort. Although opened in 1962, it didn't get to host a round of the World Championship until 1987, when Gerhard Berger won for Ferrari.

Most memorable race: Damon Hill's victory in 1994 stands out as one of the best drives, as he knew he had to beat Michael Schumacher to set up a title showdown in Adelaide and, in appalling weather conditions, he hung on.

Greatest local driver: The passionate Japanese fans would love a World Champion of their own but, for now, must simply pray for a Japanese driver capable of becoming a grand prix winner. Japan has had three of its own visit the podium, with Aguri Suzuki, Takuma Sato and Kamui Kobayashi all landing a third place in topsy-turvy races.

Rising star: It's high time that Japan had an F1 driver of its own again and it's a battle between F2 racers Nirei Fukuzumi and Tadasuke Makino to be the next in line.

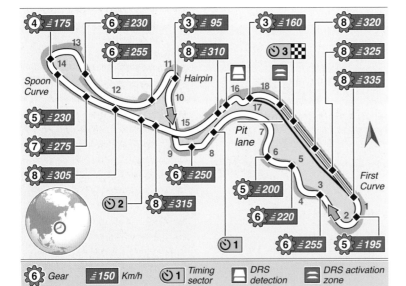

2018 POLE TIME: HAMILTON (MERCEDES),
1M27.760S, 148.015MPH/238.208KPH
2018 WINNER'S AVERAGE SPEED:
131.332MPH/211.358KPH

2018 FASTEST LAP: VETTEL (FERRARI),
1M32.318S, 140.707MPH/226.447KPH
LAP RECORD: RAIKKONEN (McLAREN),
1M31.540S 141.904MPH/228.373KPH, 2005

MEXICO CITY

Mexico's grand prix circuit has been a huge hit since its return to the F1 stage in 2015, with its packed stadium section at the end of the lap a particular cauldron of noise and passion.

There was a time in the 23-year gap between 1992 and 2015 that marked Mexico's second spell in the F1 wilderness – the first was from 1970 to 1986 – when it seemed as though this sports-crazy country would never host F1 again. It had taken to Indycar racing, which seemed a more natural away fixture for their American neighbours from the north than its fit with F1.

Yet, with a driver of its own to cheer on, in Sergio Perez, the race was back on the World Championship roster in 2015, with its facilities spruced up and, as ever, its spectators pumped up. In an instant, many asked why F1 had ever been away.

The 2.674-mile lap actually looks relatively simple on paper, with a long and wide straight to start the lap. Yet, what follows is far trickier in real life.

The first corner sequence, for example, is approached at 215mph and is a three-part affair that is never trickier than on the opening lap, when the preferred line into the first turn puts a driver on the less favourable line into the second. It remains, though, the most likely passing spot.

After another straight down to Turn 4, the Lake Esses provides a challenge. This is nothing, though, compared to the esses that greet the drivers on the homeward leg from the hairpin at Horquilla, as Turns 7, 8 and 9 are made trickier by camber change.

The nature of the lap is transformed after Turn 12, at which point this sharp right turns the track into a twisting run at the feet of giant grandstands. The drivers then go past the baseball stadium onto the lightly banked final curve: the famous Peraltada.

87

INSIDE TRACK
MEXICAN GRAND PRIX

Date:	**27 October**
Circuit name:	**Autodromo Hermanos Rodriguez**
Circuit length:	**2.674 miles/4.303km**
Number of laps:	**71**
Email:	**Rosario@cie.com.mx**
Website:	**www. autodromohermanosrodriguez.com.mx**

PREVIOUS WINNERS

1987	**Nigel Mansell** WILLIAMS
1988	**Alain Prost** McLAREN
1989	**Ayrton Senna** McLAREN
1990	**Alain Prost** FERRARI
1991	**Riccardo Patrese** WILLIAMS
1992	**Nigel Mansell** WILLIAMS
2015	**Nico Rosberg** MERCEDES
2016	**Lewis Hamilton** MERCEDES
2017	**Max Verstappen** RED BULL
2018	**Max Verstappen** RED BULL

Location: There's not a lot of space between the buildings in ever-expanding Mexico City, but the Magdalena Mixhuca park in the south-eastern suburbs has been the only ever home to the Mexican GP.

How it started: When the Rodriguez brothers, Pedro and Ricardo, burst onto the racing scene as teenagers in the early 1960s, the Mexican sporting authority seized the moment to host a race to harness this burgeoning interest. The first Mexican GP was in 1962 and its success led to it gaining World Championship status from 1963.

Most memorable race: The 2017 Mexican GP stands out for drama at the first sequence of corners when Sebastian Vettel clipped Lewis Hamilton, and Max Verstappen upstaged his more experienced rivals to take victory.

Greatest local driver: Ricardo Rodriguez would have been Mexico's greatest driver, but he died in practice here in 1962, leaving it to his brother Pedro to become the grand prix winner that Ricardo would clearly have been.

Rising star: Sergio Perez saw off compatriot Esteban Gutierrez. The next pair, Raul Guzman and Axel Matus, were in European Formula Renault last year, but not towards the front.

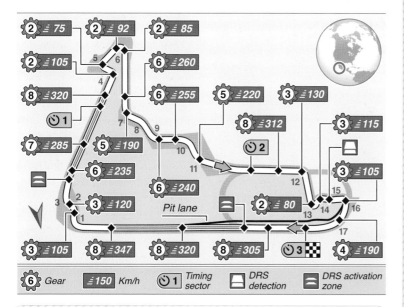

| 6 Gear | 150 Km/h | 1 Timing sector | DRS detection | DRS activation zone |

2018 POLE TIME: **RICCIARDO (RED BULL)**, 1M14.759S, 128.783MPH/207.257KPH
2018 WINNER'S AVERAGE SPEED: **115.598MPH/186.038KPH**

2018 FASTEST LAP: **BOTTAS (MERCEDES)**, 1M18.741S, 122.271MPH/196.776KPH
LAP RECORD: **BOTTAS (MERCEDES)**, 1M18.741S 122.271MPH/196.776KPH, 2018

CIRCUIT OF THE AMERICAS

The key to the attractiveness and challenge of this Texan venue is its use of considerable gradient at the start of its lap, as well as a sequence of challenging esses.

F1 circuit architect Hermann Tilke stepped up a level or two when he penned the shape of the Circuit of the Americas, a clean-sheet project in which he was encouraged to include elements of the best corners from other circuits around the world. Even better still, the Circuit of the Americas is located in rolling hills, and this gave Tilke what he needed to make the circuit really special.

The lap starts with a steep ascent to the first corner, a lefthand hairpin taken just as the drivers crest the rise. Sight lines are difficult on turn-in and getting the car into position for the tricky downhill righthander that follows is particularly difficult on the opening lap, when changing your line in response to a swerve from a rival could wreck a driver's race by leaving them with a damaged front wing. However,

with a good run, and perhaps a little luck through both of these corners on lap 1, a driver might have done half of their afternoon's passing.

What follows as the circuit gets back down onto the level are the lap's most difficult corners, a wonderful run of esse bends, before the drivers gain a little respite after Turn 9. From the Turn 11 hairpin, the track opens onto the lap's longest straight, with speeds of up to 210mph achieved before heavy braking into the sharp left at Turn 12.

The lap then changes pace again with a series of snaking corners until it opens out for five more open turns that bring the cars back onto the start/finish straight. From here, it's a flat-out blast past the pits that grows ever steeper as drivers approach the first corner again.

INSIDE TRACK
UNITED STATES GRAND PRIX

Date:	**3 November**
Circuit name:	**Circuit of The Americas**
Circuit length:	**3.400 miles/5.472km**
Number of laps:	**56**
Email:	**info@circuitoftheamericas.com**
Website:	**www.circuitoftheamericas.com**

PREVIOUS WINNERS

2012	**Lewis Hamilton**	McLAREN
2013	**Sebastian Vettel**	RED BULL
2014	**Lewis Hamilton**	MERCEDES
2015	**Lewis Hamilton**	MERCEDES
2016	**Lewis Hamilton**	MERCEDES
2017	**Lewis Hamilton**	MERCEDES
2018	**Kimi Raikkonen**	FERRARI

Location: Head south-east out of Austin and the Circuit of the Americas can be found in rolling hills just beyond the city limits.

How it started: America's seemingly eternal quest to find a fixed home may have been achieved since landing at this purpose-built circuit just outside the Texas state capital.

Most memorable race: With five wins in F1's first seven visits to CotA, Lewis Hamilton almost expects to win in Texas. The pick of his wins here so far is the one from 2017 when he had to catch and pass Sebastian Vettel's Ferrari for only the second time all season, in what was the 17th of 20 rounds, doing so at the tight lefthander at Turn 12.

Greatest local driver: No American driver can match Mario Andretti for diversity. He was World Champion for Lotus in 1978, won four Indycar titles between 1965 and 1984, the Indy 500 in 1969 and came close to taking the Le Mans 24 Hours in 1995, ending second in a Courage. The Italian/American also won races in NASCAR and American sportscar classics at Sebring and Daytona.

Rising star: With Santino Ferrucci's petulant ramming of a team-mate scuppering his career in F2 and Gustavo Menezes electing not to return from racing sports-prototypes, GP3 racers Ryan Tveter and Juan Manuel Correa are at least learning their craft in international categories beyond its borders but are not ready to advance yet.

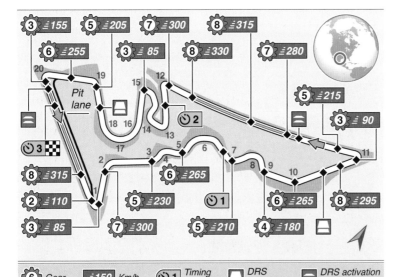

6 Gear	**150** Km/h
1 Timing sector	DRS detection
DRS activation zone	

2018 POLE TIME: HAMILTON (MERCEDES), 1M32.237S, 133.701MPH/215.171KPH
2018 WINNER'S AVERAGE SPEED: 121.916MPH/196.205KPH

2018 FASTEST LAP: HAMILTON (MERCEDES), 1M37.392S, 126.624MPH/203.782KPH
LAP RECORD: HAMILTON (MERCEDES), 1M37.392S 126.624MPH/203.782KPH, 2018

INTERLAGOS

The years haven't been kind to the infrastructure at the home of the Brazilian GP, but this super circuit still has a wonderful flow over its sloping setting. Sadly, this could be F1's last visit.

The mark of a great circuit is the way that it makes the most of its terrain. This is something that flat circuits like Silverstone and Melbourne simply cannot benefit from, but those that do, and make the most of it, like here and the Red Bull Ring, really stand out. There is nothing better than seeing a racing car driven at full tilt up hill and down dale, especially when they are cornering as they do so, to show just how nimble and dynamic they can be.

On top of this, not only does a sloping setting provide better than average viewing for spectators, but also it is augmented in Brazil by a thrilling, raucous atmosphere provided by the local fans.

Interlagos is old-school and has numerous points that would never be included in a new-build circuit, and it's all the better for it, making it more of a challenge for the drivers and more of a spectacle for the fans. Take the first corner, a hard left over a crest with a blind exit that feeds straight into the Senna S. Overtaking here is possible, if risky.

Where the cars look at their best, though, is as they come back up the slope to Ferradura, struggling for grip, before dropping down the hill again a couple more times before starting the flat-out blast for home.

The fastest point on the circuit is at the end of the lap, where the drivers carry the speed they have built all the way up the slope from Juncao, and the sensation of that speed is magnified as the pitwall rises on one side and the base of the grandstand on the other, giving them a tunnel effect as they hit 215mph.

INSIDE TRACK
BRAZILIAN GRAND PRIX

Date:	**17 November**
Circuit name:	**Autodromo Jose Carlos Pace Interlagos**
Circuit length:	**2.667 miles/4.292km**
Number of laps:	**71**
Email:	**info@gpbrazil.com**
Website:	**www.gpbrazil.com**

PREVIOUS WINNERS

2008	**Felipe Massa** FERRARI
2009	**Mark Webber** RED BULL
2010	**Sebastian Vettel** RED BULL
2011	**Mark Webber** RED BULL
2012	**Jenson Button** McLAREN
2013	**Sebastian Vettel** RED BULL
2014	**Nico Rosberg** MERCEDES
2015	**Nico Rosberg** MERCEDES
2016	**Lewis Hamilton** MERCEDES
2017	**Sebastian Vettel** FERRARI
2018	**Lewis Hamilton** MERCEDES

Location: The circuit is set in what are now the suburban hills to the south of Sao Paulo city centre, twisting around some lakes.

How it started: Opened in 1940, it took until 1972 for the first Brazilian GP to be held there as a trial that had to be passed before World Championship status would be granted. It was won by Brabham's Carlos Reutemann.

Most memorable race: Ayrton Senna kept the fans waiting years before winning in 1991. However, Rubens Barrichello's best efforts were always thwarted. He led for Ferrari in 2001, 2002, 2003 and 2004. In 2009, he led from pole, but Brawn team-mate Jenson Button got into position to usurp him for the title when, as ever, cruel fortune hit Rubens at home, this time in the form of a puncture.

Greatest local driver: Emerson Fittipaldi blazed a trail in the 1970s, winning two F1 titles, but Ayrton Senna is Brazil's finest ever. He won the F1 crown in 1988, 1990 and 1991 before being killed in the 1994 San Marino GP.

Rising star: With a flock of next generation Fittipaldis hot on his heels, Sergio Sette Camara is set to be the next Brazilian to reach F1, the 20-year-old enjoying a run of podium placings in F2 last year.

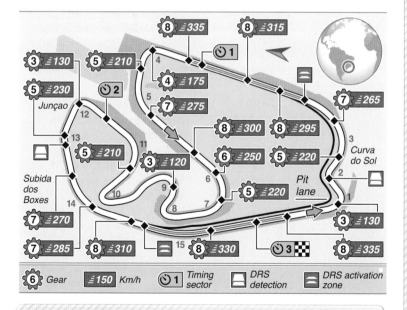

6	Gear
150	Km/h
1	Timing sector
DRS detection	DRS detection
DRS activation zone	DRS activation zone

2018 POLE TIME: HAMILTON (MERCEDES),
1M07.281S, 143.264MPH/230.561KPH
2018 WINNER'S AVERAGE SPEED:
130.851MPH/210.585KPH

2018 FASTEST LAP: BOTTAS (MERCEDES),
1M10.540S, 136.645MPH/219.909KPH
LAP RECORD: BOTTAS (MERCEDES),
1M10.540S 136.645MPH/219.909KPH, 2018

YAS MARINA

Monaco's street circuit runs along a harbourside, as does Yas Marina's, but the comparison ends there. The Abu Dhabi circuit is a very modern version on a made-to-measure layout.

Abu Dhabi raised the ante when it unveiled the Yas Marina Circuit, with its elegant marina, smart hotel draped over the track near the end of the lap and its pitlane with its exit tunnel that takes the cars under the track to rejoin on the opposite side. It made a massive statement. Money was no object. Other circuits suddenly appeared a little drab.

Yet, for all the considerable investment, the circuit has yet to find its way into F1 fans' hearts. The reason why is because it has yet to produce any great races, as something in its layout just doesn't lend itself to that.

The first corner is a place of attempted passing moves on the opening lap, but seldom after that. Instead, drivers normally wait until the chicane at Turns 5 and 6, with many a move there carrying on into Turn 7.

Making a clean exit from this hairpin is essential for ensuring a good run down the lap's longest straight. Speeds of 210mph can be hit before heavy braking is required to avoid piling into the grandstand that sits dead ahead. With a good tow, this is the lap's best place for overtaking.

The run down to Turn 11 is not dissimilar to the complex of tight turns into the chicane at Turn 8. From here, though, the track changes in feel as it becomes tighter for the homeward run, weirdly running under a broad bridge between two parts of the Viceroy Hotel. In many ways, these final corners are among the trickiest, with the last of these, Turn 21, perhaps hardest of all as a good entry from here sets a driver up for the faster section that follows all the way to Turn 5.

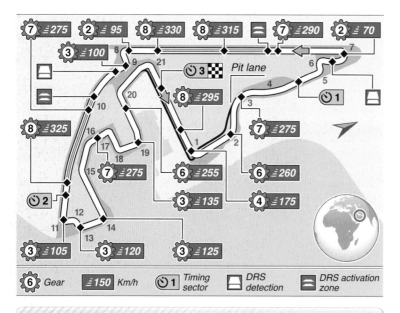

2018 POLE TIME: HAMILTON (MERCEDES), 1M34.794S, 131.062MPH/210.924KPH
2018 WINNER'S AVERAGE SPEED: 114.217MPH/183.814KPH

2018 FASTEST LAP: VETTEL (FERRARI), 1M40.867S, 123.180MPH/198.225KPH
LAP RECORD: VETTEL (RED BULL), 1M40.279S, 123.893MPH/199.387KPH

INSIDE TRACK
ABU DHABI GRAND PRIX

Date:	**1 December**
Circuit name:	**Yas Marina Circuit**
Circuit length:	**3.451 miles/5.554km**
Number of laps:	**55**
Email:	**customerservice@ yasmarinacircuit.com**
Website:	**www.yasmarinacircuit.com**

PREVIOUS WINNERS

2009	**Sebastian Vettel** RED BULL
2010	**Sebastian Vettel** RED BULL
2011	**Lewis Hamilton** McLAREN
2012	**Kimi Raikkonen** LOTUS
2013	**Sebastian Vettel** RED BULL
2014	**Lewis Hamilton** MERCEDES
2015	**Nico Rosberg** MERCEDES
2016	**Lewis Hamilton** MERCEDES
2017	**Valtteri Bottas** MERCEDES
2018	**Lewis Hamilton** MERCEDES

Location: Yas Island is situated to the east of Abu Dhabi's main island and largely has been developed as a sports complex and marina.

How it started: Abu Dhabi watched its neighbouring states build sports facilities and circuits to boost their international image and bring in tourists. Then, as befitting the senior partner on the Arabian Gulf, Abu Dhabi built one of its own that was larger and better, opening in 2009.

Most memorable race: Valtteri Bottas will always remember the 2017 Abu Dhabi GP as he not only took pole ahead of his already crowned Mercedes team-mate Lewis Hamilton, but also led all the way to the flag.

Greatest local driver: One perplexing issue regarding the races established in the Middle East has been how the host nations haven't managed to develop racing talent of their own. This is something that ought to be easy to do with the oil wealth available. The problem might be more to do with the fact that flash cars are more in their culture than racing, with the occasional driver racing GTs but none to a high level and the Middle Eastern junior single-seater series being packed with drivers from other parts of the world who want to race through the winter.

Abu Dhabi's Viceroy Hotel dwarfs the cars as they negotiate Turns 16 and 17 and turn away from the marina to complete the last four turns of the lap.

REVIEW OF THE 2018 SEASON

Ferrari threw down the gauntlet at the start of last year and Lewis Hamilton had to really fight to claim the crown, but it was enthralling to watch him rise to new heights as he moved level with Juan Manuel Fangio by landing his fifth F1 drivers' title. As the year advanced, so did Max Verstappen and Red Bull Racing, so the game looks set to change in 2019.

Ferrari have almost always been in the hunt, but seldom leading the chase since Michael Schumacher's days at its helm. At last, F1's longest running team found the pace to be at the head of the field again in 2018. This shocked previously dominant Mercedes and excited F1 fans everywhere as a great scrap looked to be lying ahead.

However, it takes more than just a quick car to win an F1 title and it became clear, as the season progressed, that Mercedes had the other elements required to maximize the pace that Lewis Hamilton could offer. In addition, Ferrari's lead driver, Sebastian Vettel, showed some fragility, never more so than when he crashed out of the lead in his home grand prix at Hockenheim. The pressure exerted by Mercedes was starting to tell.

From the midpoint of the season at the German GP, Hamilton was back in his pomp, winning eight of the last 11 rounds. In this run, only Max Verstappen truly challenged him.

While Valtteri Bottas blew hot and cold in the second Mercedes, you can forgive him for being disappointed whenever he was asked to move over to assist Hamilton's title chase. Yet, team player that he is, he obliged. Kimi Raikkonen was in a similar position at Ferrari, but continued to gather points and then seize the day to win the United States GP, his first win since 2013.

Red Bull Racing also became a team focused on one driver, with Verstappen the chosen one, especially after Daniel Ricciardo failed to agree a contract extension and told the team that he was

going to leave it for Renault. As the team came on strong in its final year with Renault engines, so too did the young Dutchman, and never more so than when he won in Mexico City for a second year running, and probably would have won in Interlagos but for a clash with Esteban Ocon.

Ricciardo deserves special praise for taking one of the cleverest and most dogged wins when he held on to the lead at Monaco despite losing around 160bhp for the majority of the race.

Beyond these top three teams, life was harder, podium finishes more difficult to come by, but to the top of this pile rose Renault for whom both Nico Hulkenberg and Carlos Sainz Jr went well enough to claim a fifth place finish.

Haas F1 really benefitted from Ferrari's exceptional engine and Romain Grosjean peaked with fourth place at the Red Bull Ring on a great day for the team as team-mate Kevin Magnusssen followed him home in fifth.

McLaren did improve in 2018, albeit only from a very low base. However, while Stoffel Vandoorne seldom finished let alone scored, Fernando Alonso did get among the points, even finishing fifth in the opening round, but racing in the midfield at best isn't the natural habitat for this exceptional driver and so it's no surprise that he has chosen to seek glory in the great races in other series like the Indianapolis 500 to add to the buzz he got from winning the Le Mans 24 Hours last year.

Force India started the year with one name and ended it with another after bankruptcy and a buy-out led to the team shedding the 59 points it had scored before the Belgian GP in order to be allowed to continue and so become Racing Point for 2019. It dropped the team from what would have been fifth overall to seventh in the constructors' championship. Esteban Ocon and Sergio Perez continued to strike sparks off each other, with the former finishing ahead on points, but the latter being able to boast of his podium finish in Azerbaijan.

Sauber had a gem in rookie Charles Leclerc who not just earned it some points but finished as high as sixth, in Baku, qualified consistently well and put a smile back on the team's face, with Marcus Ericsson going better and better through the closing races.

Scuderia Toro Rosso gave Red Bull Racing cause for optimism as it got used to the Honda engines that Red Bull's lead team will be using in 2019, but apart from Pierre Gasly's surprise fourth place finish in Bahrain and his sixth in Hungary, he and Brendon Hartley were generally racing hard to finish just outside the point-scoring positions.

Williams was in disarray, with two average but well-funded drivers struggling to wring any decent results out of a poor-handling car. The Italian GP was their only moment of celebration, when Lance Stroll and Sergey Sirtokin finished in ninth and 10th places, respectively.

Gaining victory in the opening round of any season gives a team a huge fillip. When this comes after a rival has fumbled, it's even more of a boost, as Ferrari discovered at Mercedes' expense in Melbourne after reacting more quickly to a virtual safety car.

The factor that erased Lewis Hamilton's chance of getting his 2018 campaign off to a winning start was impossible to see. It was invisible, as it was the virtual safety car that was introduced just before mid-distance after Romain Grosjean's Haas pulled to the side of the circuit with a loose front left wheel. Although this shouldn't have affected Mercedes adversely, it revealed that its number-crunching department hadn't done its sums correctly.

Hamilton had led away from pole position and run comfortably in the lead ahead of Ferrari's Kimi Raikkonen and Sebastian Vettel. Hamilton had a near 4s lead when Raikkonen pitted. It was on the following tour, lap 19, that Hamilton came in, letting Vettel take over at the front. And, in this age of using computer power rather than dead reckoning to calculate all the permutations of when a driver ought to pit – or a rival might have enough of a margin to pit and still come back out onto the track ahead – it was at this point that Mercedes came up with the wrong answer.

Hamilton was 12s behind Vettel when the virtual safety car was deployed. As far as Mercedes understood, that was fine, as they reckoned that Vettel needed to be 15s in front to be able to pit and emerge in front, so they were aghast when he pitted and yet managed to return into the lead. It was tight, by just 0.6s, but it floored Mercedes as the computer had suggested that they had him covered.

Then, over the remaining 28 laps, Vettel had more than enough in hand to win, leaving Mercedes' tactical experts feeling foolish and perplexed. To make matters worse for Mercedes, Valtteri Bottas wasn't able to collect his expected haul of points, as the Finn crashed in the third qualifying session and a five-place grid penalty for a gearbox change left him to fight forward from 15th to eighth.

The other Finn, Kimi Raikkonen was third, with Daniel Ricciardo best of the rest, finishing fourth for Red Bull on his home soil, with McLaren's Fernando Alonso 20s further back.

Double delight for Ferrari, with both Sebastian Vettel and Kimi Raikkonen up on the podium.

ALBERT PARK ROUND 1
DATE: **25 MARCH 2018**

Laps: **58** • Distance: **191.117 miles/307.574km** • Weather: **Warm & bright**

Pos	Driver	Team	Result	Stops	Qualifying Time	Grid
1	Sebastian Vettel	Ferrari	1h29m33.283s	1	1m21.838s	3
2	Lewis Hamilton	Mercedes	1h29m38.319s	1	1m21.164s	1
3	Kimi Raikkonen	Ferrari	1h29m39.592s	1	1m21.828s	2
4	Daniel Ricciardo *	Red Bull	1h29m40.352s	1	1m22.152s	8
5	Fernando Alonso	McLaren	1h30m01.169s	1	1m23.692s	10
6	Max Verstappen	Red Bull	1h30m02.228s	1	1m21.879s	4
7	Nico Hulkenberg	Renault	1h30m05.954s	1	1m23.532s	7
8	Valtteri Bottas !	Mercedes	1h30m07.622s	1	no time	15
9	Stoffel Vandoorne	McLaren	1h30m08.204s	1	1m23.853s	11
10	Carlos Sainz Jr	Renault	1h30m19.005s	1	1m23.577s	9
11	Sergio Perez	Force India	1h30m20.100s	1	1m24.005s	12
12	Esteban Ocon	Force India	1h30m33.561s	1	1m24.786s	14
13	Charles Leclerc	Sauber	1h30m49.042s	2	1m24.636s	18
14	Lance Stroll	Williams	1h30m51.571s	2	1m24.230s	13
15	Brendon Hartley	Toro Rosso	57 laps	2	1m24.532s	16
R	Romain Grosjean	Haas	24 laps/wheel nut	1	1m23.339s	6
R	Kevin Magnussen	Haas	22 laps/wheel nut	1	1m23.187s	5
R	Pierre Gasly	Toro Rosso	13 laps/power unit	0	1m25.295Ss	20
R	Marcus Ericsson	Sauber	5 laps/hydraulics	0	1m24.556s	17
R	Sergey Sirotkin	Williams	4 laps/brakes	0	1m24.922s	19

FASTEST LAP: RICCIARDO, 1M25.945S, 138.024MPH/222.128KPH ON LAP 54 • RACE LEADERS: HAMILTON 1-18, VETTEL 19-58
* 3-PLACE GRID PENALTY FOR RED FLAG INFRINGEMENT; ! 5-PLACE GRID PENALTY FOR CHANGING THE GEARBOX

BAHRAIN GP

Mercedes had stumbled in the opening race in Australia but thought that it had matters under control at Sakhir. Except that it didn't, as Ferrari helped Sebastian Vettel to make it two wins from two by risking a daring tactical strategy.

Mercedes' problems began in Melbourne, when Lewis Hamilton's gearbox sprung a leak and the damage this wreaked necessitated a change for Bahrain, which led to a five-place grid penalty at Sakhir. As the four-time World Champion had qualified only fourth fastest, this meant that he had to line up ninth, with chief rivals Ferrari filling the front row.

Barring contact, Hamilton was always going to advance from there, with Mercedes' cause being boosted by Valtteri Bottas getting the jump on Kimi Raikkonen to claim second. Hamilton passed two cars at the start, but outbraked himself at Turn 1 and fell behind not only Esteban Ocon and Nico Hulkenberg but then Fernando Alonso at Turn 8 as well. He was then clipped by Max Verstappen who was making up places from 15th, but the Dutch driver was out of the race. Thereafter, at least, things improved for Hamilton.

He gained a place when Daniel Ricciardo retired from fourth after just one lap and more by picking off Alonso, Hulkenberg, Ocon, Kevin Magnussen and Pierre Gasly to reach fourth.

Having started on soft rather than supersoft tyres, Hamilton stayed out longer than Vettel, Bottas and Raikkonen, to lead until he pitted half a dozen laps later, dropping him back to fourth. The Mercedes duo were fitted with medium compound tyres for the run to the finish and the Ferraris with less resistant softs.

Raikkonen pitted again and left too soon, hit one of his mechanics, and broke the mechanic's leg. So Hamilton reached third, but when it became clear that Vettel wasn't stopping again, Mercedes's best hope of victory was Bottas. The Finn, however, only got close enough to attack Vettel in the final two laps and wasn't able to find a way by.

Scuderia Toro Rosso received a huge boost as Gasly raced to a thoroughly deserved fourth place, using Honda engines that McLaren had suggested were so weak in 2017. Another driver smiling after the race was Sauber's Marcus Ericsson who was in the points for the first time since the 2015 Italian GP.

SAKHIR ROUND 2

DATE: 8 APRIL 2018

Laps: **57** • Distance: **191.530 miles/308.238km** • Weather: **Hot & sunny**

Pos	Driver	Team	Result	Stops	Qualifying Time	Grid
1	Sebastian Vettel	Ferrari	1h32m01.940s	1	1m27.958s	1
2	Valtteri Bottas	Mercedes	1h32m02.639s	1	1m28.124s	3
3	Lewis Hamilton *	Mercedes	1h32m08.452s	1	1m28.220s	9
4	Pierre Gasly	Toro Rosso	1h33m04.174s	2	1m29.329s	5
5	Kevin Magnussen	Haas	1h33m16.986s	2	1m29.358s	6
6	Nico Hulkenberg	Renault	1h33m40.964s	2	1m29.570s	7
7	Fernando Alonso	McLaren	56 laps	2	1m30.212s	13
8	Stoffel Vandoorne	McLaren	56 laps	2	1m30.525s	14
9	Marcus Ericsson	Sauber	56 laps	1	1m31.063s	17
10	Esteban Ocon	Force India	56 laps	2	1m29.874s	8
11	Carlos Sainz Jr	Renault	56 laps	2	1m29.986s	10
12	Charles Leclerc	Sauber	56 laps	2	1m31.420s	19
13	Romain Grosjean	Haas	56 laps	2	1m30.530s	16
14	Lance Stroll	Williams	56 laps	2	1m31.503s	20
15	Sergey Sirotkin	Williams	56 laps	2	1m31.414s	18
16	Sergio Perez !	Force India	56 laps	2	1m30.156s	12
17	Brendon Hartley !!	Toro Rosso	56 laps	2	1m30.105s	11
R	Kimi Raikkonen	Ferrari	35 laps/wheel	2	1m28.101s	2
R	Max Verstappen	Red Bull	3 laps/collision	1	no time	15
R	Daniel Ricciardo	Red Bull	1 lap/electrics	0	1m28.398s	4

FASTEST LAP: BOTTAS, 1M33.740S, 129.147MPH/207.842KPH ON LAP 22 • RACE LEADERS: VETTEL 1-17 & 26-57, BOTTAS 18-20, HAMILTON 21-25
* 5-PLACE GRID PENALTY FOR REPLACING THE GEARBOX; ! 30S PENALTY FOR OVERTAKING ON THE FORMATION LAP; !! 30S PENALTY FOR FAILING TO RE-START INFRINGEMENT

Sebastian Vettel leads away from the grid as Valtteri Bottas moves his Mercedes into second.

Daniel Ricciardo produced a drive of excellence, helped by Red Bull Racing's tactical savvy, to beat the best from both Ferrari and Mercedes in a race in which the three teams were all in with a shout of victory, but the Australian came out ahead.

There was an all-Ferrari front row, Sebastian Vettel ahead of Kimi Raikkonen, but that wasn't to last, as Valtteri Bottas demoted Raikkonen when he tried to challenge Vettel into the first corner. Pleasingly, it was all change, with Max Verstappen advancing from fifth to third when he passed first Lewis Hamilton and then Raikkonen.

Red Bull Racing's strategy was to start both drivers on ultra-soft tyres and see how long they could make them last and possibly turn the race into a one-stopper. Running to a more conservative pattern, Vettel was brought in to change from softs to mediums, but Bottas had made a better job of a similar swap a lap earlier and was ahead when the German returned.

Ferrari knew that it had to do something about this, so kept Raikkonen out and used him to slow Bottas's escape.

Then came a safety car period to shake things up. This occurred when the Toro Rossos clashed and debris needed to be cleared. Red Bull thought fastest and got both drivers to pit. This dropped Verstappen to fourth and Daniel Ricciardo to sixth, but they were now on soft tyres for the 22-lap dash to the finish and sitting right on the tails of their rivals who were now stuck on mediums. The Red Bull racers finally had a performance advantage and they made good use of it.

Ricciardo picked off Raikkonen then, when his own team-mate made a mess of passing Hamilton, he dived past into fourth.

Then came the move of the race as the Australian lined up Hamilton into the Turn 14 hairpin and made the move stick. From third, Ricciardo hunted down and passed Vettel, then set off after Bottas. The Finn was unable to resist a brilliant pass into Turn 6, and that was that. Ricciardo's ability to attack as soon as he could, while his tyres were still superior, was a joy to behold. Verstappen wasn't quite as accurate, though, and he clipped Vettel at the hairpin, leaving him in fifth place and causing the German to limp home in eighth.

Two pitstops proved to be the way to victory for Daniel Ricciardo as Red Bull came up trumps.

SHANGHAI ROUND 3

DATE: **15 APRIL 2018**

Laps: **56** • Distance: **189.559 miles/305.066km** • Weather: **Warm & bright**

Pos	Driver	Team	Result	Stops	Qualifying Time	Grid
1	**Daniel Ricciardo**	Red Bull	1h35m36.380s	2	1m31.948s	6
2	**Valtteri Bottas**	Mercedes	1h35m45.274s	1	1m31.625s	3
3	**Kimi Raikkonen**	Ferrari	1h35m46.017s	1	1m31.182s	2
4	**Lewis Hamilton**	Mercedes	1h35m53.365s	1	1m31.675s	4
5	**Max Verstappen !**	Red Bull	1h35m56.816s	2	1m31.796s	5
6	**Nico Hulkenberg**	Renault	1h35m57.432s	2	1m32.532s	7
7	**Fernando Alonso**	McLaren	1h36m07.019s	1	1m33.232s	13
8	**Sebastian Vettel**	Ferrari	1h36m11.666s	1	1m31.095s	1
9	**Carlos Sainz Jr**	Renault	1h36m12.143s	2	1m32.819s	9
10	**Kevin Magnussen**	Haas	1h36m15.974s	1	1m32.986s	11
11	**Esteban Ocon**	Force India	1h36m20.430s	2	1m33.057s	12
12	**Sergio Perez**	Force India	1h36m21.105s	2	1m32.758s	8
13	**Stoffel Vandoorne**	McLaren	1h36m25.753s	1	1m33.505s	14
14	**Lance Stroll**	Williams	1h36m31.870s	1	1m34.285s	18
15	**Sergey Sirotkin**	Williams	1h36m34.621s	2	1m34.062s	16
16	**Marcus Ericsson ***	Sauber	1h36m38.984s	1	1m34.914s	20
17	**Romain Grosjean**	Haas	1h36m41.676s	2	1m32.855s	10
18	**Pierre Gasly !**	Toro Rosso	1h36m42.710s	2	1m34.101s	17
19	**Charles Leclerc**	Sauber	1h36m58.955s	1	1m34.454s	19
R	**Brendon Hartley**	Toro Rosso	51 laps/gearbox	2	1m33.795s	15

FASTEST LAP: RICCIARDO, 1M35.785S, 127.301MPH/204.871KPH ON LAP 55 • RACE LEADERS: VETTEL 1-20, RAIKKONEN 21-26, BOTTAS 27-44, RICCIARDO 45-56
* 5-PLACE GRID PENALTY FOR FAILING TO SLOW TO DOUBLE WAVED YELLOW FLAGS; ! 10S PENALTY FOR CAUSING A COLLISION

Some races get away from a driver, others come to them and this was definitely one of the latter for Lewis Hamilton. First Sebastian Vettel slid off, then his team-mate Valtteri Bottas had a blow-out, handing the Mercedes driver the victory on a plate.

Hamilton started second behind Vettel and ran there for the first half of the race. However, Mercedes team-mate Bottas moved ahead of both by making the supersoft tyres on which he started the race last the distance.

He was looking good for a one-stop race, making that pit visit as soon as the second safety car period began. However, Vettel became overambitious on the restart and tried to pass Bottas's Mercedes into Turn 1. In a flash, as Vettel ran wide, both Hamilton and Raikkonen dived past.

Bottas was safe in the lead with just three laps to go, but he hit some debris and his right rear tyre blew, giving victory to Hamilton.

Hot-headedness in the Red Bull Racing camp culminated in the retirement of both cars after a clash between Max Verstappen and Daniel Ricciardo when they were disputing fourth into Turn 1 on lap 39. Going for a gap that never fully opened, Ricciardo hit the rear of Verstappen's car. He later admitted the collision was down to overcommitting, with Verstappen being pinged for making two blocking moves rather than the permitted one. The team reprimanded both drivers, furious that at least 22 points had gone to waste.

This, and Bottas's misery, elevated all those behind, raising Raikkonen to second. It also helped Sergio Perez who defended furiously for the last two laps to stop Vettel from taking the final place on the podium. Carlos Sainz Jr finished fifth for Renault.

Sauber was delighted with sixth place, celebrating it as others might a victory when rookie Charles Leclerc crossed the line for his first points, which were also the Swiss team's first since the 2017 Azerbaijan GP.

Showing just how hard Fernando Alonso had to work to get the recalcitrant McLaren to advance, he described his drive to be the second best Spaniard in the race, in seventh overall, as "the best race of my life" after he limped back to the pits with a pair of right side punctures after a clash with Nico Hulkenberg's Renault on the opening lap.

BAKU ROUND 4

DATE: **29 APRIL 2018**

Laps: **51** • Distance: **190.170 miles/306.049km** • Weather: **Warm & overcast**

Pos	Driver	Team	Result	Stops	Qualifying Time	Grid
1	Lewis Hamilton	Mercedes	1h43m44.291s	2	1m41.677s	2
2	Kimi Raikkonen	Ferrari	1h43m46.751s	2	1m42.490s	6
3	Sergio Perez	Force India	1h43m48.315s	2	1m42.547s	8
4	Sebastian Vettel	Ferrari	1h43m49.620s	2	1m41.498s	1
5	Carlos Sainz Jr	Renault	1h43m51.806s	2	1m43.351s	9
6	Charles Leclerc	Sauber	1h43m53.449s	2	1m44.074s	13
7	Fernando Alonso	McLaren	1h43m55.222s	2	1m44.019s	12
8	Lance Stroll	Williams	1h43m56.837s	2	1m43.585s	10
9	Stoffel Vandoorne	McLaren	1h43m58.443s	4	1m44.489s	16
10	Brendon Hartley	Toro Rosso	1h44m02.321s	3	1m57.354s	19
11	Marcus Ericsson	Sauber	1h44m02.803s	4	1m45.541s	18
12	Pierre Gasly	Toro Rosso	1h44m09.011s	2	1m44.496s	17
13	Kevin Magnussen !	Haas	1h44m24.954s	1	1m44.759s	15
14	Valtteri Bottas	Mercedes	48 laps/puncture	1	1m41.837s	3
R	Romain Grosjean *	Haas	42 laps/spun off	2	No time	20
R	Max Verstappen	Red Bull	39 laps/collision	1	1m41.994s	5
R	Daniel Ricciardo	Red Bull	39 laps/collision	1	1m41.911s	4
R	Nico Hulkenberg *	Renault	10 laps/spun off	0	1m43.066s	14
R	Esteban Ocon	Force India	0 laps/collision	0	1m42.523s	7
R	Sergey Sirotkin	Williams	0 laps/collision	0	1m43.886s	11

FASTEST LAP: BOTTAS, 1M45.149S, 127.537MPH/205.252KPH ON LAP 37 • RACE LEADERS: VETTEL 1-30, BOTTAS 31-48, HAMILTON 49-51
* 5-PLACE GRID PENALTY FOR REPLACING THE GEARBOX; ! 10S PENALTY FOR CAUSING A COLLISION

Sergio Perez was justifiably thrilled with his third place for Force India after resisting Vettel.

SPANISH GP

There was a feeling that Lewis Hamilton wasn't really racing to his potential in 2018, until the Spanish GP, where Mercedes' lead driver put this right with a performance that gave none of his rivals any hope of stealing victory from him.

If Hamilton's win in Azerbaijan a fortnight earlier had required a sizeable scoop of assistance, this victory in Spain definitely was all his own work. Afterwards, one could sense his satisfaction that he could still hit the highest notes.

Fastest in second and third practice and fastest in qualifying, Hamilton's form at the Circuit de Catalunya was solid and he made the most of starting from pole position. Unfortunately, team-mate Valtteri Bottas wasn't able to protect his tail, as Sebastian Vettel swept past him into second place around the outside at the first corner.

Then came an incident that triggered the safety car. Romain Grosjean is a driver of undoubted speed but one who continues to have mishaps. He crashed out of a good result in Baku, when running behind the safety car... Then, when he was trying to make amends in Spain, he was out as early as the third corner, spinning to avoid a wobble by team-mate Kevin Magnussen that left him to be clipped by both Nico Hulkenberg and Pierre Gasly.

The safety car period that followed lasted until lap 6, after which Hamilton controlled proceedings. Teams ran different strategies but, once all had made their stops, it was Hamilton back in front, revelling in the team having found him a superior race balance for his car. In an attempt to keep up, Vettel pushed too hard and needed to change his front left tyre. This pit visit was on lap 16 of 66 and, when the Ferrari driver came in, Mercedes decided that Bottas would cover this move. The Finn ought to have come out in front of Vettel, but a sticking right rear wheel meant that he emerged behind both Vettel and Magnussen. The Dane was passed easily, but Vettel proved to be a harder nut to crack.

Hamilton's superiority let him wait until lap 25 before he came in, and he was given an increased advantage when Raikkonen retired from second. Hamilton duly emerged second, but knew that Max Verstappen still had to pit and then led all the way to the flag.

The relief was palpable as Lewis Hamilton led home a Mercedes one-two finish in Spain.

BARCELONA ROUND 5

DATE: **13 MAY 2018**

Laps: 66 • Distance: **190.825 miles/307.104km** • Weather: **Warm & bright**

Pos	Driver	Team	Result	Stops	Qualifying Time	Grid
1	**Lewis Hamilton**	Mercedes	1h35m29.972s	1	1m16.173s	1
2	**Valtteri Bottas**	Mercedes	1h35m50.565s	1	1m16.213s	2
3	**Max Verstappen**	Red Bull	1h35m56.845s	1	1m16.816s	5
4	**Sebastian Vettel**	Ferrari	1h35m57.556s	2	1m16.305s	3
5	**Daniel Ricciardo**	Red Bull	1h36m20.030s	1	1m16.818s	6
6	**Kevin Magnussen**	Haas	65 laps	1	1m17.676s	7
7	**Carlos Sainz Jr**	Renault	65 laps	1	1m17.790s	9
8	**Fernando Alonso**	McLaren	65 laps	1	1m17.721s	8
9	**Sergio Perez**	Force India	64 laps	2	1m19.098s	15
10	**Charles Leclerc**	Sauber	64 laps	1	1m18.910s	14
11	**Lance Stroll**	Williams	64 laps	1	1m20.225s	18
12	**Brendon Hartley !**	Toro Rosso	64 laps	2	no time	20
13	**Marcus Ericsson**	Sauber	64 laps	1	1m19.493s	17
14	**Sergey Sirotkin ***	Williams	63 laps	3	1m19.695s	19
R	**Stoffel Vandoorne**	McLaren	45 laps/gearbox	1	1m18.323s	11
R	**Esteban Ocon**	Force India	38 laps/oil leak	1	1m18.696s	13
R	**Kimi Raikkonen**	Ferrari	25 laps/power unit	0	1m16.612s	4
R	**Romain Grosjean**	Haas	0 laps/collision	0	1m17.835s	10
R	**Pierre Gasly**	Toro Rosso	0 laps/collision	0	1m18.463s	12
R	**Nico Hulkenberg**	Renault	0 laps/collision	0	1m18.923s	16

FASTEST LAP: RICCIARDO, 1M18.441S, 132.748MPH/213.638KPH ON LAP 61 • RACE LEADERS: HAMILTON 1-25 & 34-66, VERSTAPPEN 26-33
* 3-PLACE GRID PENALTY FOR CAUSING A COLLISION IN PREVIOUS RACE; ! 5-PLACE GRID PENALTY FOR REPLACING THE GEARBOX

MONACO GP

Daniel Ricciardo had this race in the bag for Red Bull Racing, but then he felt that his car had lost electrical power. In fact, he'd lost 160bhp of it with 50 laps still to run, and yet somehow the Australian concealed this and hung on to still be in front at the finish.

A broad smile is never far from Daniel Ricciardo's face and he had every reason to be beaming at Monaco. First off, he was fastest in qualifying and there are few circuits at which pole position is more important. Then, at the start, he nailed his getaway to lead into Ste Devote. So far, so good. Then he changed from hypersoft Pirellis to the more resilient ultrasofts a lap after Sebastian Vettel had done the same.

Having had a 4s advantage before the Ferrari driver pitted, Ricciardo wasn't worried about not coming back out into the lead, which he did. As this set of tyres was expected to carry him all the way to the end of the race, the Australian was sitting pretty.

However, at around lap 26 of 78, Ricciardo felt a loss of power and realized that his MGU-K was no longer working. Team boss Christian Horner said that, in most circumstances, he would have thought of retiring the car, but it was leading the Monaco GP, so no...

Ricciardo's busy day in the office just got busier as he had to adapt to getting by without full power and also alter the braking now that the rear wheels were not harvesting power in the same way. Go too hard on the brakes, and Ricciardo would overheat then. On top of these travails, he also was determined not to let Vettel gain an inkling that he had a problem. One thing hugely in Ricciardo's favour was the circuit's tight layout and he was able to keep his car where he wanted it in a way that left no gaps for Vettel to dive into.

Lewis Hamilton closed in as Ricciardo backed up the field, but the Mercedes driver's tyres weren't lasting as well as his rivals' and he had to settle for third place, much as Kimi Raikkonen did for fourth.

Fifth place went to Valtteri Bottas, with Esteban Ocon and Pierre Gasly having good runs to sixth and seventh in a race in which Max Verstappen missed qualifying after crashing in practice, before coming through from last to ninth.

MONTE CARLO ROUND 6

DATE: **27 MAY 2018**

Laps: **78** • Distance: **161.734 miles/260.286km** • Weather: **Hot & sunny**

Pos	Driver	Team	Result	Stops	Qualifying Time	Grid
1	**Daniel Ricciardo**	Red Bull	1h42m54.807s	1	1m10.810s	1
2	**Sebastian Vettel**	Ferrari	1h43m02.143s	1	1m11.039s	2
3	**Lewis Hamilton**	Mercedes	1h43m11.820s	1	1m11.232s	3
4	**Kimi Raikkonen**	Ferrari	1h43m12.934s	1	1m11.266s	4
5	**Valtteri Bottas**	Mercedes	1h43m13.629s	1	1m11.441s	5
6	**Esteban Ocon**	Force India	1h43m18.474s	1	1m12.061s	6
7	**Pierre Gasly**	Toro Rosso	1h43m19.138s	1	1m12.221s	10
8	**Nico Hulkenberg**	Renault	1h43m19.646s	1	1m12.411s	11
9	**Max Verstappen !**	Red Bull	1h43m20.124s	1	no time	20
10	**Carlos Sainz Jr**	Renault	1h44m03.820s	1	1m12.130s	8
11	**Marcus Ericsson**	Sauber	1h44m04.671s	1	1m13.265s	16
12	**Sergio Perez**	Force India	1h44m05.268s	1	1m12.154s	9
13	**Kevin Magnussen**	Haas	1h44m09.630s	1	1m13.393s	19
14	**Stoffel Vandoorne**	McLaren	77 laps	2	1m12.440s	12
15	**Romain Grosjean ***	Haas	77 laps	1	1m12.728s	18
16	**Sergey Sirotkin**	Williams	77 laps	3	1m12.521s	13
17	**Lance Stroll**	Williams	76 laps	3	1m13.323s	17
R	**Charles Leclerc**	Sauber	70 laps/brakes	1	1m12.714s	14
R	**Brendon Hartley**	Toro Rosso	70 laps/collision	1	1m13.179s	15
R	**Fernando Alonso**	McLaren	52 laps/gearbox	1	1m12.110s	7

FASTEST LAP: **VERSTAPPEN, 1M14.260S, 100.520MPH/161.772KPH ON LAP 60** • RACE LEADER: **RICCIARDO 1-78**
* 3-PLACE GRID PENALTY FOR CAUSING A COLLISION IN PREVIOUS RACE; ! 5-PLACE GRID PENALTY FOR CHANGING GEARBOX & 10-PLACE GRID PENALTY FOR USING ADDITIONAL POWER UNIT

Daniel Ricciardo managed to overcome the loss of 160bhp for the major part of the race.

This was Ferrari's grand prix and Sebastian Vettel controlled it from pole position to take a clear win over Valtteri Bottas. It was all the more impressive as the German driver had suffered an abysmal time on Friday before bouncing back in style.

There are many circuits where F1's most successful team, Ferrari, has a string of wins. Yet, amazingly, the Circuit Gilles Villeneuve is not one of them, with the team hoping to score its first win in Montreal since Michael Schumacher triumphed here in 2004. With Vettel starting from pole position, there was a good chance of doing so and it was boosted when Bottas was challenged for second by Max Verstappen.

With the entire field getting through ever-critical Turns 1 and 2 on the opening lap, all seemed settled. However, that was soon to change, as Brendon Hartley had a major accident when he tried to go around the outside of Lance Stroll at Turn 5. The Williams snapped out of shape, put the Toro Rosso into the wall and both ended up in retirement in the run-off area at Turn 6.

When the subsequent safety car period ended, Vettel eased clear of Bottas. However, in this one-stop race, he only got safely clear late in the race when the Finn slid wide at Turn 1 when lapping Carlos Sainz Jr's Renault, allowing Vettel to win by 7s. Looking from the sidelines, though, it seemed that Vettel was driving only as hard as he needed to and no more.

In an event in which Lewis Hamilton was subdued, the Red Bull Racing chargers were free to challenge Bottas but the team realized that its gamble of starting its cars on Pirelli's hypersoft tyres was a mistake and they had to pit earlier than their rivals.

With Verstappen going on to claim third, Ricciardo took fourth, having demoted Hamilton when the Mercedes driver's pitstop was longer than his own as the Mercedes crew needed to remove some bodywork cooling louvres as the engine was running hot.

One of the most embarrassing events in recent F1 history came at the end of the race when the chequered flag was waved a lap early. Race control passed the wrong signal, which led to confusion and a degree of danger.

Sebastian Vettel got his year back onto a winning track, but it hadn't looked likely on Friday.

CIRCUIT GILLES VILLENEUVE ROUND 7

DATE: **10 JUNE 2018**

Laps: **68** • Distance: **184.266 miles/296.548km** • Weather: **Warm & sunny**

Pos	Driver	Team	Result	Stops	Qualifying Time	Grid
1	Sebastian Vettel	Ferrari	1h28m31.377s	1	1m10.764s	1
2	Valtteri Bottas	Mercedes	1h28m38.753s	1	1m10.857s	2
3	Max Verstappen	Red Bull	1h28m39.737s	1	1m10.937s	3
4	Daniel Ricciardo	Red Bull	1h28m52.269s	1	1m11.116s	6
5	Lewis Hamilton	Mercedes	1h28m52.963s	1	1m10.996s	4
6	Kimi Raikkonen	Ferrari	1h28m58.561s	1	1m11.095s	5
7	Nico Hulkenberg	Renault	67 laps	1	1m11.973s	7
8	Carlos Sainz Jr	Renault	67 laps	1	1m12.168s	9
9	Esteban Ocon	Force India	67 laps	1	1m12.084s	8
10	Charles Leclerc	Sauber	67 laps	1	1m12.661s	13
11	Pierre Gasly *	Toro Rosso	67 laps	1	1m13.047s	19
12	Romain Grosjean	Haas	67 laps	1	no time	20
13	Kevin Magnussen	Haas	67 laps	1	1m12.606s	11
14	Sergio Perez	Force India	67 laps	2	1m12.671s	10
15	Marcus Ericsson	Sauber	66 laps	1	1m14.593s	18
16	Stoffel Vandoorne	McLaren	66 laps	2	1m12.865s	15
17	Sergey Sirotkin	Williams	66 laps	1	1m13.643s	17
R	Fernando Alonso	McLaren	40 laps/exhaust	1	1m12.856s	14
R	Brendon Hartley	Toro Rosso	0 laps/collision	0	1m12.635s	12
R	Lance Stroll	Williams	0 laps/collision	0	1m13.590s	16

FASTEST LAP: VERSTAPPEN, 1M13.864S, 132.070MPH/212.547KPH ON LAP 65 • RACE LEADER: VETTEL 1-68
* MADE TO START FROM THE BACK OF THE GRID FOR USING ADDITIONAL POWER UNIT ELEMENTS

FRENCH GP

From race-winning hero in Canada to something close to zero in France, Sebastian Vettel slipped up on the opening lap of F1's return to Paul Ricard and this made life unusually easy for his title rival Lewis Hamilton as he raced to a clear win for Mercedes.

Traffic problems were the chief topic of conversation at F1's first grand prix outing at Paul Ricard since 1990, also France's first grand prix since 2008, but afterwards it was how championship leader Vettel had thrown away another opportunity to shine, causing a first-corner collision and opening the way for pole-sitter Hamilton to make good his escape.

Having clipped the rear of Valtteri Bottas's Mercedes to put it into a spin as they entered Turn 1, Vettel's Ferrari then hit Romain Grosjean as the field went in all directions in avoidance. French woes were then magnified at Turn 3 when Pierre Gasly spun and collected compatriot Esteban Ocon, forcing both into retirement. With debris scattered through the opening sequence of corners, the safety car was deployed and both Bottas and Vettel dived into the pits for repairs, along with both Williams drivers and Fernando Alonso.

With his closest challengers removed and Bottas wondering just what he had to do to change his awful run of luck, Hamilton was able to run the race as he pleased. It was a gift.

Max Verstappen was the best of the rest, finishing second, able to stay close to the Mercedes but not challenge it. Third might have gone to his team-mate Daniel Ricciardo, but his car was damaged by hitting debris and was unable to resist a charge from Kimi Raikkonen, who had been seventh after the Turn 1 sort-out. Raikkonen passed Ricciardo late in the race, while Vettel recovered to finish in a distant fifth place.

Carlos Sainz Jr was heading for sixth place but, with four laps to go, his Renault's MGU-K failed and he lost 160bhp – like Ricciardo suffered at Monaco where it was easier to defend – dropping him behind Kevin Magnussen and Bottas by the finish.

Charles Leclerc proved again that he is F1's coming man, as the Monegasque ace got his Sauber into the final qualifying session for the first time. Having qualified eighth, he raced to another valuable point for the Swiss team, finishing 10th.

PAUL RICARD ROUND 8
DATE: **24 JUNE 2018**

Laps: **53** • Distance: **192.432 miles/309.690km** • Weather: **Hot & sunny**

Pos	Driver	Team	Result	Stops	Qualifying Time	Grid
1	**Lewis Hamilton**	Mercedes	1h30m11.385s	1	1m30.029s	1
2	**Max Verstappen**	Red Bull	1h30m18.475s	1	1m30.705s	4
3	**Kimi Raikkonen**	Ferrari	1h30m37.273s	1	1m31.057s	6
4	**Daniel Ricciardo**	Red Bull	1h30m46.121s	1	1m30.895s	5
5	**Sebastian Vettel**	Ferrari	1h31m13.320s	2	1m30.400s	3
6	**Kevin Magnussen**	Haas	1h31m30.749s	1	1m32.930s	9
7	**Valtteri Bottas**	Mercedes	1h31m32.017s	2	1m30.147s	2
8	**Carlos Sainz Jr**	Renault	1h31m38.569s	1	1m32.126s	7
9	**Nico Hulkenberg**	Renault	1h31m43.374s	1	1m32.115s	12
10	**Charles Leclerc**	Sauber	1h31m45.258s	1	1m32.635s	8
11	**Romain Grosjean**	Haas	52 laps	1	no time	10
12	**Stoffel Vandoorne**	McLaren	52 laps	1	1m33.162s	17
13	**Marcus Ericsson**	Sauber	52 laps	1	1m32.820s	15
14	**Brendon Hartley ***	Toro Rosso	52 laps	1	1m33.025s	20
15	**Sergey Sirotkin**	Williams	52 laps	1	1m33.636s	18
16	**Fernando Alonso**	McLaren	50 laps/suspension	2	1m32.976s	16
17	**Lance Stroll**	Williams	48 laps/tyre	1	1m33.729s	19
R	**Sergio Perez**	Force India	27 laps/power unit	0	1m32.454s	13
R	**Esteban Ocon**	Force India	0 laps/collision	0	1m32.075s	11
R	**Pierre Gasly**	Toro Rosso	0 laps/collision	0	1m32.460s	14

FASTEST LAP: BOTTAS, 1M34.225S, 138.690MPH/223.201KPH ON LAP 41 • RACE LEADERS: HAMILTON 1-32 & 34-53, RAIKKONEN 33
* MADE TO START FROM THE BACK OF THE GRID FOR USING ADDITIONAL POWER UNIT ELEMENTS

Sebastian Vettel's lunge to pass Valtteri Bottas into the first corner went horribly wrong.

AUSTRIAN GP

Mercedes got it all wrong in Austria and the retirement of both of its cars handed a clear run to victory to Red Bull Racing's Max Verstappen. With the next race just a week away, the team needed to refocus to re-establish its title challenge.

The first step at any grand prix meeting is to practice well on Friday and Saturday morning, use your track time efficiently to establish a set-up that would work in qualifying and another that would be right for the race itself. Mercedes did the first and third, topping the two Friday practice sessions, but being pipped by Ferrari's Sebastian Vettel on the Saturday. Come qualifying, though, it was Mercedes back on top, with Valtteri Bottas taking pole from Lewis Hamilton. Better still for them, Vettel, third in qualifying, was penalized three places and lined up sixth after impeding Carlos Sainz Jr who ended up starting ninth.

Haas F1 had one of its better qualifying sessions, with Romain Grosjean fifth and Kevin Magnussen eighth, one place behind Daniel Ricciardo who was frustrated by giving Verstappen a tow but not getting one himself.

At the start, Hamilton and Kimi Raikkonen got past Bottas into Turn 1, but the Ferrari driver ran wide, immediately losing places to Bottas, Verstappen and Ricciardo, before reclaiming fourth before the lap was out.

Bottas's safe second place ended when his gearbox lost hydraulic pressure and he was out on lap 13. After that, place changes came according to how successful a driver was in tyre management. Most drivers pitted during the virtual safety car period triggered by Bottas's demise, but Mercedes kept Hamilton out. It was soon clear that when he did pit, Hamilton wouldn't resume in the lead. He was fourth on his return, third when Ricciardo pitted again with a tyre problem, but fell back to fourth after a second stop. Low fuel pressure forced him out, a retirement that saw him lose his World Championship lead.

Verstappen duly won as he pleased, from Raikkonen, then Vettel, for Red Bull's first win at company founder Dietrich Mateschitz's circuit. Grosjean was delighted to secure his first decent result in a while, even more so as his fourth place was the Haas team's best F1 finish. In fact, it was his first points haul after 12 races in which he drew a blank.

Red Bull's Max Verstappen chose the best place for his first win of the year: the Red Bull Ring.

RED BULL RING ROUND 9
DATE: 1 JULY 2018

Laps: **71** • Distance: **190.420 miles/306.452km** • Weather: **Warm & sunny**

Pos	Driver	Team	Result	Stops	Qualifying Time	Grid
1	Max Verstappen	Red Bull	1h21m56.024s	1	1m03.840s	4
2	Kimi Raikkonen	Ferrari	1h21m57.528s	1	1m03.464s	3
3	Sebastian Vettel *	Ferrari	1h21m59.205s	1	1m03.660s	6
4	Romain Grosjean	Haas	70 laps	1	1m03.892s	5
5	Kevin Magnussen	Haas	70 laps	1	1m04.051s	8
6	Esteban Ocon	Force India	70 laps	1	1m04.845s	11
7	Sergio Perez	Force India	70 laps	1	1m05.279s	15
8	Fernando Alonso !!!	McLaren	70 laps	1	1m05.058s	20
9	Charles Leclerc !	Sauber	70 laps	1	1m04.979s	17
10	Marcus Ericsson	Sauber	70 laps	1	1m05.479s	18
11	Pierre Gasly	Toro Rosso	70 laps	1	1m04.874s	12
12	Carlos Sainz Jr	Renault	70 laps	2	1m04.725s	9
13	Sergey Sirotkin	Williams	69 laps	2	1m05.322s	16
14	Lance Stroll **	Williams	69 laps	2	1m05.286s	13
15	Stoffel Vandoorne	McLaren	65 laps/gearbox	2	1m05.271s	14
R	Lewis Hamilton	Mercedes	62 laps/fuel pressure	2	1m03.149s	2
R	Brendon Hartley!!	Toro Rosso	54 laps/suspension	0	1m05.366s	19
R	Daniel Ricciardo	Red Bull	53 laps/exhaust	2	1m03.996s	7
R	Valtteri Bottas	Mercedes	13 laps/hydraulics	0	1m03.130s	1
R	Nico Hulkenberg	Renault	11 laps/power unit	0	1m05.019s	10

FASTEST LAP: RAIKKONEN, 1M06.957S, 144.257MPH/232.160KPH ON LAP 71 • RACE LEADERS: HAMILTON 1-25, VERSTAPPEN 26-71
* 3-PLACE GRID PENALTY FOR IMPEDING ANOTHER DRIVER; ** 10S PENALTY FOR IGNORING BLUE FLAGS; ! 5-PLACE GRID PENALTY FOR REPLACING THE GEARBOX; !! REQUIRED TO START FROM BACK OF GRID FOR USING ADDITIONAL POWER UNIT ELEMENTS; !!! REQUIRED TO START FROM BACK OF GRID DUE TO NEW-SPEC PARTS BEING FITTED UNDER PARC FERME CONDITIONS

BRITISH GP

Ferrari left Silverstone with a massive smile on its face, as Sebastian Vettel triumphed to go back into the championship lead, which is certainly not the way that a frustrated Lewis Hamilton felt after his charge from the back of the field to second place.

After the first nine grands prix, the honours were even between the top three teams, with Ferrari, Mercedes and Red Bull Racing having claimed three wins apiece. At Silverstone, Ferrari moved ahead.

Vettel qualified second to Hamilton, but it was the Ferrari driver who completed lap 1 in the lead, as Hamilton's Mercedes had suffered too much wheelspin and was only second into the first corner. It got worse from there, as he was hit and put into a spin, two corners later, when Kimi Raikkonen locked up down the inside line. From 18th at the end of lap 1, all Hamilton could do was keep pressing on. And this he did, reaching sixth after just 10 laps. From there, progress was harder. For his part, Raikkonen was hit with a 10s penalty which he served at the end of his first pitstop.

Silverstone's reputation as a high-speed track that can bite was magnified following big accidents in practice to both Romain Grosjean and Brendon Hartley. The Frenchman hit the barriers at Abbey and the Kiwi at Brooklands after his Toro Rosso's front right suspension failed. Both needed new monocoques. Sadly, Grosjean would suffer further damage in the race when he and Carlos Sainz Jr collided at Copse, eliminating both.

They weren't the only victims of this incident. Valtteri Bottas's chances of winning were holed as Mercedes had elected for their drivers to pit just once and he was exposed on medium tyres as Vettel was able to pit a second time under the safety car and come out on soft tyres for the final stint. The German made his move into the lead with six laps to go, diving past Bottas into Brooklands. It got worse as the struggling Finn dropped to fourth when Hamilton and Raikkonen drove past too.

Charles Leclerc's impressive rookie season looked set to yield sixth place, but a loose wheel scuppered that.

Williams' dreadful season failed to improve at its home race. Indeed, both drivers had spins in qualifying and started the race from the pitlane with older rear wings.

SILVERSTONE ROUND 10

DATE: **8 JULY 2018**

Laps: **52** • Distance: **190.262 miles/306.198km** • Weather: **Hot & sunny**

Pos	Driver	Team	Result	Stops	Qualifying Time	Grid
1	Sebastian Vettel	Ferrari	1h27m29.784s	2	1m25.936s	2
2	Lewis Hamilton	Mercedes	1h27m32.048s	1	1m25.892s	1
3	Kimi Raikkonen	Ferrari	1h27m33.436s	2	1m25.990s	3
4	Valtteri Bottas	Mercedes	1h27m38.667s	1	1m26.217s	4
5	Daniel Ricciardo	Red Bull	1h27m39.284s	2	1m27.099s	6
6	Nico Hulkenberg	Renault	1h27m58.004s	1	1m27.901s	11
7	Esteban Ocon	Force India	1h27m59.714s	1	1m28.194s	10
8	Fernando Alonso	McLaren	1h28m00.899s	2	1m28.139s	13
9	Kevin Magnussen	Haas	1h28m02.972s	1	1m27.244s	7
10	Sergio Perez	Force India	1h28m04.492s	2	1m27.928s	12
11	Stoffel Vandoorne	McLaren	1h28m05.558s	2	1m29.096s	17
12	Lance Stroll !	Williams	1h28m07.890s	1	no time	19
13	Pierre Gasly *	Toro Rosso	1h28m08.913s	2	1m28.343s	14
14	Sergey Sirotkin !	Williams	1h28m17.897s	1	1m29.252s	18
15	Max Verstappen	Red Bull	46 laps/brakes	2	1m26.602s	5
R	Romain Grosjean	Haas	37 laps/collision	1	1m27.455s	8
R	Carlos Sainz Jr	Renault	37 laps/collision	2	1m28.456s	16
R	Marcus Ericsson	Sauber	31 laps/spun off	1	1m28.391s	15
R	Charles Leclerc	Sauber	18 laps/wheel	1	1m27.879s	9
R	Brendon Hartley !!	Toro Rosso	1 lap/power unit	0	no time	20

FASTEST LAP: VETTEL, 1M30.696S, 145.296MPH/233.831KPH ON LAP 47   RACE LEADERS: VETTEL 1-20, 22-33 & 47-52, BOTTAS 21 & 34-46
* 5 SECOND PENALTY FOR CAUSING A COLLISION; ! STARTED FROM THE PITLANE FOR CAR BEING MODIFIED UNDER PARC FERME CONDITIONS;
!! STARTED FROM THE PITLANE FOR CHANGING A SURVIVIAL CELL & USING EXTRA POWER UNIT ELEMENTS

Lewis Hamilton chased Sebastian Vettel, but it proved to be the Ferrari driver's day.

GERMAN GP

Lewis Hamilton made the most of a slip up in the rain by Sebastian Vettel to celebrate the occasion of extending his Mercedes contract by two years with a clear victory that restored his championship lead, and gave him a 17-point advantage.

It appeared as if this really wasn't going to be Hamilton's meeting as, despite being able to announce that his contract had been extended to the end of the 2020 season - it had been a formality - his Mercedes was hit by a hydraulic failure in the second qualifying session. It left him lining up 14th on the grid and, worse still, title rival Vettel qualified his Ferrari on pole. Damage limitation, it seemed, was all Hamilton had left to focus on.

Vettel duly powered into the lead from the start, with Valtteri Bottas doing his best to keep up, but gradually falling back as Vettel cruised clear. While it was status quo at the front, with Kimi Raikkonen third, Max Verstappen fourth and Kevin Magnussen fifth, Hamilton was progressing up the order. By lap 10, he was up to seventh, then kept climbing to reach third by lap 30.

Daniel Ricciardo was also climbing the order, having had to start from the back row of the grid, reaching sixth before his Red Bull pulled up with an engine problem.

With Raikkonen having been told to pit early, on lap 14, Vettel was kept out until lap 25 before his stop, but emerged behind the Finn and it took some angry talk on the radio to encourage the team to get Raikkonen to let him by. Once back in front, he had everything under control, but then came rain on lap 44, catching Vettel out as he reached the stadium on lap 52 and slid, ignominiously, into the gravel, bringing out the safety car.

Bottas and Raikkonen chose to pit, but Hamilton elected, at the very last second, to stay out and took the lead. In the latter stages, on considerably older tyres than his rivals, Hamilton had to fight to keep Bottas back, but did so.

The drama wasn't over for Hamilton as the stewards investigated whether he might be disqualified for making that decision not to pit under a safety car and crossed the line that separated the pitlane from the track. In the end, they cautioned Hamilton but let the result stand.

This image will haunt Sebastian Vettel, as it shows him sliding his Ferrari out of the lead.

HOCKENHEIM ROUND 11

DATE: 22 JULY 2018

Laps: **67** • Distance: **190.424 miles/306.458km** • Weather: **Warm & cloudy with showers**

Pos	Driver	Team	Result	Stops	Qualifying Time	Grid
1	**Lewis Hamilton**	Mercedes	1h32m29.845s	1	1m13.012s	14
2	**Valtteri Bottas**	Mercedes	1h32m34.380s	2	1m11.416s	2
3	**Kimi Raikkonen**	Ferrari	1h32m36.577s	2	1m11.547s	3
4	**Max Verstappen**	Red Bull	1h32m37.499s	3	1m11.822s	4
5	**Nico Hulkenberg**	Renault	1h32m56.7454s	3	1m12.560s	7
6	**Romain Grosjean**	Haas	1h32m58.716s	3	1m12.544s	6
7	**Sergio Perez**	Force India	1h33m00.401s	1	1m12.774s	10
8	**Esteban Ocon**	Force India	1h33m01.595s	1	1m13.720s	15
9	**Marcus Ericsson**	Sauber	1h33m02.207s	1	1m13.736s	13
10	**Brendon Hartley**	Toro Rosso	1h33m04.042s	2	1m14.045s	16
11	**Kevin Magnussen**	Haas	1h33m04.764s	3	1m12.200s	5
12	**Carlos Sainz Jr ****	Renault	1h33m12.914s	3	1m12.692s	8
13	**Stoffel Vandoorne**	McLaren	1h33m16.462s	4	1m14.401s	18
14	**Pierre Gasly ***	Toro Rosso	66 laps	2	1m13.749s	20
15	**Charles Leclerc**	Sauber	66 laps	3	1m12.717s	9
16	**Fernando Alonso**	McLaren	65 laps/gearbox	3	1m13.657s	11
R	**Lance Stroll**	Williams	53 laps/brakes	2	1m14.206s	17
R	**Sebastian Vettel**	Ferrari	51 laps/accident	1	1m11.212s	1
R	**Sergey Sirotkin**	Williams	51 laps/oil leak	2	1m13.702s	12
R	**Daniel Ricciardo ***	Red Bull	27 laps/engine	0	1m13.318s	19

FASTEST LAP: HAMILTON, 1M15.545S, 135.439MPH/217.968KPH ON LAP 66 • RACE LEADERS: VETTEL 1-25 & 39-51, BOTTAS 26-28 & 52, RAIKKONEN 29-38, HAMILTON 53-67

* MADE TO START FROM BACK OF GRID FOR USING ADDITIONAL POWER UNIT ELEMENTS; ** 10S PENALTY FOR OVERTAKING UNDER SAFETY CAR CONDITIONS

HUNGARIAN GP

Ferrari had been expected to take victory in Hungary, but a brilliant lap to take pole position in driving rain gave Lewis Hamilton just what he needed to put Mercedes at the front of the field on this twisty track and he then stayed ahead in the dry on race day.

The teams were all flagging, ready for their summer break when they reached the 12th round of the year, in Hungary. A chance to draw breath would be welcomed by all and there would be a chance for one team, Force India, to draw new breath as it entered administration. Normally, this spells the end for F1 teams, but there was a queue of potential purchasers lined up, so the team felt confident that better times would be ahead.

Sebastian Vettel was in fine form through practice. The first qualifying session was all about him too and he topped session two, as well, when rain hit. The rain was heavier still in the final session and Mercedes's drivers managed it better, with Hamilton taking pole ahead of Valtteri Bottas. Vettel ended up fourth, behind team-mate Kimi Raikkonen and suddenly a new script was required.

The Hungaroring is notoriously hard to pass on and so Hamilton knew that he just had to get the start right and he'd be in a strong position, but one in which he knew he'd have to defend from Vettel. What blew the race for the German was that the ultrasoft Pirelli tyres proved more durable than Ferrari had reckoned and Hamilton made them last further into the race than they'd expected.

Vettel stayed out for a further 14 laps before changing his softs for ultrasofts. However, his desire to attack immediately was thwarted as a slow stop brought him out behind Bottas and this allowed Hamilton to open up a gap of 24s. Eventually, on lap 65, Vettel got through into second place, even surviving a clout when Bottas fought back at the next corner, but Hamilton was long gone. Bottas, his car damaged and his tyres shot, slipped back to fifth.

Toro Rosso had reason to be pleased as both drivers qualified in the top 10 and Pierre Gasly came home sixth thanks to brilliant tyre management, while Brendon Hartley was frustrated to have been bottled up behind Carlos Sainz Jr, who was on the harder, slower tyre and delayed him.

HUNGARORING ROUND 12

DATE: **29 JULY 2018**

Laps: **70** • Distance: **190.531 miles/306.630km** • Weather: **Very hot & sunny**

Pos	Driver	Team	Result	Stops	Qualifying Time	Grid
1	**Lewis Hamilton**	Mercedes	1h37m16.427s	1	1m35.658s	1
2	**Sebastian Vettel**	Ferrari	1h37m33.550s	1	1m36.210s	4
3	**Kimi Raikkonen**	Ferrari	1h37m36.528s	2	1m36.186s	3
4	**Daniel Ricciardo**	Red Bull	1h38m02.846s	1	1m36.442s	12
5	**Valtteri Bottas ***	Mercedes	1h38m16.427s	1	1m35.918s	2
6	**Pierre Gasly**	Toro Rosso	1h38m29.700s	1	1m37.591s	6
7	**Kevin Magnussen**	Haas	69 laps	1	1m39.858s	9
8	**Fernando Alonso**	McLaren	69 laps	1	1m35.214s	11
9	**Carlos Sainz Jr**	Renault	69 laps	1	1m36.743s	5
10	**Romain Grosjean**	Haas	69 laps	1	1m40.593s	10
11	**Brendon Hartley**	Toro Rosso	69 laps	1	1m38.128s	8
12	**Nico Hulkenberg**	Renault	69 laps	2	1m36.506s	13
13	**Esteban Ocon**	Force India	69 laps	1	1m19.142s	17
14	**Sergio Perez**	Force India	69 laps	1	1m19.200s	18
15	**Marcus Ericsson**	Sauber	68 laps	1	1m37.075s	14
16	**Sergey Sirotkin**	Williams	68 laps	1	1m19.301s	19
17	**Lance Stroll !**	Williams	68 laps	1	no time	20
R	**Stoffel Vandoorne**	McLaren	49 laps/gearbox	1	1m18.782s	15
R	**Max Verstappen**	Red Bull	5 laps/power unit	0	1m38.032s	7
R	**Charles Leclerc**	Sauber	0 laps/collision	0	1m18.817s	16

FASTEST LAP: RICCIARDO, 1M20.012S, 122.481MPH/197.115KPH ON LAP 46 • RACE LEADERS: HAMILTON 1-25 & 40-70, VETTEL 26-39
* 10S PENALTY FOR CAUSING A COLLISION; ! MADE TO START FROM PITLANE FOR CAR BEING MODIFIED UNDER PARC FERME CONDITIONS

Lewis Hamilton didn't just win in Hungary, he dominated, leaving the Ferraris far behind.

BELGIAN GP

The outcome of the first race back after F1's summer break was demoralizing for Lewis Hamilton. Not only because he was beaten by Sebastian Vettel, but also because he was beaten easily and Ferrari seemed to have found an extra gear.

In the decades to come, F1 fans won't remember the Belgian GP for possibly being a pivotal point in the 2018 title battle between Lewis Hamilton and Sebastian Vettel, when the pendulum swung firmly in Ferrari's favour. Instead, because the incident was so dramatic, we will remember it for the spectacular and fortunately injury-free first corner accident.

This was triggered by Nico Hulkenberg out-braking himself into La Source just after the start and his Renault hitting the back of Fernando Alonso's so hard that he propelled it to hit Daniel Ricciardo's rear wing and then fly into the air, clipping the top of Charles Leclerc's Sauber. Fortunately, 2018 was the year that all cars had to have a halo fitted, so the Monegasque driver was saved from terrible injury or worse.

The run up the hill towards the right/left flick at Les Combes was terrific television on the first racing lap, as Vettel powered past poleman Hamilton, then had the Mercedes use his tow to get back at him. This, though, was covered by Vettel moving to the inside line where they both tripped over each other and the chasing Force Indias pulled either side to make it four abreast. Sadly, there was debris to clear at La Source, so the safety car was scrambled and this battle was thwarted.

On the restart, Vettel had matters under control, helped by the fact that his Ferrari power unit was simply better than the one in Hamilton's Mercedes. Max Verstappen demoted the two Force Indias and that was how the top three remained to the finish, with Vettel making winning by 11s look easy.

Valtteri Bottas was best of the rest, advancing to fourth from 17th on the grid. The 18 points gathered by Perez and Ocon for finishing fifth and sixth for Racing Point Force India immediately moved this rebooted team ahead of Williams to rise from the bottom of the table after its name change forced it to shed the 59 points gathered through the season's first 12 grands prix.

Nico Hulkenburg hit Fernando Alonso and launched his McLaren onto Charles Leclerc's Sauber.

SPA-FRANCORCHAMPS ROUND 13 DATE: 26 AUGUST 2018

Laps: **44** • Distance: **191.414 miles/308.052km** • Weather: **Warm & bright**

Pos	Driver	Team	Result	Stops	Qualifying Time	Grid
1	Sebastian Vettel	Ferrari	1h23m34.476s	1	1m58.905s	2
2	Lewis Hamilton	Mercedes	1h23m45.537s	1	1m58.179s	1
3	Max Verstappen	Red Bull	1h24m05.848s	1	2m02.769s	7
4	Valtteri Bottas !	Mercedes	1h24m43.081s	2	no time	17
5	Sergio Perez	Force India	1h24m45.499s	1	2m01.894s	4
6	Esteban Ocon	Force India	1h24m53.996s	1	2m01.851s	3
7	Romain Grosjean	Haas	1h25m00.429s	1	2m02.122s	5
8	Kevin Magnussen	Haas	1h25m02.115s	1	2m04.933s	9
9	Pierre Gasly	Toro Rosso	1h25m20.368s	1	1m43.844s	10
10	Marcus Ericsson	Sauber	43 laps	1	1m44.301s	13
11	Carlos Sainz Jr *	Renault	43 laps	1	1m44.489s	19
12	Sergey Sirotkin	Williams	43 laps	1	1m44.998s	15
13	Lance Stroll	Williams	43 laps	1	1m45.134s	16
14	Brendon Hartley	Toro Rosso	43 laps	1	1m43.865s	11
15	Stoffel Vandoorne *	McLaren	43 laps	2	1m45.307s	20
R	Daniel Ricciardo	Red Bull	28 laps/accident	1	2m02.939s	8
R	Kimi Raikkonen	Ferrari	8 laps/accident	1	2m02.671s	6
R	Charles Leclerc	Sauber	0 laps/accident	0	1m44.062s	12
R	Fernando Alonso	McLaren	0 laps/accident	0	1m44.917s	14
R	Nico Hulkenberg *	Renault	0 laps/accident	0	no time	18

FASTEST LAP: BOTTAS, 1M46.286S, 147.408MPH/237.231KPH ON LAP 32 • RACE LEADER: VETTEL 1-44
* MADE TO START FROM BACK OF GRID FOR USING ADDITIONAL POWER UNIT; ! 5S PENALTY FOR CAUSING A COLLISION

ITALIAN GP

On form, this was a race that Sebastian Vettel was expected to win but, to Ferrari's horror, there was to be no home victory as the Italian team had erred with its tyre choice and the team was humiliated as Lewis Hamilton triumphed for Mercedes.

It's a great feeling to be heading to your home race confident that victory will be yours, and especially so for Ferrari, for whom the *tifosi* are the world's most passionate fans. Everything was all set for Monza to be swamped by a sea of waving red flags. First stop was pole position and that went to Ferrari, albeit to Kimi Raikkonen, rather than Vettel. In the race, though, Ferrari's tyre choice simply didn't work and Hamilton came good to hit them where it really hurts: in the championship table.

Why? How? Why here of all places? These were the questions bouncing around as the *tifosi* began their post-mortems. The first answer was that Ferrari didn't manage qualifying particularly well, allowing Raikkonen to get a tow from Vettel rather than the other way around, and this was enough for the Finn to take pole. That had ramifications at the start of the race.

The second answer was Hamilton attacked from third on the grid with intent. Raikkonen was in no mood to let his team-mate pass for the lead at the first chicane on the opening lap and put him slightly off line, which meant that he lost momentum. This allowed Hamilton to get alongside Vettel when he tried again at the second chicane. They clashed and Vettel not only suffered a damaged front wing, but also spun to the tail of the field.

All he could from there was to push for the best possible result. In the end, he was fifth past the chequered flag, but it did get better. Max Verstappen was fourth on the road, but a 5s penalty for colliding with Valtteri Bottas dropped him to fifth, behind Vettel, who thus collected 12 points.

Hamilton, on the other hand, ran a different strategy to Raikkonen, making his one stop to change from supersoft tyres to softs eight laps later. He was helped by a long opening stint from team-mate Bottas keeping Raikkonen in check. This meant that Hamilton caught the Finn with nine laps to go as his Ferrari suffered with blistered tyres, before diving back into the lead at the first chicane.

MONZA ROUND 14

DATE: **2 SEPTEMBER 2018**

Laps: **53** • Distance: **190.587 miles/306.720km** • Weather: **Hot & sunny**

Pos	Driver	Team	Result	Stops	Qualifying Time	Grid
1	Lewis Hamilton	Mercedes	1h16m54.484s	1	1m19.294s	3
2	Kimi Raikkonen	Ferrari	1h17m03.189s	1	1m19.119s	1
3	Valtteri Bottas	Mercedes	1h17m08.550s	1	1m19.656s	4
4	Sebastian Vettel	Ferrari	1h17m10.635s	2	1m19.280s	2
5	Max Verstappen **	Red Bull	1h17m12.692s	1	1m20.615s	5
6	Esteban Ocon	Force India	1h17m52.245s	1	1m21.099s	8
7	Sergio Perez	Force India	1h17m53.182s	1	1m21.888s	14
8	Carlos Sainz Jr	Renault	1h18m12.624s	1	1m21.041s	7
9	Lance Stroll	Williams	52 laps	1	1m21.627s	10
10	Sergey Sirotkin	Williams	52 laps	1	1m21.732s	12
11	Charles Leclerc	Sauber	52 laps	1	1m21.889s	15
12	Stoffel Vandoorne	McLaren	52 laps	1	1m22.085s	17
13	Nico Hulkenberg !! *	Renault	52 laps	2	no time	20
14	Pierre Gasly	Toro Rosso	52 laps	1	1m21.350s	9
15	Marcus Ericsson !	Sauber	52 laps	2	1m22.048s	18
16	Kevin Magnussen	Haas	52 laps	1	1m21.669s	11
R	Daniel Ricciardo *	Red Bull	23 laps/clutch	1	no time	19
R	Fernando Alonso	McLaren	9 laps/electrical	0	1m22.568s	13
R	Brendon Hartley	Toro Rosso	0 laps/collision	0	1m21.934s	16
DQ	Romain Grosjean †	Haas	1h17m50.804s	1	1m20.936s	6

FASTEST LAP: HAMILTON, 1M22.497S, 157.079MPH/252.794KPH ON LAP 30 RACE LEADERS: RAIKKONEN 1-19 & 36-44, HAMILTON 20-28 & 45-53, BOTTAS 29-35

! 10-PLACE GRID PENALTY FOR USING AN ADDITIONAL POWER UNIT; !! 10-PLACE GRID PENALTY FOR CAUSING A COLLISION IN PREVIOUS RACE; * MADE TO START FROM BACK OF GRID FOR USING AN ADDITIONAL POWER UNIT; ** 5S PENALTY FOR CAUSING A COLLISION; † DISQUALIFIED FROM SIXTH PLACE FINISH FOR CAR HAVING ILLEGAL FLOOR

Lewis Hamilton made an early move on Sebastian Vettel, then tyre choice helped him to win.

SINGAPORE GP

Ferrari needed to atone after its diappointing home race at Monza and the team was on top throughout practice, only to get beaten in qualifying and the race as well as Lewis Hamilton moved to the top, with Max Verstappen impressive in second.

Qualifying on the front row is more than usually important at Singapore's Marina Bay Circuit, and practice form suggested that this should help swing the pendulum Ferrari's way, but Sebastian Vettel wasn't laughing after qualifying ended, as both Hamilton and Verstappen had outpaced him. This was unexpected, and Hamilton's lap was so good that it beat the team's best estimate by more than half a second. His race engineer called it "epic". Furthermore, the Dutchman's setting of the second quickest lap was remarkable as Red Bull had been afflicted by inconsistent power delivery from its recently upgraded Renault power units that were apparently affected by the heat and humidity.

So, Hamilton had the best starting spot and made it pay by taking the lead at the start, but Vettel struck hard with a great move to pass Verstappen at Turn 7. However, Ferrari undid all that by calling Vettel in for his first stop on lap 14 - the first of the frontrunners to do so - and, with Verstappen waiting another three laps, that great passing move was negated.

The win, with Vettel third, gave Hamilton a huge smile and a 40-point lead.

Sergio Perez earned the wrath of the Force India team for a clumsy move on the opening lap in which he put team-mate Esteban Ocon into a wall and out of the race at Turn 3, costing the team what could have been a useful helping of points.

Fernando Alonso's run to seventh made him the best of the rest behind the three top class teams for the second time in a troubled season and he was delighted with that.

Off the pace all meeting, the Haas team gained some succour when Kevin Magnussen, running near the back, made a third pitstop and slotted on a set of hyper-soft tyres to go out and score both his and the team's first ever fastest lap. Conversely, team-mate Romain Grosjean was in trouble - again - this time for ignoring blue flags as he ran down the order and was told that his next penalty will result in a one-race ban.

Sebastian Vettel was first to pit, but it didn't work for the Ferrari driver as he stayed third.

MARINA BAY ROUND 15

DATE: **16 SEPTEMBER 2018**

Laps: **61** • Distance: **191.821 miles/308.706km** • Weather: **Very hot & humid**

Pos	Driver	Team	Result	Stops	Qualifying Time	Grid
1	**Lewis Hamilton**	Mercedes	1h51m11.611s	1	1m36.015s	1
2	**Max Verstappen**	Red Bull	1h51m20.572s	1	1m36.334s	2
3	**Sebastian Vettel**	Ferrari	1h51m51.556s	1	1m36.628s	3
4	**Valtteri Bottas**	Mercedes	1h52m03.541s	1	1m36.702s	4
5	**Kimi Raikkonen**	Ferrari	1h52m04.612s	1	1m36.794s	5
6	**Daniel Ricciardo**	Red Bull	1h52m05.593s	1	1m36.996s	6
7	**Fernando Alonso**	McLaren	1h52m54.622s	1	1m38.641s	11
8	**Carlos Sainz Jr**	Renault	60 laps	1	1m38.716s	12
9	**Charles Leclerc**	Sauber	60 laps	1	1m38.747s	13
10	**Nico Hulkenberg**	Renault	60 laps	1	1m38.588s	10
11	**Marcus Ericsson**	Sauber	60 laps	1	1m39.453s	14
12	**Stoffel Vandoorne**	McLaren	60 laps	1	1m39.864s	18
13	**Pierre Gasly**	Toro Rosso	60 laps	1	1m39.691s	15
14	**Lance Stroll**	Williams	60 laps	1	1m41.334s	20
15	**Romain Grosjean ***	Haas	60 laps	1	1m38.320s	8
16	**Sergio Perez**	Force India	60 laps	3	1m37.985s	7
17	**Brendon Hartley**	Toro Rosso	60 laps	2	1m39.809s	17
18	**Kevin Magnussen**	Haas	59 laps	3	1m39.644s	16
19	**Sergey Sirotkin**	Williams	59 laps	2	1m41.263s	19
R	**Esteban Ocon**	Force India	0 laps/collision	0	1m38.365s	9

FASTEST LAP: MAGNUSSEN, 1M41.905S, 111.138MPH/178.860KPH ON LAP 50 RACE LEADERS: HAMILTON 1-14 & 27-61, VERSTAPPEN 15-17, RAIKKONEN 18-21, RICCIARDO 22-26
* 5S PENALTY FOR IGNORING BLUE FLAGS

RUSSIAN GP

There is nothing wrong with team tactics, and they have always been part of the sport, but the request for Valtteri Bottas to let Lewis Hamilton through into the lead at Sochi was handled clumsily and left a sour taste for the pair when they stood on the podium.

After a loss of form through the summer, Valtteri Bottas came good again and bagged pole. Then, after a clean start, he led the race, with Hamilton holding down second place. When Bottas was the first of the leading group to pit, Sebastian Vettel copied a lap later, but Hamilton remained on track, picking up his pace. This ought to have led to him emerging from his pitstop in the lead, but he came across Sergey Sirotkin's Williams on his in-lap. The delay was enough to not only allow Bottas to stay in the lead but to let Vettel challenge for second. Indeed, the Ferrari driver had his nose in front when they arrived at Turn 1.

Hamilton was livid, aware that his race had got a whole lot harder. Fired up, he put the pressure on for the next two laps and Vettel was robust in his defence, but unable to resist for long, with Hamilton going by into Turn 4 on lap 16.

Kimi Raikkonen didn't pit for a further two laps and then the lead went to Max Verstappen, one of a number of drivers made to start from the rear of the grid for having additional power unit elements fitted to his car. He was on an entirely different strategy, running a long first stint and then a short second stint, so stayed at the head of the pack until pitting on lap 43.

Before then, however, team orders had been implemented. This happened on lap 25 of the 53-lap race when Bottas, Hamilton and Vettel were running line astern and Hamilton told Mercedes that his tyres were blistering. Concerned about Vettel being so close, they told Bottas to move aside and he let Hamilton through at Turn 13. The win gave Hamilton a World Championship lead of 50 points with 125 to play for.

There was considerable sympathy for Bottas as this would have been his first win of the year, but after the race, Vettel, himself no stranger to team orders, defended Mercedes' call, describing it as a "no brainer" decision.

SOCHI ROUND 16

DATE: **30 SEPTEMBER 2018**

Laps: **53** • Distance: **192.463 miles/309.740km** • Weather: **Hot & bright**

Pos	Driver	Team	Result	Stops	Qualifying Time	Grid
1	Lewis Hamilton	Mercedes	1h27m25.181s	1	1m31.532s	2
2	Valtteri Bottas	Mercedes	1h27m27.726s	1	1m31.387s	1
3	Sebastian Vettel	Ferrari	1h27m32.668s	1	1m31.943s	3
4	Kimi Raikkonen	Ferrari	1h27m41.724s	1	1m32.237s	4
5	Max Verstappen *!	Red Bull	1h27m56.197s	1	no time	19
6	Daniel Ricciardo *!	Red Bull	1h28m45.632s	1	no time	18
7	Charles Leclerc	Sauber	1h29m03.571s	1	1m33.419s	7
8	Kevin Magnussen	Haas	52 laps	1	1m33.181s	5
9	Esteban Ocon	Force India	52 laps	1	1m33.413s	6
10	Sergio Perez	Force India	52 laps	1	1m33.563s	8
11	Romain Grosjean	Haas	52 laps	1	1m33.704s	9
12	Nico Hulkenberg	Renault	52 laps	1	no time	12
13	Marcus Ericsson	Sauber	52 laps	2	1m35.196s	10
14	Fernando Alonso !	McLaren	52 laps	1	1m35.504s	16
15	Lance Stroll	Williams	52 laps	1	1m36.437s	14
16	Stoffel Vandoorne *	McLaren	51 laps	1	1m35.977s	15
17	Carlos Sainz Jr	Renault	51 laps	1	no time	11
18	Sergey Sirotkin	Williams	51 laps	1	1m35.612s	13
R	Pierre Gasly !	Toro Rosso	4 laps/brakes	0	no time	17
R	Brendon Hartley ^!	Toro Rosso	4 laps/brakes	1	1m35.037s	20

FASTEST LAP: BOTTAS, 1M35.861S, 136.463MPH/219.617KPH ON LAP 50 RACE LEADERS: BOTTAS 1-11, HAMILTON 12-14 & 43-53, RAIKKONEN 15-18, VERSTAPPEN 19-42

* 5-PLACE GRID PENALTY FOR REPLACING GEARBOX; ^ 10-PLACE GRID PENALTY FOR USING ADDITIONAL POWER UNIT ELEMENTS; ! MADE TO START FROM REAR OF GRID FOR USING ADDITIONAL POWER UNIT ELEMENTS

Valtteri Bottas was asked to let Lewis Hamilton past when Sebastian Vettel closed in.

JAPANESE GP

When the pressure ought to have been coming back at Lewis Hamilton, Ferrari dropped the ball and this left him free to dominate from pole to give himself a 67-point lead with 100 points left to play for in the final four rounds.

The biggest question mark as summer turned to autumn was how Ferrari went from having the fastest car to Mercedes taking control and Sebastian Vettel in particular falling down the order in the final four rounds.

Acknowledging that Mercedes had clearly stepped up its development and found more pace, Ferrari actually appeared to be slower than they were before the Russian GP and clearly didn't know how to react. Team principal Maurizio Arrivabene blamed "an inexperienced team" for making poor tyre choices. The outcome was that its championship challenger, Sebastian Vettel, lined up only eighth on the grid while Hamilton was wearing a smile as he started from pole.

With team-mate Valtteri Bottas starting alongside him, Hamilton led away, but Vettel made considerable progress on the opening lap, rising to fourth. Seven laps later, ambition overrode experience as Vettel tried to push his Ferrari inside Max Verstappen's Red Bull at Spoon Curve, which is almost never a passing place. They touched and both left the track but, crucially, Vettel spun. This put him all the way back to last place.

With Verstappen able only to keep in touch with Bottas, who was again riding shotgun for Hamilton, the order stayed like that for the podium positions all the way to the chequered flag.

Daniel Ricciardo was the only other driver even vaguely in touch, finishing fourth after advancing from 15th on the grid following an engine problem in qualifying. There was then a half-minute gap to Kimi Raikkonen, with Vettel a further 19s back after his fightback from last place to sixth. His tail may have been between his legs, but Vettel remained unrepentant about attempting the move on Verstappen. He pointed out that he couldn't afford to let the Mercedes duo get any further ahead.

In the battle to be best of the rest, Sergio Perez beat Romain Grosjean, with the Haas driver being pursued by Esteban Ocon.

It's a Mercedes one-two as they race to the first corner, with Bottas guarding Hamilton.

SUZUKA ROUND 17

DATE: 7 OCTOBER 2018

Laps: **53** • Distance: **191.053 miles/307.471km** • Weather: **Hot & overcast**

Pos	Driver	Team	Result	Stops	Qualifying Time	Grid
1	**Lewis Hamilton**	Mercedes	1h27m17.062s	1	1m27.760s	1
2	**Valtteri Bottas**	Mercedes	1h27m29.981s	1	1m28.059s	2
3	**Max Verstappen**	Red Bull	1h27m31.357s	1	1m29.057s	3
4	**Daniel Ricciardo**	Red Bull	1h27m36.557s	1	no time	15
5	**Kimi Raikkonen**	Ferrari	1h28m08.060s	1	1m29.521s	4
6	**Sebastian Vettel**	Ferrari	1h28m26.935s	1	1m32.192s	8
7	**Sergio Perez**	Force India	1h28m36.441s	1	1m37.229s	9
8	**Romain Grosjean**	Haas	1h28m44.260s	1	1m29.761s	5
9	**Esteban Ocon ***	Force India	1h28m45.117s	1	1m30.126s	11
10	**Carlos Sainz Jr**	Renault	52 laps	1	1m30.490s	13
11	**Pierre Gasly**	Toro Rosso	52 laps	1	1m30.093s	7
12	**Marcus Ericsson !**	Sauber	52 laps	1	1m31.213s	20
13	**Brendon Hartley**	Toro Rosso	52 laps	1	1m30.023s	6
14	**Fernando Alonso**	McLaren	52 laps	1	1m30.573s	18
15	**Stoffel Vandoorne**	McLaren	52 laps	1	1m31.041s	19
16	**Sergey Sirotkin**	Williams	52 laps	2	1m30.372s	17
17	**Lance Stroll**	Williams	52 laps	2	1m30.714s	14
R	**Charles Leclerc**	Sauber	38 laps/crash damage	2	1m29.864s	10
R	**Nico Hulkenberg**	Renault	37 laps/handling	1	1m30.361s	16
R	**Kevin Magnussen**	Haas	8 laps/crash damage	1	1m30.226s	12

FASTEST LAP: VETTEL, 1M32.318S, 140.707MPH/226.447KPH ON LAP 53 • RACE LEADER: HAMILTON 1-53
* 3-PLACE GRID PENALTY FOR FAILING TO SLOW DURING A RED FLAG PERIOD;
! 15-PLACE GRID PENALTY FOR REPLACING GEARBOX & USING ADDITIONAL POWER UNIT ELEMENTS

UNITED STATES GP

This was a proper, old-fashioned grand prix, so it was fitting that victory went to the oldest driver in the field: Kimi Raikkonen. Lewis Hamilton had hoped to wrap up the title, but a second pitstop left him unable to rise above third position.

Hamilton's checklist was full of ticks when he lined up on the grid. Having been fastest in two of the three practice sessions, then taken pole position. Better still for his hopes of clinching the championship in Texas was the grid penalty for rival Sebastian Vettel for not slowing sufficiently when the red flag was flown in practice. It dropped him to fifth.

At the start, Hamilton realised, to his horror, that Raikkonen had found enough grip from Pirelli's ultrasoft tyres to get alongside him as they accelerated up the hill to Turn 1, was on the inside line and so able to take the lead.

Ferrari's fortunes were mixed, because although Vettel had passed Daniel Ricciardo, he then ran wide at Turn 12 and the Australian got back in front. Then, at Turn 13, Vettel lost control as he tried to fight back, slid into the Red Bull, then spun, which dropped him right down the order.

Ricciardo then affected the outcome of the race when his Red Bull's Renault engine fell silent and he pulled off, triggering a virtual safety car period. Mercedes decided that Hamilton would do what Raikkonen didn't, so he pitted. Emerging 9s behind, Bottas let him back into second, but Raikkonen was excellent in defending the lead. Eventually, with his ultrasofts worn, Raikkonen pitted on lap 21. Hamilton stayed out on his softs until lap 37, but was fourth when he came back out. Bottas let him by and Hamilton closed in on Max Verstappen. But this was to be as far as he would advance, his race compromised by making two stops to his rivals one.

On the podium, Raikkonen had every reason to crack a rare smile, as this was his first win since the 2013 Australian GP, thus ending a winless run of 111 starts.

After the race, both Esteban Ocon and Kevin Magnussen were disqualified. The French racer had exceeded the 100 litres/hour fuel limit on the opening lap and the Dane for using more than his race allowance of 105 litres.

CIRCUIT OF THE AMERICAS
ROUND 18
DATE: **21 OCTOBER 2018**

Laps: **56** • Distance: **191.634 miles/308.405km** • Weather: **Warm & bright**

Pos	Driver	Team	Result	Stops	Qualifying Time	Grid
1	**Kimi Raikkonen**	Ferrari	1h34m18.643s	1	1m32.307s	2
2	**Max Verstappen !**	Red Bull	1h34m19.924s	1	no time	18
3	**Lewis Hamilton**	Mercedes	1h34m20.985s	2	1m32.237s	1
4	**Sebastian Vettel ***	Ferrari	1h34m36.865s	1	1m32.298s	5
5	**Valtteri Bottas**	Mercedes	1h34m43.387s	1	1m32.616s	3
6	**Nico Hulkenberg**	Renault	1h35m45.583s	1	1m34.215s	7
7	**Carlos Sainz Jr**	Renault	1h35m53.637s	1	1m34.566s	11
8	**Sergio Perez ^**	Force India	1h35m59.723s	1	1m34.594s	10
9	**Brendon Hartley**	Toro Rosso	55 laps	1	no time	20
10	**Marcus Ericsson**	Sauber	55 laps	1	1m35.536s	16
11	**Stoffel Vandoorne**	McLaren	55 laps	2	1m35.735s	17
12	**Pierre Gasly !!**	Toro Rosso	55 laps	2	no time	19
13	**Sergey Sirotkin**	Williams	55 laps	2	1m35.362s	14
14	**Lance Stroll**	Williams	54 laps	3	1m35.480s	15
R	**Charles Leclerc**	Sauber	31 laps/crash damage	1	1m34.420s	9
R	**Daniel Ricciardo**	Red Bull	8 laps/electrical	0	1m33.494s	4
R	**Romain Grosjean**	Haas	2 laps/collision	1	1m34.250s	8
R	**Fernando Alonso**	McLaren	1 lap/collision	0	1m35.294s	13
DQ	**Esteban Ocon**	Force India	Too much fuel	1	1m34.145s	6
DQ	**Kevin Magnussen**	Haas	Fuel mass flow	1	1m34.732s	12

FASTEST LAP: HAMILTON, 1M37.392S, 126.624MPH/203.782KPH ON LAP 40 • RACE LEADERS: RAIKKONEN 1-10, 12-21 & 38-56, HAMILTON 11 & 22-37
* 3-PLACE GRID PENALTY FOR RED FLAG INFRINGEMENT; ! 5-PLACE GRID PENALTY FOR CHANGING GEARBOX;
^ 5-PLACE GRID PENALTY FOR CHANGING GEARBOX AND MADE TO START FROM BACK OF GRID FOR USING ADDITIONAL POWER UNITS;
!! MADE TO START FROM BACK OF GRID FOR USING ADDITIONAL POWER UNITS

Kimi Raikkonen remembered how to win, despite it being five years since his last victory.

MEXICAN GP

This was the race at which Lewis Hamilton was all at sea with his tyres, but fourth place, as Max Verstappen won easily, was enough for him to take the title and to pull level with Juan Manuel Fangio as a five-time World Champion.

What happened in the race was always going to be secondary to the end result of Hamilton landing the title, which is hard luck on Verstappen, who was the best of the best in Mexico for the second year in a row.

The Dutch ace got the better of his Red Bull team-mate Daniel Ricciardo at the start, with Hamilton also powering past the poleman on the lengthy run to the first corner. From there, Verstappen stretched his advantage, and Hamilton was soon struggling on tyres that were wearing more quickly than was ideal.

As well as watching his tyres, Hamilton had an eye out for Sebastian Vettel, who got past Ricciardo into third at mid-distance and then passed Hamilton too. This was fine, as Hamilton knew that he needed to finish only seventh if Vettel won to be sure of claiming the title and he would be World Champion in any case if the German didn't win the race.

However, it showed how much that Hamilton cared as he complained about the lack of grip coming from his tyres. Every race was there to be won in his mind and anything less was a failure. Perhaps on this occasion he simply wanted to be sure he could finish in the top three so that he could celebrate on the podium, but his Mercedes' lack of grip was vexing him.

On lap 47, with Ricciardo pushing him, Hamilton ran off the circuit at the first corner and got on the radio to the team, asking for fresh rubber.

Vettel also made a second pitstop and then set about trying to depose the first and second running Red Bulls. On lap 62, Vettel was gifted one of those places when Ricciardo's wretched run of retirements continued, this time with a hydraulic failure. Verstappen was not to be denied though, and he finished 17s clear of Vettel.

With Kimi Raikkonen also moving ahead of Hamilton, there was to be no podium celebration, but there was plenty of partying in the paddock.

Max Verstappen led away, and there was nothing that Hamilton could do to keep up.

MEXICO CITY ROUND 19

DATE: **28 OCTOBER 2018**

Laps: **71** • Distance: **189.738 miles/305.354km** • Weather: **Cloudy & overcast**

Pos	Driver	Team	Result	Stops	Qualifying Time	Grid
1	**Max Verstappen**	Red Bull	1h38m28.851s	2	1m14.785s	2
2	**Sebastian Vettel**	Ferrari	1h38m46.167s	2	1m14.970s	4
3	**Kimi Raikkonen**	Ferrari	1h39m18.765s	1	1m15.330s	6
4	**Lewis Hamilton**	Mercedes	1h39m47.589s	2	1m14.894s	3
5	**Valtteri Bottas**	Mercedes	70 laps	2	1m15.160s	5
6	**Nico Hulkenberg**	Renault	69 laps	1	1m15.827s	7
7	**Charles Leclerc**	Sauber	69 laps	1	1m16.189s	9
8	**Stoffel Vandoorne**	McLaren	69 laps	1	1m16.966s	15
9	**Marcus Ericsson**	Sauber	69 laps	1	1m16.513s	10
10	**Pierre Gasly !**	Toro Rosso	69 laps	2	no time	20
11	**Esteban Ocon**	Force India	69 laps	2	1m16.844s	11
12	**Lance Stroll**	Williams	69 laps	2	1m17.689s	17
13	**Sergey Sirotkin**	Williams	69 laps	1	1m17.886s	19
14	**Brendon Hartley**	Toro Rosso	69 laps	2	1m17.184s	14
15	**Kevin Magnussen**	Haas	69 laps	1	1m17.599s	16
16	**Romain Grosjean ***	Haas	68 laps	2	1m16.911s	18
R	**Daniel Ricciardo**	Red Bull	61 laps/hydraulics	1	1m14.759s	1
R	**Sergio Perez**	Force India	38 laps/brakes	1	1m17.167s	13
R	**Carlos Sainz Jr**	Renault	28 laps/electrical	1	1m16.084s	8
R	**Fernando Alonso**	McLaren	3 laps/accident	0	1m16.871s	12

FASTEST LAP: BOTTAS, 1M18.741S, 122.270MPH/196.776KPH ON LAP 65 • RACE LEADERS: VERSTAPPEN 1-13 & 18-71, VETTEL 14-17
* 3-PLACE GRID PENALTY FOR CAUSING A COLLISION AT THE PREVIOUS RACE;
! 5-PLACE GRID PENALTY FOR CHANGING THE GEARBOX AND 15-PLACE PENALTY FOR USING ADDITIONAL POWER UNIT ELEMENTS

BRAZILIAN GP

This should have been Max Verstappen's race, but his brilliant drive for Red Bull Racing was wrecked when Force India's Esteban Ocon tried to unlap himself after a pitstop and tipped the Dutchman out of the lead, leaving the way clear for Hamilton to win.

Lewis Hamilton took pole, with Sebastian Vettel second, but the Ferrari driver was never able to challenge in the race. Instead, it was Red Bull's Verstappen who was the thorn in Hamilton's side.

The early laps belonged to Hamilton, with team-mate Valtteri Bottas getting past Vettel before the first corner to ride shotgun for the first 10 laps until Verstappen passed him. The Dutch racer got to within 1.5s of the race leader but then Mercedes brought Hamilton in way earlier than his rivals, doing so after 19 laps. Indeed, he came in for his one planned pitstop eight laps before Vettel and fully 16 before Verstappen. Hamilton, in second place, was ahead of Verstappen when he rejoined, but only by 2.5s and was on tyres that had less life in them. The chase was on.

Not only did Verstappen close on the Mercedes, but within four laps he motored past into first place just as his team-mate Daniel Ricciardo pitted from the lead. Then Verstappen started to escape, right to the point that one of the most memorable moments of the season occurred when he was tipped into a spin, not by Hamilton but by a driver attempting to unlap himself... This was Ocon, who was just out of the pits on even fresher rubber and elected to dive by into the second corner, where Verstappen didn't feel like making space for him, and they spun. Hamilton didn't need a second invitation to take back a lead he hadn't looked likely to be able to regain.

This left Hamilton free to chalk up his 10th win of the year, but he had to fight all the way, as Verstappen was closing in on fresher Pirelli tyres, added to which Hamilton's engine was losing power occasionally. At flagfall, though, Hamilton had done just enough to win by 1.5s and Mercedes had further reason to celebrate, as it collected sufficient points to land its fifth consecutive constructors' championship, a truly impressive feat.

INTERLAGOS ROUND 20

DATE: **11 NOVEMBER 2018**

Laps: **71** • Distance: **190.083 miles/305.909km** • Weather: **Bright & warm**

Pos	Driver	Team	Result	Stops	Qualifying Time	Grid
1	**Lewis Hamilton**	Mercedes	1h27m09.066s	1	1m07.281s	1
2	**Max Verstappen**	Red Bull	1h27m10.535s	1	1m07.778s	5
3	**Kimi Raikkonen**	Ferrari	1h27m13.830s	1	1m07.456s	4
4	**Daniel Ricciardo ***	Red Bull	1h27m14.259s	1	1m07.780s	11
5	**Valtteri Bottas**	Mercedes	1h27m32.009s	2	1m07.441s	3
6	**Sebastian Vettel**	Ferrari	1h27m36.063s	2	1m07.374s	2
7	**Charles Leclerc**	Sauber	1h27m53.265s	1	1m08.492s	7
8	**Romain Grosjean**	Haas	1h28m00.296s	1	1m08.517s	8
9	**Kevin Magnussen**	Haas	1h28m01.923s	1	1m08.659s	10
10	**Sergio Perez**	Force India	70 laps	1	1m08.741s	12
11	**Brendon Hartley**	Toro Rosso	70 laps	1	1m09.280s	16
12	**Carlos Sainz Jr**	Renault	70 laps	2	1m09.269s	15
13	**Pierre Gasly**	Toro Rosso	70 laps	1	1m09.029s	9
14	**Stoffel Vandoorne ^^**	McLaren	70 laps	1	1m09.601s	20
15	**Esteban Ocon ! ^**	Force India	70 laps	2	1m08.770s	18
16	**Sergey Sirotkin**	Williams	69 laps	1	1m10.381s	14
17	**Fernando Alonso ^^**	McLaren	69 laps	1	1m09.402s	17
18	**Lance Stroll**	Williams	69 laps	2	1m09.441s	19
R	**Nico Hulkenberg**	Renault	32 laps/overheating	0	1m08.834s	13
R	**Marcus Ericsson**	Sauber	20 laps/handling	1	1m08.296s	6

FASTEST LAP: BOTTAS, 1M10.540S, 136.645MPH/219.909KPH ON LAP 65 • RACE LEADERS: HAMILTON 1-18 & 44-71, VERSTAPPEN 19-35 & 40-43, RICCIARDO 36-39

* 5-PLACE GRID PENALTY FOR USING A SIXTH TURBOCHARGER; ! 5-PLACE GRID PENALTY FOR REPLACING THE GEARBOX; ^ 10S PENALTY FOR INCIDENT WITH VERSTAPPEN; ^^ 5-SECOND PENALTY FOR IGNORING BLUE FLAGS

Disaster for Max Verstappen as Esteban Ocon collides while trying to take a lap back.

ABU DHABI GP

It was fitting that Lewis Hamilton rounded out his season with victory, as this was a year in which he reached new heights. However, it was far from straightforward, as he had to fight his way back to the front after a tactical switch early in the race.

Any hopes that the final race would be a clean run to the chequered flag were scuppered halfway around the opening lap when Nico Hulkenberg and Romain Grosjean clashed at Turn 9 and the Renault driver ended up inverted, his car briefly on fire. Fortunately, he was able to climb out unharmed once the car had been righted by marshals.

Then, on the seventh lap, Kimi Raikkonen had the engine shut down on his Ferrari. This triggered a virtual safety car period and caused the teams to consider changing their tactics. Hamilton's one planned pitstop was duly moved forward and this early stop dropped him to fifth. It meant he was going to have to nurse his second set of tyres through to the end of the race while still pushing hard enough to pass those who came in later. Hamilton managed to do this, regaining the lead with 22 laps to go when the late-stopping Daniel Ricciardo pitted.

Vettel finished second, a suitable result for the driver completing the year as runner-up, but he had to work for it as he was being caught by Max Verstappen who, in turn, was being caught by Ricciardo. However, Pierre Gasly's smoke-emitting Toro Rosso then delayed the Red Bull racers and this confined them to third and fourth.

Despite starting from the front row, Valtteri Bottas could finish only fifth after making two pitstops in a race plagued by brake problems and so fell from fourth to fifth in the standings.

The next two places went to drivers changing teams for 2019, with Carlos Sainz Jr finishing sixth before moving from Renault and Charles Leclerc again impressing as he finished seventh for Sauber.

Much attention was paid to Fernando Alonso in his last F1 race, for now at least, but he missed out on the final point by a single place as McLaren struggled. Not that it made any difference to him, after a career that landed him two F1 titles and should have had landed him more.

Lewis Hamilton celebrates after having to work hard for his 11th and final win of the year.

YAS MARINA ROUND 21

DATE: **25 NOVEMBER 2018**

Laps: **55** • Distance: **189.738 miles/305.355km** • Weather: **Clear & warm**

Pos	Driver	Team	Result	Stops	Qualifying Time	Grid
1	**Lewis Hamilton**	Mercedes	1h39m40.382s	1	1m34.794s	1
2	**Sebastian Vettel**	Ferrari	1h39m42.963s	1	1m35.125s	3
3	**Max Verstappen**	Red Bull	1h39m53.088s	1	1m35.589s	6
4	**Daniel Ricciardo**	Red Bull	1h39m55.761s	1	1m35.401s	5
5	**Valtteri Bottas**	Mercedes	1h40m28.339s	2	1m34.956s	2
6	**Carlos Sainz Jr**	Renault	1h40m52.930s	1	1m36.982s	11
7	**Charles Leclerc**	Sauber	1h41m11.171s	1	1m36.237s	8
8	**Sergio Perez**	Force India	1h41m11.657s	1	1m37.541s	14
9	**Romain Grosjean**	Haas	54 laps	1	1m36.192s	7
10	**Kevin Magnussen**	Haas	54 laps	1	1m37.309s	13
11	**Fernando Alonso ^**	McLaren	54 laps	1	1m37.743s	15
12	**Brendon Hartley**	Toro Rosso	54 laps	1	1m37.994s	16
13	**Lance Stroll**	Williams	54 laps	1	1m36.682s	20
14	**Stoffel Vandoorne**	McLaren	54 laps	1	1m38.577s	18
15	**Sergey Sirotkin**	Williams	54 laps	1	1m38.635s	19
R	**Pierre Gasly**	Toro Rosso	46 laps/engine	1	1m38.166s	17
R	**Esteban Ocon**	Force India	44 laps/engine	1	1m36.540s	9
R	**Marcus Ericsson**	Sauber	24 laps/power unit	0	1m37.132s	12
R	**Kimi Raikkonen**	Ferrari	6 laps/engine	0	1m35.365s	4
R	**Nico Hulkenberg**	Renault	0 laps/accident	0	1m36.542s	10

FASTEST LAP: **VETTEL, 1M40.867S, 123.171MPH/198.225KPH ON LAP 54** • RACE LEADERS: HAMILTON 1-7 & 34-55, BOTTAS 8-16, RICCIARDO 17-33
^ 5-SECOND PENALTY FOR MISSING CHICANE

Lewis Hamilton finished the F1 season in style by winning the Abu Dhabi Grand Prix.

FINAL RESULTS 2018

POS	DRIVER	NAT		CAR-ENGINE	R1	R2	R3	R4	R5
1	LEWIS HAMILTON	GBR		Mercedes F1 W09	2P	3	4	1	1P
2	SEBASTIAN VETTEL	GER		Ferrari SF71H	1	1P	8P	4P	4
3	KIMI RAIKKONEN	FIN		Ferrari SF71H	3	R	3	2	R
4	MAX VERSTAPPEN	NED		Red Bull-Tag Heuer RB14	6	R	5	R	3
5	VALTTERI BOTTAS	FIN		Mercedes F1 W09	8	2F	2	14F	2
6	DANIEL RICCIARDO	AUS		Red Bull-Tag Heuer RB14	4F	R	1F	R	5F
7	NICO HULKENBERG	GER		Renault RS18	7	6	6	R	R
8	SERGIO PEREZ	MEX		Force India-Mercedes VJM11	11	16	12	3	9
9	KEVIN MAGNUSSEN	DEN		Haas-Ferrari VF-18	R	5	10	13	6
10	CARLOS SAINZ JR	SPA		Renault RS18	10	11	9	5	7
11	FERNANDO ALONSO	SPA		McLaren-Renault MCL33	5	7	7	7	8
12	ESTEBAN OCON	FRA		Force India-Mercedes VJM11	12	10	11	R	R
13	CHARLES LECLERC	MON		Sauber-Ferrari C37	13	12	19	6	10
14	ROMAIN GROSJEAN	FRA		Haas-Ferrari VF-18	R	13	17	R	R
15	PIERRE GASLY	FRA		Toro Rosso-Honda STR13	R	4	18	12	R
16	STOFFEL VANDOORNE	BEL		McLaren-Renault MCL33	9	8	13	9	R
17	MARCUS ERICSSON	SWE		Sauber-Ferrari C37	R	9	16	11	13
18	LANCE STROLL	CDN		Williams-Mercedes FW41	14	14	14	8	11
19	BRENDON HARTLEY	NZL		Toro Rosso-Honda STR13	15	17	20	10	12
20	SERGEY SIROTKIN	RUS		Williams-Mercedes FW41	R	15	15	R	14

SCORING

1st	25 points
2nd	18 points
3rd	15 points
4th	12 points
5th	10 points
6th	8 points
7th	6 points
8th	4 points
9th	2 points
10th	1 point

POS	TEAM-ENGINE	R1	R2	R3	R4	R5
1	MERCEDES	2/8	2/3	2/4	1/14	1/2
2	FERRARI	1/3	1/R	3/8	2/4	4/R
3	RED BULL-TAG HEUER	4/6	R/R	1/5	R/R	3/5
4	RENAULT	7/10	6/11	6/9	5/R	7/R
5	HAAS-FERRARI	R/R	5/13	10/17	13/R	6/R
6	McLAREN-RENAULT	5/9	7/8	7/13	7/9	8/R
7	FORCE INDIA-MERCEDES*	11/12	10/16	11/12	3/R	9/R
8	SAUBER-FERRARI	13/R	9/12	16/19	6/11	10/13
9	TORO ROSSO-HONDA	15/R	4/17	18/R	10/12	12/R
10	WILLIAMS-MERCEDES	14/R	14/15	14/15	8/R	11/14

* All points earned by Force India before the Belgian GP were forfeit so that the team was allowed to change ownership.

SYMBOLS AND GRAND PRIX KEY

ROUND 1............AUSTRALIAN GP		ROUND 6..............MONACO GP	ROUND 11...............GERMAN GP	ROUND 16...............RUSSIAN GP
ROUND 2...............BAHRAIN GP		ROUND 7.............CANADIAN GP	ROUND 12..........HUNGARIAN GP	ROUND 17.............JAPANESE GP
ROUND 3...............CHINESE GP		ROUND 8................FRENCH GP	ROUND 13..............BELGIAN GP	ROUND 18......UNITED STATES GP
ROUND 4............AZERBAIJAN GP		ROUND 9..............AUSTRIAN GP	ROUND 14..............ITALIAN GP	ROUND 19..............MEXICAN GP
ROUND 5...............SPANISH GP		ROUND 10.............BRITISH GP	ROUND 15...........SINGAPORE GP	ROUND 20............BRAZILIAN GP
				ROUND 21............ABU DHABI GP

DQ DISQUALIFIED   **F** FASTEST LAP   **NC** NOT CLASSIFIED   **NS** NON-STARTER   **P** POLE POSITION   **R** RETIRED   **W** WITHDRAWN

R6	R7	R8	R9	R10	R11	R12	R13	R14	R15	R16	R17	R18	R19	R20	R21	TOTAL
3	5	1P	R	2P	1F	1P	2P	1F	1P	1	1P	3PF	4	1P	1P	408
2	1P	5	3	1F	RP	2	1	4	3	3	6F	4	2	6	2F	320
4	6	3	2F	3	3	3	R	2P	5	4	5	1	3	3	R	251
9F	3F	2	1	15	4	R	3	5	2	5	3	2	1	2	3	249
5	2	7F	RP	4	2	5	4F	3	4	2PF	2	5	5F	5F	5	247
1P	4	4	R	5	R	4F	R	R	6	6	4	R	RP	4	4	170
8	7	9	6	6	5	12	R	13	10	12	R	6	6	R	R	69
12	14	R	7	10	7	14	5	7	16	10	7	8	R	10	8	62
13	13	6	5	9	11	7	8	16	18F	8	R	DQ	15	9	10	56
10	8	8	12	R	12	9	11	8	8	17	10	7	R	12	11	53
R	R	16	8	8	16	8	R	R	7	14	14	R	R	17	11	50
6	9	R	6	7	8	13	6	6	R	9	9	DQ	11	14	R	49
18	10	10	9	R	15	R	R	11	9	7	R	R	7	7	7	39
15	12	11	4	R	6	10	7	DQ	15	11	8	R	16	8	9	37
7	11	R	11	13	14	6	9	14	13	R	11	12	10	13	R	29
14	16	12	15	11	13	R	15	12	12	16	15	11	8	15	14	12
11	15	13	10	R	9	15	10	15	11	13	12	10	9	R	R	9
17	R	17	14	12	R	17	13	9	14	15	17	14	12	18	13	6
19	R	14	R	R	10	11	14	R	17	R	13	9	14	11	12	4
16	17	15	13	14	R	16	12	10	19	18	16	13	13	16	15	1

R6	R7	R8	R9	R10	R11	R12	R13	R14	R15	R16	R17	R18	R19	R20	R21	TOTAL
3/5	2/5	1/7	R/R	2/4	1/2	1/5	2/4	1/3	1/4	1/2	1/2	3/5	4/5	1/5	1/5	655
2/4	1/6	3/5	2/3	1/3	3/R	2/3	1/R	2/4	3/5	3/4	5/6	1/4	2/3	3/6	2/R	571
1/9	3/4	2/4	1/R	5/15	4/R	4/R	3/R	5/R	2/6	5/6	3/4	2/R	1/R	2/4	3/4	419
8/10	7/8	8/9	12/R	6/R	5/12	9/12	11/R	8/13	8/10	12/17	10/R	6/7	6/R	12/R	6/R	122
13/15	12/13	6/11	4/5	9/R	6/11	7/10	7/8	16/DQ	15/18	8/11	8/R	DQ/R	15/16	8/9	9/10	93
14/R	16/R	12/16	8/15	8/11	13/R	8/R	15/R	12/R	7/12	14/16	14/15	11/R	8/R	14/17	11/14	62
6/12	9/14	R/R	6/7	7/10	7/8	13/14	5/6	6/7	16/R	9/10	7/9	8/DQ	11/R	10/15	8/R	52
11/18	10/15	10/13	9/10	R/R	9/15	15/R	10/R	11/15	9/11	7/13	12/R	10/R	7/9	7/R	7/R	48
7/12	11/R	14/R	11/R	13/R	10/14	6/11	9/14	14/R	13/17	R/R	11/13	9/12	10/14	11/13	12/R	33
16/17	17/R	15/17	13/14	12/14	R/R	16/17	12/13	9/10	14/19	15/18	16/17	13/14	12/13	16/18	13/15	7

FORMULA ONE RECORDS

Rubens Barrichello showed flashes of speed in his first year of F1 with Jordan in 1993, and raced on until the end of 2011 when he retired from Williams after contesting a record 325 grands prix.

MOST STARTS

DRIVERS

325	Rubens Barrichello	(BRA)	175	Jacques Laffite	(FRA)		Adrian Sutil	(GER)
314	Fernando Alonso	(SPA)	171	Niki Lauda	(AUT)	126	Jack Brabham	(AUS)
308	Michael Schumacher	(GER)	165	Jacques Villeneuve	(CDN)	123	Ronnie Peterson	(SWE)
307	Jenson Button	(GBR)	163	Thierry Boutsen	(BEL)	119	Pierluigi Martini	(ITA)
294	Kimi Raikkonen	(FIN)	162	Mika Hakkinen	(FIN)	118	Valtteri Bottas	(FIN)
270	Felipe Massa	(BRA)		Johnny Herbert	(GBR)	116	Damon Hill	(GBR)
256	Riccardo Patrese	(ITA)	161	Ayrton Senna	(BRA)		Jacky Ickx	(BEL)
	Jarno Trulli	(ITA)	159	Heinz-Harald Frentzen	(GER)		Alan Jones	(AUS)
247	David Coulthard	(GBR)	158	Martin Brundle	(GBR)	114	Keke Rosberg	(FIN)
230	Giancarlo Fisichella	(ITA)		Nico Hulkenberg	(GER)		Patrick Tambay	(FRA)
229	Lewis Hamilton	(GBR)		Olivier Panis	(FRA)	112	Denny Hulme	(NZL)
220	Sebastian Vettel	(GER)	155	Sergio Perez	(MEX)		Jody Scheckter	(RSA)
216	Mark Webber	(AUS)	152	John Watson	(GBR)	111	Heikki Kovalainen	(FIN)
210	Gerhard Berger	(AUT)	150	Daniel Ricciardo	(AUS)		John Surtees	(GBR)
208	Andrea de Cesaris	(ITA)	149	Rene Arnoux	(FRA)	109	Philippe Alliot	(FRA)
206	Nico Rosberg	(GER)	147	Eddie Irvine	(GBR)		Mika Salo	(FIN)
204	Nelson Piquet	(BRA)		Derek Warwick	(GBR)	108	Elio de Angelis	(ITA)
201	Jean Alesi	(FRA)	146	Carlos Reutemann	(ARG)	106	Jos Verstappen	(NED)
199	Alain Prost	(FRA)	145	Romain Grosjean	(FRA)	104	Jo Bonnier	(SWE)
194	Michele Alboreto	(ITA)	144	Emerson Fittipaldi	(BRA)		Pedro de la Rosa	(SPA)
187	Nigel Mansell	(GBR)	135	Jean-Pierre Jarier	(FRA)		Jochen Mass	(GER)
185	Nick Heidfeld	(GER)	132	Eddie Cheever	(USA)	100	Bruce McLaren	(NZL)
180	Ralf Schumacher	(GER)		Clay Regazzoni	(SWI)			
176	Graham Hill	(GBR)	128	Mario Andretti	(USA)			

CONSTRUCTORS

970	Ferrari		Midland, then Spyker,	381	Red Bull (*nee* Stewart, then
843	McLaren		then Force India)		Jaguar Racing)
762	Williams	492	Lotus	365	Mercedes GP (*nee* BAR, then
634	Renault* (*nee* Toleman, then	464	Sauber (including BMW Sauber)		Honda Racing, then Brawn GP)
	Benetton, then Renault II, Lotus II	418	Tyrrell	230	March
	& Renault III)	409	Prost (nee Ligier)	197	BRM
588	Toro Rosso (*nee* Minardi)	394	Brabham	132	Osella
497	Racing Point (*nee* Jordan, then	383	Arrows	129	Renault

MOST WINS

DRIVERS

91 Michael Schumacher (GER)	**16** Stirling Moss (GBR)	Jody Scheckter (RSA)
73 Lewis Hamilton (GBR)	**15** Jenson Button (GBR)	**9** Mark Webber (AUS)
52 Sebastian Vettel (GER)	**14** Jack Brabham (AUS)	**8** Denny Hulme (NZL)
51 Alain Prost (FRA)	Emerson Fittipaldi (BRA)	Jacky Ickx (BEL)
41 Ayrton Senna (BRA)	Graham Hill (GBR)	**7** Rene Arnoux (FRA)
32 Fernando Alonso (SPA)	**13** Alberto Ascari (ITA)	Juan Pablo Montoya (COL)
31 Nigel Mansell (GBR)	David Coulthard (GBR)	Daniel Ricciardo (AUS)
27 Jackie Stewart (GBR)	**12** Mario Andretti (USA)	**6** Tony Brooks (GBR)
25 Jim Clark (GBR)	Alan Jones (AUS)	Jacques Laffite (FRA)
Niki Lauda (AUT)	Carlos Reutemann (ARG)	Riccardo Patrese (ITA)
24 Juan Manuel Fangio (ARG)	**11** Rubens Barrichello (BRA)	Jochen Rindt (AUT)
23 Nelson Piquet (BRA)	Felipe Massa (BRA)	Ralf Schumacher (GER)
Nico Rosberg (GER)	Jacques Villeneuve (CDN)	John Surtees (GBR)
22 Damon Hill (GBR)	**10** Gerhard Berger (AUT)	Gilles Villeneuve (CDN)
21 Kimi Raikkonen (FIN)	James Hunt (GBR)	
20 Mika Hakkinen (FIN)	Ronnie Peterson (SWE)	

CONSTRUCTORS

234 Ferrari	**17** BRM	**3** March
181 McLaren	**16** Cooper	Wolf
114 Williams	**15** Renault	**2** Honda
87 Mercedes GP (including Honda Racing, Brawn GP)	**10** Alfa Romeo	**1** BMW Sauber
79 Lotus	**9** Ligier	Eagle
59 Red Bull (including Stewart)	Maserati	Hesketh
48 Renault* (including Benetton, Renault II, Lotus II & Renault III)	Matra	Penske
	Mercedes	Porsche
35 Brabham	Vanwall	Shadow
23 Tyrrell	**4** Racing Point (including Jordan, Force India)	Toro Rosso

Ferrari racer John Surtees, seen here leading Dan Gurney's Brabham in the 1964 Italian GP, is the only world champion on two wheels and four.

Michael Schumacher's fifth consecutive drivers' title for Ferrari, in 2004, came in a season in which he racked up a record 13 race victories.

DRIVERS

	Driver	Year
13	Michael Schumacher	2004
11	Lewis Hamilton	2014
	Lewis Hamilton	2018
	Michael Schumacher	2002
	Sebastian Vettel	2011
10	Lewis Hamilton	2015
	Lewis Hamilton	2016
9	Lewis Hamilton	2017
	Nigel Mansell	1992
	Nico Rosberg	2016
	Michael Schumacher	1995
	Michael Schumacher	2000
	Michael Schumacher	2001
8	Mika Hakkinen	1998
	Damon Hill	1996
	Michael Schumacher	1994
	Ayrton Senna	1988
7	Fernando Alonso	2005
	Fernando Alonso	2006
	Jim Clark	1963
	Alain Prost	1984
	Alain Prost	1988
	Alain Prost	1993
	Kimi Raikkonen	2005
	Ayrton Senna	1991
	Jacques Villeneuve	1997
6	Mario Andretti	1978
	Alberto Ascari	1952
	Jim Clark	1965
	Juan Manuel Fangio	1954
	Damon Hill	1994
	James Hunt	1976
	Nigel Mansell	1987
	Kimi Raikkonen	2007
	Nico Rosberg	2015
	Michael Schumacher	1998
	Michael Schumacher	2003
	Michael Schumacher	2006
	Ayrton Senna	1989
	Ayrton Senna	1990

CONSTRUCTORS

	Constructor	Year
19	Mercedes GP	2016
16	Mercedes GP	2014
	Mercedes GP	2015
15	Ferrari	2002
	Ferrari	2004
	McLaren	1988
12	McLaren	1984
	Mercedes GP	2017
	Red Bull	2011
	Williams	1996
11	Benetton	1995
	Mercedes GP	2018
10	Ferrari	2000
	McLaren	2005
	McLaren	1989
	Williams	1992
	Williams	1993
9	Ferrari	2001
	Ferrari	2006
	Ferrari	2007
	McLaren	1998
	Red Bull	2010
	Williams	1986
	Williams	1987
8	Benetton	1994
	Brawn GP	2009
	Ferrari	2003
	Lotus	1978
	McLaren	1991
	McLaren	2007
	Renault	2005
	Renault	2006
	Williams	1997
7	Ferrari	1952
	Ferrari	1953
	Ferrari	2008
	Lotus	1963
	Lotus	1973
	McLaren	1999
	McLaren	2000
	McLaren	2012
	Red Bull	2012
	Tyrrell	1971
	Williams	1991
	Williams	1994

MOST POLE POSITIONS

DRIVERS

83	Lewis Hamilton	(GBR)		Nelson Piquet	(BRA)		James Hunt	(GBR)	
68	Michael Schumacher	(GER)	22	Fernando Alonso	(SPA)		Ronnie Peterson	(SWE)	
65	Ayrton Senna	(BRA)	20	Damon Hill	(GBR)	13	Jack Brabham	(AUS)	
55	Sebastian Vettel	(GER)	18	Mario Andretti	(USA)		Graham Hill	(GBR)	
33	Jim Clark	(GBR)		Rene Arnoux	(FRA)		Jacky Ickx	(BEL)	
	Alain Prost	(FRA)		Kimi Raikkonen	(FIN)		Juan Pablo Montoya	(COL)	
32	Nigel Mansell	(GBR)	17	Jackie Stewart	(GBR)		Jacques Villeneuve	(CDN)	
30	Nico Rosberg	(GER)	16	Felipe Massa	(BRA)	12	Gerhard Berger	(AUT)	
29	Juan Manuel Fangio	(ARG)		Stirling Moss	(GBR)		David Coulthard	(GBR)	
26	Mika Hakkinen	(FIN)	14	Alberto Ascari	(ITA)	11	Mark Webber	(AUS)	
24	Niki Lauda	(AUT)		Rubens Barrichello	(BRA)	10	Jochen Rindt	(AUT)	

CONSTRUCTORS

219	Ferrari	31	Renault	3	Racing Point (including Jordan, Force India)		
154	McLaren	14	Tyrrell		Shadow		
128	Williams	12	Alfa Romeo		Toyota		
107	Lotus	11	BRM	2	Lancia		
101	Mercedes GP (including Brawn GP, Honda Racing, BAR)		Cooper	1	BMW Sauber		
60	Red Bull	10	Maserati		Toro Rosso		
39	Brabham	9	Ligier				
34	Renault* (including Toleman, Benetton, Renault II, Lotus II & Renault III)	8	Mercedes				
		7	Vanwall				
		5	March				
		4	Matra				

Ayrton Senna claimed his first pole at the start of 1985, for Lotus, and carried on until he had achieved a then record 65.

FASTEST LAPS

DRIVERS

76	Michael Schumacher	(GER)	21	Gerhard Berger	(AUT)	13	Alberto Ascari	(ITA)
46	Kimi Raikkonen	(FIN)	20	Nico Rosberg	(GER)		Alan Jones	(AUS)
41	Lewis Hamilton	(GBR)	19	Damon Hill	(GBR)		Riccardo Patrese	(ITA)
	Alain Prost	(FRA)		Stirling Moss	(GBR)		Daniel Ricciardo	(AUS)
36	Sebastian Vettel	(GER)		Ayrton Senna	(BRA)	12	Rene Arnoux	(FRA)
30	Nigel Mansell	(GBR)		Mark Webber	(AUS)		Jack Brabham	(AUS)
28	Jim Clark	(GBR)	18	David Coulthard	(GBR)		Juan Pablo Montoya	(COL)
25	Mika Hakkinen	(FIN)	17	Rubens Barrichello	(BRA)	11	John Surtees	(GBR)
24	Niki Lauda	(AUT)	16	Felipe Massa	(BRA)	10	Mario Andretti	(USA)
23	Juan Manuel Fangio	(ARG)	15	Clay Regazzoni	(SWI)		Valtteri Bottas	(FIN)
	Nelson Piquet	(BRA)		Jackie Stewart	(GBR)		Graham Hill	(GBR)
22	Fernando Alonso	(SPA)	14	Jacky Ickx	(BEL)			

CONSTRUCTORS

247	Ferrari	54	Renault* (including Toleman, Benetton, Renault II & Lotus II)	14	Alfa Romeo
154	McLaren			13	Cooper
133	Williams	40	Brabham	12	Matra
71	Lotus	22	Tyrrell	11	Prost (including Ligier)
66	Mercedes GP (including Brawn GP, BAR & Honda Racing)	18	Renault	9	Mercedes
		15	BRM	7	March
60	Red Bull		Maserati		Racing Point (inc Jordan, Force India)

POINTS (this figure is gross tally, ie. including scores that were later dropped)

DRIVERS

3018	Lewis Hamilton	(GBR)	535	David Coulthard	(GBR)	281	Emerson Fittipaldi	(BRA)
2745	Sebastian Vettel	(GER)	529	Sergio Perez	(MEX)		Riccardo Patrese	(ITA)
1899	Fernando Alonso	(SPA)	485.5	Nelson Piquet	(BRA)	277.5	Juan Manuel Fangio	(ARG)
1816	Kimi Raikkonen	(FIN)	482	Nigel Mansell	(GBR)	275	Giancarlo Fisichella	(ITA)
1594.5	Nico Rosberg	(GER)	474	Nico Hulkenberg	(GER)	274	Jim Clark	(GBR)
1566	Michael Schumacher	(GER)	420.5	Niki Lauda	(AUT)	273	Robert Kubica	(POL)
1235	Jenson Button	(GBR)	420	Mika Hakkinen	(FIN)	261	Jack Brabham	(AUS)
1167	Felipe Massa	(BRA)	385	Gerhard Berger	(AUT)	259	Nick Heidfeld	(GER)
1047.5	Mark Webber	(AUS)	381	Romain Grosjean	(FRA)	255	Jody Scheckter	(RSA)
986	Daniel Ricciardo	(AUS)	360	Damon Hill	(GBR)	248	Denny Hulme	(NZL)
963	Valtteri Bottas	(FIN)		Jackie Stewart	(GBR)	246.5	Jarno Trulli	(ITA)
798.5	Alain Prost	(FRA)	329	Ralf Schumacher	(GER)	241	Jean Alesi	(FRA)
670	Max Verstappen	(NED)	310	Carlos Reutemann	(ARG)	235	Jacques Villeneuve	(CDN)
658	Rubens Barrichello	(BRA)	307	Juan Pablo Montoya	(COL)	228	Jacques Laffite	(FRA)
614	Ayrton Senna	(BRA)	289	Graham Hill	(GBR)			

CONSTRUCTORS

7735.5	Ferrari	1514	Lotus	333	Cooper
5185.5	McLaren	1331	Racing Point (including Jordan, Midland, Spyker, Force India)	312	Renault
4876	Mercedes GP (including BAR, Honda Racing, Brawn GP)			278.5	Toyota
		858	Sauber (including BMW Sauber)	171.5	March
4395.5	Red Bull (including Stewart, Jaguar Racing)	854	Brabham	169	Haas
		617	Tyrrell	167	Arrows
3566	Williams	451	Toro Rosso	155	Matra
2732.5	Renault* (including Toleman, Benetton, Renault II & Lotus II)	439	BRM		
		424	Prost (including Ligier)		

The points tallies of Gerhard Berger, Alain Prost and Nelson Piquet, shown in 1987, look small but the allocation was less generous in their day.

CHAMPIONSHIP TITLES

DRIVERS

7	Michael Schumacher	(GER)		Alberto Ascari	(ITA)		Denis Hulme	(NZL)
5	Juan Manuel Fangio	(ARG)		Jim Clark	(GBR)		James Hunt	(GBR)
	Lewis Hamilton	(GBR)		Emerson Fittipaldi	(BRA)		Alan Jones	(AUS)
4	Alain Prost	(FRA)		Mika Hakkinen	(FIN)		Nigel Mansell	(GBR)
	Sebastian Vettel	(GER)		Graham Hill	(GBR)		Kimi Raikkonen	(FIN)
3	Jack Brabham	(AUS)	1	Mario Andretti	(USA)		Jochen Rindt	(AUT)
	Niki Lauda	(AUT)		Jenson Button	(GBR)		Keke Rosberg	(FIN)
	Nelson Piquet	(BRA)		Giuseppe Farina	(ITA)		Nico Rosberg	(FIN)
	Ayrton Senna	(BRA)		Mike Hawthorn	(GBR)		Jody Scheckter	(RSA)
	Jackie Stewart	(GBR)		Damon Hill	(GBR)		John Surtees	(GBR)
2	Fernando Alonso	(SPA)		Phil Hill	(USA)		Jacques Villeneuve	(CDN)

CONSTRUCTORS

16	Ferrari	1	Benetton
9	Williams		Brawn
8	McLaren		BRM
7	Lotus		Matra
5	Mercedes GP		Tyrrell
4	Red Bull		Vanwall
2	Brabham		
	Cooper		
	Renault		

NB. To avoid confusion, the Lotus stats listed are based on the team that ran from 1958 to 1994, whereas those listed as Renault* are for the team based at Enstone that started as Toleman in 1981, became Benetton in 1986, then Renault II in 2002, Lotus II in 2012 and Renault again in 2016. The Renault listings are for the team that ran from 1977 to 1985, the stats for Red Bull Racing include those of the Stewart Grand Prix and Jaguar Racing teams from which it evolved, and those for Mercedes GP for the team that started as BAR in 1999, then ran as Honda GP from 2006 and as Brawn GP in 2009. Racing Point's stats include those of Jordan, Midland, Spyker and Force India, while Scuderia Toro Rosso's include those of its forerunner Minardi.

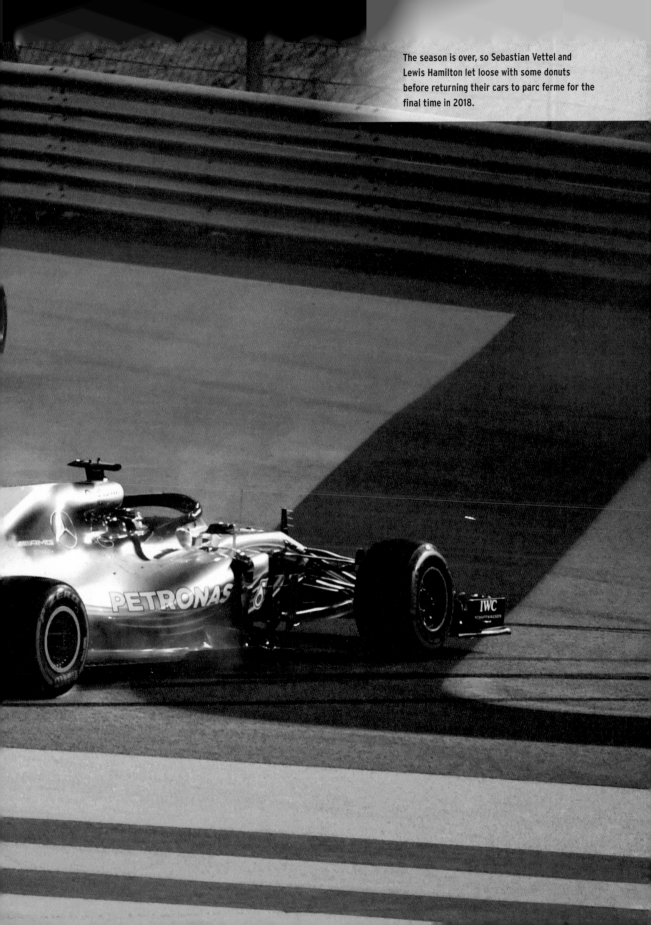

The season is over, so Sebastian Vettel and Lewis Hamilton let loose with some donuts before returning their cars to parc ferme for the final time in 2018.

2019 FILL-IN CHART

DRIVER	TEAM	Round 1 – 17 March AUSTRALIAN GP	Round 2 – 31 March BAHRAIN GP	Round 3 – 14 April CHINESE GP	Round 4 – 28 April AZERBAIJAN GP	Round 5 – 12 May SPANISH GP	Round 6 – 26 May MONACO GP	Round 7 – 9 June CANADIAN GP	Round 8 – 23 June FRENCH GP	Round 9 – 30 June AUSTRIAN GP
LEWIS HAMILTON	Mercedes									
VALTTERI BOTTAS	Mercedes									
SEBASTIAN VETTEL	Ferrari									
CHARLES LECLERC	Ferrari									
MAX VERSTAPPEN	Red Bull									
PIERRE GASLY	Red Bull									
NICO HULKENBERG	Renault									
DANIEL RICCIARDO	Renault									
ROMAIN GROSJEAN	Haas F1									
KEVIN MAGNUSSEN	Haas F1									
CARLOS SAINZ JR	McLaren									
LANDO NORRIS	McLaren									
SERGIO PEREZ	Racing Point									
LANCE STROLL	Racing Point									
KIMI RAIKKONEN	Sauber									
ANTONIO GIOVINAZZI	Sauber									
DANIIL KVYAT	Toro Rosso									
ALEX ALBON	Toro Rosso									
ROBERT KUBICA	Williams									
GEORGE RUSSELL	Williams									

SCORING SYSTEM: 25, 18, 15, 12, 10, 8, 6, 4, 2, 1 POINTS
FOR THE FIRST 10 FINISHERS IN EACH GRAND PRIX

Round 10 – 14 July BRITISH GP	Round 11 – 28 July GERMAN GP	Round 12 – 4 Aug HUNGARIAN GP	Round 13 – 1 Sept BELGIAN GP	Round 14 – 8 Sept ITALIAN GP	Round 15 – 22 Sept SINGAPORE GP	Round 16 – 29 Sept RUSSIAN GP	Round 17 – 13 Oct JAPANESE GP	Round 18 – 27 Oct MEXICAN GP	Round 19 – 3 Nov UNITED STATES GP	Round 20 – 17 Nov BRAZILIAN GP	Round 21 – 1 Dec ABU DHABI GP	POINTS TOTAL

After an incredible season that landed him his fifth F1 title, Lewis Hamilton sprays Champagne in a massed Mercedes team celebration in the Yas Marina paddock, with the joy clear to be seen in every face as the photographers capture the moment.

The publishers would like to thank the following sources for their kind permission to reproduce the pictures in this book.

ALL PHOTOGRAPHY © MOTORSPORT IMAGES: /Jerry Andre/Sutton Images: 8-9, 13, 22, 23, 27, 28-29, 33, 38, 40, 100, 105, 110; /Sam Bloxham/LAT Images: 59R, 103, 108; /Hasan Bratic/Sutton Images: 104; /Charles Coates/LAT Images: 43; /Glenn Dunbar/LAT Images: 24, 41, 59B, 74-75, 98, 106; /Steve Etherington/LAT Images: 6-7, 95, 99, 113, 128; /Simon Galloway/Sutton Images: 112, 124-125; /James Gasperotti/Sutton Images: 91; /Manuel Goria/Sutton Images: 20, 26, 34, 45, 109, 111, 115; /Andy Hone/LAT Images: 12, 21, 31, 32, 44, 52, 97; /Daniel Kalisz/Sutton Images: 94; /LAT Images: 25, 49, 59T, 61TR, 63TL, 63R, 63B, 118, 121, 123; /Zak Mauger/LAT Images: 3, 30, 46-47, 48, 55, 61B, 66-67, 96, 102, 107; /Joe Portlock/LAT Images: 64-65; /Rainer Schlegelmilch: 61R; /Alastair Staley/LAT Images: 51, 63TR; /Sutton Images: 15, 35, 39, 53, 59L, 61TL, 119, 120; /Mark Sutton/Sutton Images: 11, 36, 50, 54, 101; /Steven Tee/LAT Images: 5, 10, 14, 16, 17, 18-19, 37, 42, 56-57, 92-93, 114

Every effort has been made to acknowledge correctly and contact the source and/ or copyright holder of each picture and Carlton Books Limited apologizes for any unintentional errors or omissions that will be corrected in future editions of this book.